# dirtbag billionaire

## How Yvon Chouinard Built Patagonia, Made a Fortune, and Gave It All Away

## DAVID GELLES

*Simon & Schuster*

NEW YORK   AMSTERDAM/ANTWERP   LONDON
TORONTO   SYDNEY/MELBOURNE   NEW DELHI

Simon & Schuster
1230 Avenue of the Americas
New York, NY 10020

First Simon & Schuster hardcover edition September 2025

SIMON & SCHUSTER and colophon are registered trademarks of Simon & Schuster, LLC

Simon & Schuster strongly believes in freedom of expression and stands against censorship in all its forms. For more information, visit BooksBelong.com.

For information about special discounts for bulk purchases, please contact Simon & Schuster Special Sales at 1-866-506-1949 or business@simonandschuster.com.

The Simon & Schuster Speakers Bureau can bring authors to your live event. For more information or to book an event, contact the Simon & Schuster Speakers Bureau at 1-866-248-3049 or visit our website at www.simonspeakers.com.

Interior design by Paul Dippolito

Manufactured in the United States of America

1   3   5   7   9   10   8   6   4   2

Library of Congress Cataloging-in-Publication Data has been applied for.

ISBN 978-1-6680-3226-8
ISBN 978-1-6680-3228-2 (ebook)

*For Ali*

*Thank you for the adventure of a lifetime*

# Contents

*Introduction*     1

**CHAPTER 1**   A Rhythm All His Own     11

**CHAPTER 2**   Dirtbags     36

**CHAPTER 3**   Pushing the Limits     59

**CHAPTER 4**   Patagoniacs     82

**CHAPTER 5**   Winning Back the Wild     105

**CHAPTER 6**   A Critical Time     132

**CHAPTER 7**   Leaps of Faith     155

**CHAPTER 8**   Leadership     181

**CHAPTER 9**   Fights     210

**CHAPTER 10**   Giving It All Away     237

**CHAPTER 11**   The Next 50 Years     261

*Acknowledgments*     281

*Notes*     283

*Index*     295

# Introduction

As I watched him cast his fly into a remote river at the foot of the Andes, it occurred to me that Yvon Chouinard, five years shy of his 90th birthday, might finally be at peace.

For the better part of a century, a restless energy had propelled this compact, enigmatic, brilliant, cantankerous man to the ends of the Earth and the frontiers of business, making him a legend and earning him a fortune. Although he came from humble origins and never graduated from college, Chouinard assembled a staggering list of accomplishments that enshrined him as one of his generation's greatest outdoorsmen and one of its most successful businessmen. As a pioneering rock climber, Chouinard put up first ascents on some of the most challenging granite walls in the world. As a kayaker, he navigated first descents of perilous rivers. As a surfer, he sought out virgin waves on pristine beaches. He scaled glaciers in the Arctic, stalked wild tigers in Siberia, and got lost in the mountains of Bhutan. He almost fell to his death in Wyoming. He nearly died in an avalanche in China. He almost drowned in Chile. He revolutionized the sport of rock climbing twice; first by establishing previously unfathomable routes and then with his reinvention of just about every piece of climbing equipment. He helped invent the sport of ice climbing, devising tools and techniques for scaling frozen waterfalls. And he became one of the world's finest anglers, catching rainbow trout with an ease that confounded even the most seasoned fishing guides.

Chouinard founded two companies, each of which survived more than a half century. Chouinard Equipment, his climbing gear business, was no longer under his control but lived on as Black Diamond and remained a major force in the outdoor gear market. Patagonia, his apparel company, was bigger than ever, boasting sales of more than $1 billion a year. As an executive, Chouinard developed a reputation as both an uncompromising craftsman with an intuitive knack for design and a visionary leader who was decades ahead of his time. Under his stewardship, Patagonia became one of the most progressive companies in the world, setting the agenda for the rest of corporate America with its commitment to childcare, its embrace of work-life balance, its focus on sustainability, and its political activism. All this success, however, left Chouinard antsy and agitated at the end of his career. The fact that he was a living legend wasn't really what irked him.

It was the money.

Maintaining full control of Patagonia for so long enabled Chouinard to live the life he wanted, spending decades exploring Earth's wildest places and creating a different sort of corporation in the process. It gave him the means to become a major funder of large-scale conservation projects. But in his waning years, Chouinard's ownership of a multibillion-dollar company had become a burden. He was a billionaire on paper. Financial magazines estimated his net worth to be $1.2 billion, a ludicrous sum to a man who still cooked with the same cast-iron skillet he had acquired 50 years ago, lived in a log cabin cluttered with secondhand furniture, and didn't own a cell phone or a computer. Labeling him a billionaire was blasphemous, an affront to everything he stood for, and he wouldn't be able to relax until he remedied this cosmic clerical error.

For decades, Chouinard tried to figure out what to do with Patagonia. What did succession planning look like at a company that didn't play by the rules? How could he get rid of his wealth while keeping control of his company? Chouinard and his inner circle, along with some high-priced estate planners, dreamed up different arrangements that could accomplish several seemingly contradictory goals at once. Chouinard wanted to find a way to funnel the bulk of Patagonia's profits—more than $100 million a year—to combating the environmental crisis. He also wanted to ensure the company remained independent and wouldn't be taken over. Most importantly, he wanted to make sure no one could ever call him a billionaire again.

It took years of work, but after several false starts, they finally landed on an acceptable solution. And so it was that on a mild day in September of 2022, after months of planning, Chouinard made his big reveal. With his employees gathered at Patagonia's headquarters in Ventura, California, the Pacific Ocean so close they could smell the salt in the air, he announced his audacious plan: he was giving the whole company away.

Using a complex new structure of trusts and nonprofit entities, Chouinard and his family renounced their claim to a multibillion-dollar fortune, locking up the equity of the company in a way that would make a hostile takeover all but impossible and ensuring that all future profits would go toward protecting the planet. He was not cashing out. There would be no initial public offering, no sale to private equity, no acquisition by a larger rival. Patagonia would continue operating more or less unchanged, and it would now have more money than ever to invest in conservation and activism. Chouinard had notched one last first, devising an innovative governance structure to safeguard a most unusual company. And crucially, with the signing of some paperwork, his net worth plummeted. He was a billionaire no more.

As the Patagonia staff learned the news, I was in the *New York Times* newsroom, publishing an article that detailed the ownership change. For months, I had been talking with Chouinard, his family, and members of Patagonia's board, working to understand the complexities of the transaction, as well as their motives and aspirations. I'd first met Chouinard a decade earlier while researching my first book, *Mindful Work*, interviewing him about how Zen Buddhism had influenced his career. Then, as a reporter for the *Times*, I'd written about Patagonia's environmental activism and its efforts to get out the vote, and interviewed its CEOs for a column I wrote on executive leadership.

Covering Patagonia was a welcome respite from my usual work. As a business journalist, I've written about my fair share of charlatans and criminals, exposing Silicon Valley con artists, investigating what went wrong at Boeing after two deadly crashes, and interviewing Ponzi schemer Bernie Madoff in prison. Not long before I broke the news about Chouinard giving away Patagonia, I published *The Man Who Broke Capitalism*, a book that revealed how Jack Welch, the former CEO of General Electric, had turned corporate America on its head by prioritizing profits no matter the cost to workers, customers, or society at large. All of which made what Chouinard and Patagonia were doing that much more remarkable. As the rest of the business world was swept away in the rush to maximize shareholder value, here was a founder, and a company, swimming upstream.

Many books offer pat lessons and actionable strategies for getting ahead in business. This narrative doesn't lend itself to that sort of tidy analysis. The story of Patagonia isn't a self-help treatise. It's more like a Zen koan. And at the center of the story is a man who was a revolutionary three times over: in sports, commerce, and charity.

Early in his life, Chouinard earned renown as a dirtbag climber—a term affectionately bestowed on poor, itinerant outdoorsmen so uninterested in material possessions they are happy to sleep in the dirt. He then became one of the finest mountaineers of his generation, putting up new ascents on some of the world's most treacherous rock walls and redesigning climbing gear.

As an executive, he created a company that defied conventional logic at every turn, pioneering a more responsible model of commerce. Patagonia distinguished itself with its commitment to sustainability, generous childcare benefits, creative marketing, and beloved outdoor clothing. It also made Chouinard a billionaire.

But Chouinard's most daring feat came at the end of his career. At the pinnacle of his success he did the unthinkable, relinquishing ownership of the company and renouncing his wealth. In doing so, he found an elegant answer to the questions that had been vexing him for his whole life and blazed a new trail for other charitable capitalists. He was an adventurer, a businessman, and a philanthropist, with each identity informing the others until the end.

Which isn't to say that Chouinard is perfect. As a boss, he could be a micromanager at times, aloof at others, and he cycled through executives, often sowing chaos at his own company. He could be mercurial, indecisive, and elitist. He is intensely private, has no patience for small talk, and is pessimistic in his old age.

Nor is Patagonia perfect. It is a for-profit company making clothes that people might want but don't really need. It strives to take good care of its employees but employs low-wage workers in the developing world to spend long days in loud, hot factories. It aspires to save the planet but uses fossil fuels that are contributing to climate change and toxic materials that are polluting the very environment it is trying to protect. It celebrates feats of extreme athleticism but makes much of its money selling T-shirts to city slickers.

Patagonia's own leaders are keenly aware of the hypocrisy embedded in their work. The fact that they are contributing to the same problems they are trying to solve drives them mad, and it also pushes them to find solutions to seemingly intractable conundrums. Their failings are a source of both agony and inspiration. And they channel this frustration with their own imperfections into a drive for constant improvement. The self-critical corporation is a rare beast. But as we will see, the company's contradictions, and its efforts to wrestle with these competing priorities, are central to its success.

Despite all these inconsistencies, and maybe because of them, Patagonia managed to become something more than a corporation. It's a philosophy, a way of being, a subculture, one that represents an alternative vision of what it means to be a part of the modern economy. For many, it's a beacon of hope, proof that it is possible to do well by doing good. From its enlightened human resources practices, to the way it spends its profits, to the exacting criteria it expects its suppliers to uphold, Patagonia has set an exceedingly high bar for the rest of corporate America.

It also helped develop a new set of standards for other companies to follow. Patagonia was involved in establishing progressive business groups including the Conservation Alliance, the Textile Exchange, 1% for the Planet, the Sustainable Apparel Coalition, the B Corp movement, and Time to Vote. And Patagonia throws its weight around when it comes to politics. It gets involved in local, state, and federal elections, donates money to help elect Democratic candidates, and has sued the president of the United States. While Patagonia is an apparel maker first, it's really everything about the company that doesn't have to do with clothing that makes the brand so exceptional.

*Dirtbag Billionaire* unspools chronologically, beginning with a close look at Chouinard's early life, daring exploits, and accidental turn to business. The aperture then widens to include the story of Patagonia's extraordinary growth, chronicling its ups and downs as a homespun business became a multinational powerhouse. As both Chouinard and his company become more influential, we see the emergence of a different kind of capitalism, one defined not exclusively by profits but by a commitment to making a positive impact in the world as well. Finally, we go behind the scenes as Chouinard embarks on a groundbreaking act of philanthropy and gives it all away.

To report this book, I spent two years following Chouinard and the Patagonia team. I interviewed current and former employees and spent time sifting through the company archives and the Chouinard family scrapbooks in Ventura, California. I tested the latest ski gear deep in the backcountry of Montana and tried out the company's wetsuits at a legendary surf break in Chile. I wandered through fields of regenerative grains with Patagonia's food team in Minnesota and toured a Patagonia factory in Peru. I retraced Chouinard's steps on some of his most famous journeys, including an expedition to the spires of Mount Fitz Roy that inspired the Patagonia logo. I hiked into remote valleys that had been turned into national parks thanks to Chouinard's conservation efforts. And I spent time with Chouinard himself—cooking with him at home in Wyoming, fishing with him in Argentina, and taking a road trip with him on a South American highway he had first traversed 56 years earlier.

The experience of writing this book was more than just an academic exercise for me. I'm no climber, but I've spent a good amount of time in the backcountry, and Chouinard's obsession with preserving unspoiled wilderness made intuitive sense to me. Few things stir the soul, quiet the mind, and invoke a sense of awe like being hundreds of miles away from civilization, surrounded by mountains, hearing nothing but wind passing through the trees. By following the Patagonia team into some wild places, my own connection with the natural world deepened. And by hanging out with Chouinard, my fishing game improved.

Researching Patagonia was also an opportunity to test my conviction that business can be a force for good. It's easy to be cynical about our highly unequal economy, and it's vital—especially as a journalist—to be critical of for-profit corporations. But it's just as important to shine a light on what's working. Without stories that provide some glimmer of hope, we forfeit the possibility of being inspired. Without good role models, we're left without a playbook for effecting positive change in the world. Not every company can be Patagonia, and no one can re-create Chouinard's wildly abundant life. Yet all businesses and everyone who works has much to learn from the way the Patagonia team forged a new path through the wilds of late capitalism.

One late spring afternoon, days into a fishing trip in Argentina, I sat on the banks of a river and watched Chouinard cast his line over and over again. We were in a valley, surrounded on three sides by the snowcapped Andes. Golden grasses waved in the breeze, a rainbow spanned the sky, and pink flamingos and black-necked swans floated nearby. Standing alone, water up to his hips, Chouinard whipped his rod behind him. Then, with hardly any movement at all, he flicked his arm and sent his fly soaring into the air, landing it with pinpoint accuracy in a tiny pocket of foam where imperceptible currents merged. It bobbed for a moment, then the line went taut, his rod bent, and he reeled in a majestic rainbow trout. Balancing on the smooth river stones, Chouinard, then 85 years old, grabbed the fish, expertly removed the hook from its cheek, tossed the trout back in the water, and cast again.

His whole life had led to this moment. A man who could have had anything, who walked away from billions of dollars, who scaled mountains, lost friends, and built empires, Chouinard, in the twilight of his life, wanted nothing more than to be alone on a river, rod and reel in hand, immersed in the beauty of the natural world.

# CHAPTER 1

# A Rhythm All His Own

## "Invent My Own Game"

Lush with wild blueberry bushes and honeysuckle, thick with balsam fir and white oak, the woods around Lewiston, Maine, were largely untouched by modernity in 1938. Porcupines and skunks foraged in the underbrush. Muskrats and moose roamed the forest. Meadow mice and woodchucks scuttled away to hibernate when the first freeze set in. Beavers holed up in their lodges, rationing the lilies and bark they had stored for winter. Here, in this unremarkable corner of North America, the natural world proceeded much as it had for thousands of years, with plants and animals mostly left to go about their business. Around the world, from the Andean peaks of South America to the wild rivers of Eastern Europe, it was much the same story. Just over two billion humans inhabited Earth at the time, roughly a quarter of the nearly ten billion now straining the planet's resources. There was no question that the world was changing fast. The Industrial Revolution had kick-started an era of technological innovation, the global population was booming, and World War II was around the corner. But for this fleeting moment, global average temperatures were effectively unchanged since the end of the last ice age, not yet having experienced the rapid warming brought about by the relentless burning of coal, oil, and gas. The oceans had not yet begun heating up, bleaching corals and confounding the migratory patterns of whales and their prey. Thousands of now-extinct species were still alive, from the golden toad to the Javan tiger. The mass disappearance of insects, portending a future absent of pollinators, had not yet commenced. Microplastics were not omnipresent in our lakes, our clouds, and our bodies. Sea levels had not yet begun to rise as the inexorable effects of glacial melting kicked in. Drought-fueled megafires were not regularly turning the skies orange, choking cities with acrid smoke. Though it was less than a century ago, just a blip in the long history of planet Earth, it was, in many ways, a world vastly different from the one we inhabit today. And it was into this greener, quieter world that Yvon Chouinard was delivered.

Chouinard's paternal grandfather, Jacques, was a farmer and the descendent of Canadian fur trappers. In the first years of the 20th century, searching for better lives, Jacques and his wife, Celanire, moved the family from Tingwick, Quebec, to Lisbon, Maine. They brought with them a few possessions and eleven children, among them Gerard Lorenzo Chouinard. Gerard had finished just three years of school when he was put to work on the family farm.

The Chouinards had little trouble finding their way. A community of French-speaking Canadian immigrants welcomed them, and work was easy to come by. Before long, the boys took jobs at Lisbon's main employer, the Worumbo Woolen Mill. The family moved into a spacious house surrounded by a small farm, with a vegetable garden, a chicken coop, a couple cows, several pigs, and a barn stuffed with grain and hay. Jacques was a font of practical wisdom and taught his children, including Gerard, how to milk a cow, sharpen a scythe, and clean the stalls of a barn. As

Gerard grew into a man, he learned to fix the looms in the mill. By the time he was a teenager, he could fix just about everything else, too. He worked as a plumber, an electrician, and a carpenter, learning how to unclog pipes, repair fans, and keep furnaces hot in the dead of winter. It was a hands-on, practical sort of wisdom that Gerard would eventually pass on to his youngest son.

When Gerard was 23, he married a young woman named Yvonne Lizotte at Lisbon's lone Catholic church, St. Anne's. They soon had their first child, Gerald, who was known as Jeff. Four years later, they had a daughter, Rachael, and two years after that, another daughter, Doris. Then on November 9, 1938, Yvonne traveled to nearby Lewiston and gave birth to another son. The boy came home from the hospital without a name. Jeff suggested they call him Yvon. The best wrestler in Canada at the time was named Yvon Robert, he said, producing a magazine featuring an article about "the French Canadian Lion" to prove his point. The family agreed, and the boy was given the name Yvon Vincent Chouinard.

Chouinard learned to climb before he could walk. A priest who lived upstairs in the house his parents rented rewarded him with a spoonful of honey every time he crawled up the steps, and the toddler clambered up that wooden mountain over and over again. As soon as Chouinard could walk, he ventured outside. He wandered the woods, pacing the loamy soil and exploring the riverbanks, listening to the animals, and learning how to read the leaves, understand the weather, smell the rain coming. Jeff taught him how to fish, and Chouinard found joy in pulling small brook trout from little creeks near the house, eventually graduating to hauling pickerel out of the nearby Androscoggin River. It was a childhood unmediated by technology, and it instilled in Chouinard an abiding love of nature. Not yet fully appreciating what the 20th century had in store, he dreamed of following in the footsteps of his French Canadian forebears and becoming a fur trapper.

The family didn't have much money, and Chouinard learned the virtues of being both thrifty and tough. During World War II, Chouinard's brother, Jeff, joined the navy and was sent to a base in San Diego. Back home in Maine, rationing set in, and the family lost ready access to staples like sugar, beef, and pork. Instead, they sustained themselves largely from the family farm. When protein got scarce, they slaughtered a horse. In one of his formative memories, Chouinard looked on as his father performed his own dental work to save money. Sitting next to the wood-burning stove in the kitchen and taking slugs from a bottle of whiskey, Gerard produced his electrician's pliers and pulled out a few of his own teeth.

Yvonne had always wanted to escape Lisbon. She sent away for travel brochures from the Chamber of Commerce, collecting pamphlets that extolled the virtues of sunny Arizonan cities and storing them in a shoebox under her bed. She finally got the nerve to act when, in January of 1946, Jeff sent the family a box of fresh oranges from California. Along with the succulent fruit was a note encouraging them to move West. By March, Yvonne had decided they would do just that. She was tired of the long Maine winters, convinced that the warm, dry climate would be better for Gerard's increasingly problematic asthma, and didn't want her children to end up working in the mill. At Yvonne's insistence, the family sold most of their possessions, including furniture that Gerard had made by hand, and packed up as much food as they could. Then they squeezed into their Chrysler and headed toward the Pacific Ocean with $5,000 in a jar and the mattresses strapped to the car's roof.

Over the next few weeks, the family drove through the industrial hubs of the East, crossed the Mississippi, made their way across the Great Plains, and slipped into the vast American West. Though they didn't have much, Chouinard, who was not yet 10 at the time, managed to get a lesson in charitable giving along the way. Driving along Route 66 in the Southwest, they passed a group of impoverished Hopi children on the side of the road. Yvonne told Gerard to pull over, and Chouinard watched as his mother gave away the preserved corn she had brought along for the journey. Material possessions never mattered much to his parents, and they would never matter much to Chouinard, either.

The family finally arrived in Burbank, California, and Chouinard started at the local public school the next day. There was an immediate problem, though. Having been raised among the Quebecois in rural Maine, he could not speak English. The language barrier, combined with the fact that he was the shortest child in his class, made him an outcast from the start. Chouinard found it traumatic. After just a few days, he ran away, disappearing into the wilds of greater Los Angeles. It didn't take long for him to return, but the die was set: Chouinard was an outsider.

His parents transferred him to a parochial school, where he had more help learning English, but his academics didn't improve. Over the course of his first full year, he got straight Ds. Outside the classroom, however, Chouinard thrived. He rode his bicycle for miles, snuck onto private golf courses, and hung out beneath the willow trees on the banks of Toluca Lake, catching bluegills and bass with wooden plugs he had carved by hand. In later years he roamed further, exploring Griffith Park and the Los Angeles River and trapping crawdads, occasionally hunting cottontail rabbits with a bow and arrow. In search of a swimming hole in the city, he sometimes splashed around in a pond created from possibly toxic outfall from the Walt Disney Corporation's film development labs. And while he maintained his aversion to school, his

English improved and he became a voracious reader; still harboring dreams of becoming a fur trader, he combed the local libraries for every book on trapping he could find.

By the early 1950s, the perils of the modern world were getting harder to escape. Los Angeles was sprawling outward, sending concrete tendrils of freeways into the golden hills. At school, Chouinard learned to drop and cover under his desk in case the Cold War got hot and a thermonuclear bomb detonated in Southern California. Sometimes at night, when the wind shifted and he could hear the roar of the planes from the Burbank airport, he cowered in his bedroom, fearful that World War III had begun. And still it was nature, not the latest technologies, that sustained his interest.

In 1951, along the rocky shoreline near La Jolla, Chouinard put his head underwater with a face mask for the first time. He was instantly hooked and began free diving for lobster and abalone. To improve his endurance, Chouinard practiced holding his breath during math class. This was before the widespread availability of wetsuits, so to stay warm in the water, he wore an old wool flight suit he picked up at an army surplus store. To reduce his buoyancy, he designed an improvised weight belt from an old ammunition satchel and filled it with lead pellets melted down from car batteries.

Though he was adept in the wild, Chouinard did not grow any more comfortable socializing as high school rolled around. He had acne, was short, and remained uninterested in academics. He spent his time outside, or reading about the outdoors, or better yet, reading about the outdoors while outside. He couldn't dance and was petrified by girls. On the night of his high school prom, he skipped out and spent the evening wading through the Los Angeles River, catching frogs.

Although Chouinard didn't fit in with the jocks, he was a gifted athlete. At baseball and basketball practices, he was one of the best players on the field. But in front of a crowd, he choked. Paralyzed by the pressure to perform, he couldn't make a play. It didn't take long for him to forswear team sports. "I hated head-to-head competition," he said. At this early age, he was already understanding his gifts and his limitations. He wasn't going to fit in; that much was clear. But that didn't mean he couldn't succeed on his own terms. "Rather than force myself to be a basketball player, I'd rather invent my own game," he said. "Then I can always be a winner. If you set the rules, you're going to win."

## "Lucky Nobody Got Killed"

Although team sports weren't for him, Chouinard found the right mix of camaraderie and athleticism when he was introduced to falconry, the ancient art of training birds of prey. On May 2, 1953, Chouinard attended the inaugural meeting of the Southern California Falconry Club, joining a band of locals with a shared curiosity for this eccentric activity. The group began exploring the hills outside Los Angeles, searching for nests. To reach some of the inaccessible aeries, Chouinard learned to scamper down sheer walls, clinging to the rock, and keeping his toes perched on inch-wide ledges. Pushing into even more remote terrain, he began using ropes to climb down sheer cliffs. Using a thick manila cord stolen from the local telephone company, he secured the line to a boulder at the top of a wall, then lowered himself down, hand over hand. When Chouinard captured birds, he learned to tame them, positioning the falcons on his wrist over and over again until they fell asleep. He then trained them to hunt and return home. Chouinard had already placed his faith in nature; now he was getting nature to place its faith in him.

In time, members of the club began tagging hawks for the government, which was beginning to monitor bird populations in the area as the suburbs encroached on their habitat. Tom Cade, a biology student at the University of California, Los Angeles, who went on to help to save the peregrine falcon—the fastest animal on earth—from the brink of extinction, took it one step further and began breeding falcons in captivity. And when volunteers were needed for the delicate, treacherous work of restoring those eggs to nests in the wild, Chouinard raised his hand.

From there, it was a straight path to rock climbing. One of the adults in the club, Don Prentice, taught Chouinard how to rappel. Wrapping the rope around his waist and over his shoulder, Chouinard learned how to descend with ease, pushing off with his legs and letting rope out as he fell, then bringing himself to a stop as he returned to the wall. He came to love the feeling of dangling from a rope, bouncing off the face of a cliff, feeling like a Slinky flipping down a set of stairs.

Chouinard and the others were soon making their own rappelling gear, replete with leather padding in key spots, which allowed them to zip down the walls faster and faster. Once, Chouinard almost died after his ropes got tangled around his neck. But the close call didn't faze him, and he kept seeking out bigger thrills. Along with other members of the falconry club, he hopped on freight trains passing through Burbank and hopped off in Chatsworth, on the other end of the San Fernando Valley. There, on 100-foot cliffs, Chouinard began to test the limits of rappelling. Instead of descending a cliff in 20 bounces, he tried to descend with as few hops as possible, launching off the wall and falling 50 feet before coming to a stop. Chouinard was beginning to push his physical limits, finding his edge. "It was lucky nobody got killed," he said.

One day in 1954, Chouinard and Cade drove out to Lompoc to look for some nests. Alone in the hot, dry hills, they came across a handful of paper-thin eggs that had been crushed before they were hatched. It was an early indication that DDT, the toxic insecticide in widespread use at the time, was devastating the peregrine population. Following their discovery, the Falconry Club helped campaign for the first California regulations protecting the birds. The law passed, and in the years that followed, the population began to recover. Although he played only a minor role in the campaign, this marked Chouinard's first dalliance with public policy and activism, and demonstrated to him that even small actions could have a big impact.

After so much time rappelling down walls, Chouinard began wondering what it would be like to go the other direction, too. Rock climbing was in its infancy as a sport in the mid-'50s, but Chouinard's interest was piqued. He and a few of the club's other members began exploring the Tehachapi Mountains, a range that marks the boundary between the San Joaquin Valley and the Mojave Desert. Those cliffs were fun enough, but Chouinard and his compatriots quickly outgrew them and began seeking out larger peaks to scale. But to go farther, Chouinard would need a car.

On this front, he was lucky. Chouinard came of age when it wasn't uncommon for young men to learn how to repair automobiles. Mechanics was the one class he took seriously in high school, and when he was 16, he scrounged together enough money to buy a broken down, two-door 1929 Ford Model A, which he learned to repair on the fly. He fixed the ruptured gas line by coating some shoelaces with soap and wrapping them around the tube. When he got a flat, he stuffed the tire with hay and kept going. That Ford had a top speed of roughly 35 miles an hour, but it got better mileage than a new Cadillac. It was so simple, Chouinard liked to say, you could fix it with duct tape and bubble gum; it was, in other words, perfect.

With a car of his own, Chouinard set off on a summer road trip. He had little experience driving, and even less living independently. Still, even though he was a minor, his parents let him roam free. The West was still sparsely populated in the years following World War II, all open road and tumbleweed. Jackrabbits raced alongside his car. Swarms of insects battered his windshield. But the Ford was reliable and kept him moving. In the Mojave Desert, he breezed past new Buicks overheating on the side of the road, their hoods popped and steam hissing out from the radiators. After a week, he arrived at the Wind River Range in Wyoming and met up with Prentice. His friend from the falconry club had taught him to rappel down cliffs and was now going to teach him and a few other newbies how to scale mountains.

Chouinard had never done any serious rock climbing at this point. Now he was staring at Gannett Peak, the tallest point in Wyoming, almost 14,000 feet of towering, ancient granite. Chouinard was enraptured. As the party prepared for their ascent, Prentice delivered a brief tutorial on the basics of rock climbing, including how to use carabiners. It was all new to most of the group, including Chouinard, and the consensus was that they should follow the gullies, traversing a relatively safe route. But Chouinard had no patience for what seemed like the easy way up and struck out on his own. Wearing Sears, Roebuck work boots and hauling his own rope, Chouinard summited Gannett Peak alone, on his first try, a remarkable feat for a novice. When he reached the summit, thunder and lightning were blowing in, and he raced down through the snowfields, outrunning the storm.

From the Wind River Range, Chouinard drove to the Tetons—a majestic series of peaks that slices across northern Wyoming. He turned up at campsites unannounced, talking his way into joining more experienced mountaineers on ever more ambitious ascents. He was a quick study and soon fell in with some of the best climbers of the day, including TM Herbert, Royal Robbins, and Tom Frost. They put up more first ascents in the Tetons. They scaled Stoney Point and Tahquitz Rocks, the site of a waterfall near Palm Springs. And they began making forays into Yosemite Valley in California, home to some of the biggest granite walls in the world.

Money was scarce, so Chouinard learned to make do with almost nothing at all. He eschewed a tent, instead curling up in a sleeping bag under the stars. If it rained, he wedged himself beneath a boulder or found a dense stand of trees for shelter. On multiday climbs, he affixed his hammock to the wall, sleeping soundly in a canvas bag hanging hundreds of feet in the air. When the weather was severe, he used an old shower curtain as an improvised tent. For several summers in the Tetons, he made his home in an abandoned incinerator on the banks of Jenny Lake, at the site of a defunct facility built by the Civilian Conservation Corps, a New Deal program that put Americans to work helping preserve lands owned by the government. While climbing in Canada, Chouinard and his fellow vagabonds would wait until other climbers set out for the day, then raid their camp and forage for whatever food they had left behind.

In the wilderness, Chouinard hunted and ate porcupines, grouse, and squirrels. To supplement his meager diet, he turned to fishing, finding utility in his boyhood hobby. He often made do on 50 cents to $1 a day, eating little more than potatoes or oatmeal. Once, on his way to the Rockies, he and his friend Ken

Weeks bought a case of dented cans of cat food, five cents apiece, and ate them over the course of a summer. Another time, he absconded to Mexico for a month, sustaining himself on tropical fruit and fish, chasing away scorpions, and using votive candles from the nearby church to wax his surfboard. "I was a dirtbag climber," he said. "I had no money whatsoever. I was eating cat food, ground squirrels. I would sneak into yards to steal fruit."

Chouinard was on the fringes of society, and he loved it. He embraced the life of the dirtbag, reveling in the knowledge that the activity he found most fulfilling—climbing up granite walls—had no social or economic value. Climbing was an act of rebellion as he saw it, from a conventional life and from society at large. While other young adults were headed off to work, Chouinard determined that his time was better spent in the woods.

Yet even as he became a fixture on the rough-edged climbing scene, Chouinard remained a quiet presence in person. At just 5 feet, 4 inches, he had none of the imposing physicality of a big-time athlete. It could be hard to catch his eye, and he often appeared dour or discontented. Rather than socialize, he often retreated to his books. Chouinard compiled a small library by transcendentalist and environmentalist authors including John Muir, Ralph Waldo Emerson, and Henry David Thoreau. He read widely, getting familiar with the works of the French alpinist Gaston Rébuffat and the Austrian climber Hermann Buhl. And while he wasn't religious, he found in this self-designed curriculum a sort of unifying worldview. Nature was to be revered. Conventional wisdom was to be ignored. The modern world was not to be trusted.

Most of all, he climbed. He scaled named peaks and unnamed hills, in fair weather and foul. During one of these summers in the Tetons, he had his first serious brush with death. It happened when he and a friend named Bob Kamps were attempting a first ascent of a formation called Crooked Thumb. Chouinard was tired. At one point, there was a particularly difficult stretch ahead, but he decided to go for it anyway. He lunged for a loose piece of rock, and the stone gave out from under his fingertips. In an instant, he plummeted 160 feet. The rope caught him and absorbed some of the shock, but he sustained a gash in his leg that cut to the bone. It was getting late, and the pair had to scramble off the wall and down through the forest, while blood leaked from his leg. The next day, he went to a doctor, who spent an hour pulling pine needles, leaves, and dirt out of his wound.

Chouinard was sidelined for a month. More than the physical injury, it was his miscalculation that gnawed at him. It wasn't just that he had gotten hurt. It was that he had made the wrong decision and almost got himself killed. For years after that, whenever Chouinard went climbing and found himself in a similar situation, with small holds or overhangs, a memory of the fall materialized. His legs shook and his hands clammed up. But he couldn't walk away from climbing altogether. Despite the shredded fingertips, throbbing muscles, and strained joints, he missed the transcendent experience of being on the wall. And while it took him three years to fully regain his confidence, he was soon at it again, this time going even higher. In climbing, Chouinard had found not just a hobby but an identity. It was more than a sport, it was a puzzle, a community, and a grueling physical challenge. It was a way of life, and it would eventually become his livelihood.

## "His Gear Stood Out"

Chouinard would do just about anything for a buck after graduating from high school. He baled hay. He earned a few dollars guiding climbs. And sometimes, he helped out his brother, Jeff, who had taken a job as the head of personal security for Howard Hughes, the eccentric aerospace engineer and film mogul. When Jeff needed extra muscle, Chouinard would lend a hand. At times, this involved trailing Hughes's various romantic interests. For another stretch, Chouinard was tasked with guarding an empty yacht Hughes wanted to buy. A notorious germophobe, Hughes wanted to make sure that no one set foot on the boat before he took possession of it, so Chouinard was there for weeks, 16 hours a day, mostly napping in his car. In between odd jobs, Chouinard flirted with higher education, taking a couple years of geography classes at a junior college in the San Fernando Valley, but he never graduated. It was hardly the makings of a real career.

His vocation, as it turned out, was at his fingertips. As Chouinard became a more proficient climber, he began using pitons: metal spikes that could be driven into cracks in a wall and used to secure a rope. With a knifelike blade coming to a point at one end, and a ring on the other, pitons are the simplest pieces of hardware. Climbers hammered pitons into cracks as they made their way up the wall, attached a carabiner, secured their rope, and repeated the maneuver, making their way up ever-larger walls one placement at a time. But as Chouinard and his climbing partners attempted bigger feats, they discovered that their gear had its limitations. First, there was the issue of weight. A multiday ascent up a big wall in Yosemite could require dozens of pitons, and hauling that much hardware was exhausting. Smaller, lighter ones would be desirable, if they could be found. Then there was the matter of durability. At the time, most pitons were being imported from Europe and were made with relatively soft metals. When they were hammered into Yosemite's towering walls, they got bent out of shape and were impossible to reuse. Ultimately, Chouinard decided he needed to make his own gear. At the very least, doing so would give him control of the equipment he was counting on to save his life. Perhaps he could make some money at it, too.

In 1957, still living with his parents in Burbank, Chouinard went to a junkyard and bought a used 138-pound anvil and a coal-fired forge. He brought them home, procured some hammers and tongs, and with his father's help, converted a chicken coop in the backyard into a workshop. "Crazy as it was, his parents were supportive from the very beginning," said Karen Frishman, a long-time friend of the family. "They didn't understand what he was doing, but there was never any sense that they wished he wouldn't do this."

Chouinard knew his way around tools from his days rebuilding the Ford, but he had never pounded steel before. So once again, he turned to books. Just as he had when he was reading up on falconry, he went to the library and checked out a volume on blacksmithing. Before long, Chouinard was crafting his first pitons. He would heat the coal forge to 400 degrees Fahrenheit, roasting steel splinters until they glowed the color of molten lava. Once they could get no hotter, he would extract them with a pair of iron tongs and place them on the anvil, then hammer them into the precise shape he desired. For raw materials, he improvised— the first pitons he made were fashioned from an old steel blade he salvaged from a harvester. It was an innovation born from necessity, and it wouldn't be the last time Chouinard repurposed an item. For the rest of his career, he was constantly on the lookout for unusual materials that might serve a new purpose.

Chouinard had some guidance as he learned this new craft. A few other local climbers were making their own gear, among them John Salathé, a mystic Swiss climber who scaled walls to get closer to God. Salathé had more or less invented the reusable piton and

25

passed on some of his wisdom to Chouinard, who proved a quick study. Once he had grown comfortable with the anvil, Chouinard could make two steel pitons an hour. And once he had tested his gear—using it on his own ascents of Californian cliffs—he began selling the pitons for $1.50 each. This was substantially more than the imported European ones, which went for 15 to 30 cents apiece and were made of iron, a softer metal. But Chouinard was chan-neling a virtue he had inherited from his father. "He taught me that when you buy a tool, you buy the absolute best tool you can get and keep it for the rest of your life," Chouinard said. "That's much better than buying a cheap tool and having it break, buying another one, having that break."

Chouinard started making the pitch to his fellow climbers that his gear was worth the extra expense and quickly won some converts. His pitons were stiffer, so they could be removed with-out getting deformed. And because one piton could be reused many times, it was an economical investment. Moreover, on lon-ger climbs, it wasn't practical to carry dozens of pitons up a wall. Better, climbers realized, to carry just a handful that you could reuse over and over again. As his pitons began to sell, Choui-nard learned an important lesson that would inform his whole career: if he made the very best product, consumers would pay a premium. Initially, this was true with an extremely specialized crowd, a small band of extreme climbers. They needed the best gear; their lives depended on it. But as his market expanded from the niche to the mainstream, the same principle held fast. It might cost more to make quality jackets and sweaters and bags, but the customers who cared about functionality and durability would spend more if the craftsmanship was there.

Not wanting to let work get in the way of his recreation, Choui-nard took his piton production on the road, packing up his anvil and supplies in the back of his car and setting up shop wherever he happened to be. More often than not, that was by the beach. By the mid-'50s Chouinard had taken up surfing. Like falconry, free diving, and rock climbing, surfing was a niche sport at the time. But the waves were intoxicating, and Chouinard taught himself how to ride them one wipeout at a time. Since new surfboards weren't widely available, Chouinard had to make his own gear for this new pursuit as well. One day he dropped by General Veneer, a flooring store in Los Angeles, spent a few dollars on balsa wood planks, came home, and shaped himself a surfboard. With a board in hand, he drove up and down the California coast looking for waves, camping near the beach, then pulling out his tools to work for a few hours each day. As his inventory grew, he would stockpile the gear for months, waiting until big-wall climbing season, when he would venture into the mountains and sell his wares to fellow climbers.

While Chouinard's ambitions were growing, it was hard scraping out a living $1.50 at a time. Fortunately, as he began tinkering with new pieces of climbing gear, he stumbled his way into another market. After the piton, the next breakthrough came when Chouinard endeavored to make a lighter carabiner—a reusable clip that is an indispensable part of a climber's ensemble. But making carabiners would be more complicated than pounding out spikes on the anvil. To make the cast metal clips, he needed a special piece of machinery from Alcoa, the industrial manufacturer. So, sporting a full beard, sandals, and well-worn Levi's, he went to the company's offices in Los Angeles and bought a custom aluminum forging die, paying for it with $825.35 he borrowed from his parents. His brother Jeff was skeptical of the investment. "I thought, 'What kind of a business is a forge, for God's sake?'" Yet in Chouinard's hands, the forging die proved profitable. With a drill press and a grinder, he set to work making his own carabiners, one by one. They were a hit with other climbers, and before long, Chouinard had recruited a few buddies to help him in the production process, and they were selling the carabiners as fast as they could make them.

Against all odds, Chouinard was becoming a businessman. He had no interest in running a company. Inasmuch as he had a job, he considered himself a blacksmith. Nor was the work particularly lucrative. He was making hardly any money, with a total profit margin of just 1 percent a year. Yet Chouinard couldn't help himself. He needed the pitons and the carabiners. He was a savvy enough climber to know how to improve on the existing gear and was a skilled enough craftsman to make the improvements himself. It may have been a small operation, but Chouinard was making an impression. While there were fewer than a thousand serious climbers in the United States, Chouinard made most of them his customers, one by one. "Chouinard's equipment was that much better," said Royal Robbins, the world's finest climber at the time. "His gear stood out because of its inventiveness and its quality."

The more audacious Chouinard became as a mountaineer, the more innovative he became as a designer. In 1960, Chouinard tried to scale Kat Pinnacle, a formation in Yosemite National Park, with his climbing partner Tom Frost. As they made their way up, they found that the cracks on the wall were too narrow to accommodate traditional pitons. They needed something smaller, thinner, and sturdier than anything on the market. Not even Chouinard's best pitons sufficed. After giving it a good try, the men aborted their climb.

They soon came back with a postage stamp–sized piton they had fashioned by taking a power hacksaw blade, breaking off the end, and fitting their sling into the blade's hole. They made it most of the way up, but as Chouinard attempted to hammer the blade into a crack near the top, it shattered into pieces, forcing them to abort the climb again. The failure offered an additional insight: this piton needed to be made not of the everyday steel Chouinard usually used, but of an exceptionally durable alloy. That led Chouinard and Frost to collaborate and design an entirely new piece of gear. Just half an inch long, composed of chrome-nickel steel, and the width of a razor blade, they called it the Realized Ultimate Reality Piton, or RURP, and put it into production.

The RURPs started selling briskly, and quite by accident, Chouinard found himself managing material costs, profit margins, and inventory. He also found a new business partner in Frost. And yet in his relentless quest for constant improvement, his friends saw in him something more profound. "A poetic soul, Chouinard really rather disdains the analytical mind, for he hates to see beautiful things ripped and torn," Robbins said. "He has the kind of mind which would make a good artist but a poor chess player. Maddeningly creative, Chouinard has invented more techniques and devices in climbing than anyone I know."

Out on the walls, Chouinard's reputation was starting to precede him. Many climbers, hearing stories about Yvon Chouinard, thought he was a woman until they met him, figuring his name was spelled "Yvonne." They were surprised when Chouinard, brawny and sometimes sporting a beard, appeared and started darting up difficult lines. They were equally amazed when Chouinard opened the trunk of his car to reveal a cache of handmade pitons and carabiners.

As the seasons passed and he kept putting up new routes, Chouinard became a fixture at Camp 4 in Yosemite National Park, the epicenter of the climbing subculture. Yet even there, he was an outsider among outsiders. While others paid the requisite fees to pitch their tents at the prepared campsites, Chouinard and his friends slept among the boulders in the woods after they had overstayed their two-week permit, calling themselves the Valley Cong, a reference to the rebel Viet Cong forces in Vietnam.

It all went to his head for a while. Other climbers remember Chouinard coming off as elitist. He had little patience for neophytes or weak athletes, and at times equated physical fitness with moral superiority. Keen to preserve Yosemite in its Eden-like state, he at one point proposed limiting climbing in the valley to only the best, creating an invitation-only Yosemite Climbing Club. Only those with "outstanding climbing ability" and with an interest in "raising the standards" would be allowed in. It was impractical, of course, but it spoke to his belief that under the right circumstances, it might be possible to limit the impact of humanity on the natural world and protect wild places from overdevelopment. Decades later, a similar spirit would animate his conservation efforts around the globe.

More than his gear, however, it was his climbing that brought Chouinard renown. With a friend named Fred Beckey, he notched a series of difficult first ascents in Canada in 1961, including new routes on Mount Edith Cavell in the Rockies, Mount Sir Donald in the Selkirks, and the South Howser Tower in the Bugaboos. In June of 1962, Chouinard and another excellent climber, TM Herbert, attempted a new line up the north face of Sentinel Rock, a regal peak in Yosemite that looms above Camp 4. The pair made it a good bit of the way up but ran out of bolts and had to retreat. Three months later they returned, and—using those first pitons Chouinard had forged from the harvester blade—this time they made it. It was an audacious first ascent and is now known as the Chouinard-Herbert route.

Between climbing, surfing, and blacksmithing, Chouinard developed a rhythm all his own. He spent the winters hammering away in California, crafting pitons and carabiners when he wasn't catching waves. When it began to warm up in the spring, he hit the road, selling his wares out of the back of his car. When he was sold out, he ditched the car and went to the Tetons. Then he found his way to the Shawangunks in New York and finally hitchhiked back to California for another winter with the anvil.

Although the postwar boom years in America were a moment of breakneck technological progress, Chouinard wanted nothing to do with it. New plastics were revolutionizing what could be made and what things were made of. NASA was sending men to space and, ultimately, to the moon. The most promising companies in the country were those discovering new chemicals, new synthetic materials, and new gadgets and putting all that newness to work. But at this moment of limitless innovation, with the future being invented before his eyes, what did Chouinard do? He went back to the Bronze Age.

## "Destroying Our Home Planet"

It was the fall of 1962, and Chouinard had to get home. He had been in upstate New York for months, climbing the Shawangunks. Now it was time to return to California and resume work at the anvil. But he didn't have a ride. A solution presented itself when he heard about a 1952 Pontiac that a car-delivery service needed driven to New Mexico. He signed up for the job but quickly discovered he had a problem: the car was a lemon. It sputtered its way across the country and was barely running when he got it to Albuquerque. There, the woman who took possession of it accused him of conning her by delivering a busted car and reported him to the police.

Chouinard and his traveling companion, Chuck Pratt, were jailed for 72 hours in Grants, New Mexico, kept in a cell where the concrete floors were covered in vomit. Once released, they were briefly taken in by a Christian rescue mission. From there, he and Pratt train hopped west to Winslow, Arizona, where they were arrested again, this time for vagrancy. They spent 18 days in jail, each in their own 5-by-6-foot cell. On the days when Chouinard was able to join a work detail, he helped operate a garbage truck and foraged for scraps of food. Finally, Chouinard was released and made his way home, only to learn that he'd been drafted by the army.

With his congenital aversion to authority and an abiding pacifism cultivated during his time in nature, Chouinard tried to get out of it. He had a mild heart arrhythmia and asked a doctor to write the draft board a letter excusing him from military service. The doctor refused. When he was summoned for his physical, he drank a bottle of soy sauce, hoping it would cause his blood pressure to spike. Instead, it made him vomit. The doctor saw through the ruse and gave him the all-clear, and Chouinard, an antiauthoritarian vagabond who could barely tolerate a classroom, was headed to basic training.

He was sent off to Fort Ord, in California. There, he was told that if he won a physical fitness competition among 200 of his fellow draftees, he would be granted a three-day leave. He wasn't the most muscular man on the base, nor the most patriotic. But his time in the mountains had made him fit and determined, and he won the competition through sheer force of will, just so he could have a few days to himself to climb. Back home for a spell before being deployed, Chouinard married his girlfriend, Carol Lamb, who was known as "Peanut." It was a hasty wedding, and the couple spent almost no time together before Chouinard was shipped to Huntsville, Alabama.

Chouinard joined the army during a brief window of relative peace. The Korean War was over, and Americans had not yet begun fighting in Vietnam. Because he had listed his profession as blacksmith upon enlisting, he was assigned to be a mechanic on guided-missile systems. After a few months, he was on his way to a base in Korea. It was difficult to get any leave, so Chouinard began acting oddly and causing trouble, going on hunger strikes and failing to salute his superiors, stopping just short of getting thrown in the brig. He finally became enough of a headache that he was given a simple task—turning a generator on in the morning and off at night. The rest of the day, Chouinard wandered off base and found granite walls to climb around Seoul. He had his climbing gear shipped over from the States and made friends with local climbers who kept a change of civilian clothes for him. Before long, Chouinard was putting up first ascents in the nearby hills. "It was almost like not being in the army," he said. When he did have to work, he tried to use it to his advantage. Scouring the base's library, he found books on engineering and metallurgy, trying to better understand mechanical engineering and machine shops. He was preparing for the day he was discharged, eager to get back to his anvil and start improving his craft.

Eventually the army sent Chouinard back to San Francisco, where he was assigned to a post in the Presidio, a sprawling base overlooking the Pacific Ocean, and told to maintain a baseball diamond. It was not particularly demanding work, but Chouinard found a way to get out of this assignment, too, this time with the help of a man who would become Chouinard's best friend, professional foil, and sometimes rival: Doug Tompkins.

Tompkins was in many ways Chouinard's opposite. The descendant of pilgrims who arrived in America on the *Mayflower*, Tompkins was raised in New York City by doting parents who ran an upscale antique furniture business. He grew up helping his father pilot a private plane and learned to read navigational maps while he was still a boy. Whereas Chouinard inhabited the fringes of polite society, Tompkins was born into the country's upper crust and was fluent in the language of money, business, and power.

Yet in other ways, the men were kindred spirits. Like Chouinard, Tompkins was a rebellious youth and was also bookish and athletic. And by the time he reached his 20s, he too was a dirtbag. He first met Chouinard while climbing in the Shawangunks and hanging out with a group of unruly climbers who called themselves the Vulgarian Mountain Club and had a reputation for climbing in the nude.

Over the next 50 years, the lives and careers of Chouinard and Tompkins ran in parallel, intertwining, aligning, and sometimes diverging. As Chouinard went on to build Patagonia, Tompkins founded one of the most successful clothing brands of the '80s, Esprit. As Chouinard got rich, Tompkins got richer. And as Chouinard began to dabble in conservation and environmental activism, Tompkins went all in, buying up large parcels of land in South America and waging fierce political battles to create national parks. Tompkins would bail out Patagonia in its darkest hour and ultimately marry the woman who ran Patagonia during its formative years. And in the last years of Chouinard's life, he would draw inspiration from Tompkins as he considered what to do with his own fortune.

All the while, Tompkins and Chouinard egged each other on, testing out new ideas and pushing their physical limits. While their values were deeply aligned, they had profoundly different views about how to run a business and how to spend their winnings. Tompkins was a maximalist, looking to grow his companies, make a killing, and live like a king. Chouinard was a minimalist, opting to refrain from excessive growth, proceed cautiously when it came to financial matters, and live like a pauper. It was a friendship that made a dent in the universe, and to fully understand the story of Chouinard and Patagonia, it's essential to understand the story of Tompkins and Esprit.

At this early stage in their relationship, however, with both men living in San Francisco, Tompkins mostly helped Chouinard play hooky. On many a morning, Tompkins called up Chouinard's superior officer at the Presidio and pretended to be a general, demanding that Chouinard get to the library in 10 minutes. Tompkins would then swing by on his motorcycle and pick up Chouinard, and the two would spend the day roaming the Bay Area. They would drive across the Golden Gate Bridge and into the golden hills of Marin County, gazing out to the Pacific Ocean from the wild cliffs of Northern California.

In long talks on these day trips, they shared a foundational epiphany that would shape both their lives. Humans, they realized, were messing up the environment. With overdevelopment, industry, and the mundane but resource-intensive work of simply getting by, everyone on Earth was playing a role in the ecosystem's destruction, and everyone, Chouinard and Tompkins came to believe, had a responsibility to make things better. "Early on, we recognized that we humans were destroying our home planet," Chouinard said, "and that each of us, in our own way, was responsible to protect and restore the wild nature that we loved."

# CHAPTER 2

# Dirtbags

## "Modern Yosemite Climbing"

Discharged from the army, his marriage to Peanut a bust, Chouinard returned to the one place that made sense: his anvil. Back
home in Burbank, he brought a new level of organization to his
nascent business, hiring a handful of his climbing friends to help
with production and shipping. With a wider array of pitons and
carabiners on offer, he made his first catalog—a one-sheet mimeographed price list. At the bottom of the sheet, a note cautioned
potential buyers not to anticipate prompt customer service during
the climbing season: "Don't expect speedy delivery in the months
of May, June, July, August and September."

It was an unorthodox approach to business, but it worked.
Chouinard's gear was unsurpassed in quality, and climbing afficio-
nados were willing to pay up. Yet even as Chouinard began to scale
up his boutique operation, an emerging global supply chain was
beginning to put pressure on domestic companies. Cheap foreign
labor, new trade routes, and improved logistics began to make
overseas manufacturing more attractive. Back in his hometown of
Lisbon, the Worumbo Woolen Mill shut its doors 100 years after
it had opened. The mill's owner, J. P. Stevens & Co., Inc., said it

was no longer economically viable to compete against cheap imports from abroad. Globalization had arrived in the once-bucolic woods of Maine, and some 591 people were out of work overnight. It was the beginning of a sweeping transformation in American manufacturing that would upend global commerce and, though he didn't yet know it, shape much of Chouinard's own career. In the immediate, however, Chouinard was unconcerned with foreign trade. He was just trying to scale bigger walls.

One of the rare climbs that got Chouinard nervous came when Robbins proposed an audacious ascent up the North American Wall of El Capitan, a sheer granite slab that is one of the most striking features in Yosemite Valley. The North American Wall, so named because it is roughly the shape of the continent, is a flat sheet of black diorite with perilously few holds. Half a century before Chouinard attempted his climb, John Muir wrote reverently of the formation: "It is 3,300 feet high, a plain, severely simple, glacier-sculpted face of granite, the end of one of the most compact and enduring of the mountain ridges, unrivaled in height and breadth and flawless strength." Along with Robbins and Chouinard, Tom Frost and Chuck Pratt joined the team, setting out on October 22, 1964, for what they knew would be a multiday ascent. As they took their first steps, Chouinard saw a soaring peregrine falcon illuminated by the morning sun. On the valley floor below, Salathé and other climbers watched the quartet begin their journey.

It was tough going from the start. Chouinard was fresh out of the army but complained he wasn't in great shape. Frost fell on the second pitch when a flake of granite broke away. Conditions on the wall were inhospitable. The men were hauling 200 pounds of food and water, plus bushels of gear hand-crafted by Chouinard. They slept in hammocks that hung from the wall, resting on ledges just 16 inches wide when they could find them. They sustained themselves on bread, cheese, and salami, and rationed a quart and a half of water each day. At times, the rock was too hot to touch. After five days, Chouinard's fingers were swollen, and his wrists were sore from the incessant hammering. On the sixth day, a TV crew in a news helicopter hovered off the wall and the expedition made the nightly news. Chouinard later learned that his parents had seen the segment, and for the first time finally understood what their son meant when he said he was a rock climber.

A week into the ascent, Chouinard was running out of steam. "Two meals a day of one square inch of salami, a tiny square of cheese and a handful of gorp is just not enough," he wrote in his journal while on the wall. That night, it rained and snowed, soaking them in their hammocks. Robbins worried that Chouinard was in over his head. But on October 30, after some close calls, Chouinard reached the summit, with the other three following close behind. It was the first ascent of the North American Wall, and a remarkable test of the men's fortitude. "We learned that our minds and bodies never stopped adjusting to the situation," Chouinard reflected not long after the climb. "We were able to live and work and sleep in comparative comfort in a vertical environment. When the food and water ran low, we found that we could obtain an enormous amount of energy from eating just ten raisins. We reached the summit feeling as if we could go on for another ten days."

At the time, it was widely regarded as the hardest climb ever done, and Chouinard used the experience to describe a new approach to the sport of rock climbing. "The new philosophy is characterized by small expeditions going into remote areas and trying new and extremely difficult routes with a minimum of equipment, no support parties nor fixed ropes to the ground; living for days and weeks at a time on the climb and leaving no signs of their presence behind," he wrote in the *American Alpine Journal* in 1965. "This purer form of climbing takes more of a complete effort, more personal adjustment, and involves more risk, but being more idealistic, the rewards are greater."

Another essay Chouinard wrote at the time, "Modern Yosemite Climbing," went even further in articulating his emerging worldview. Coming in at more than 4,000 words, the article was at once technical and poetic, practical and profound. He offered tips on how to insert pitons into Yosemite's notoriously confounding granite cracks. "Just why is Yosemite climbing so different?" he wrote. "Why does it have techniques, ethics and equipment all of its own? The basic reason lies in the nature of the rock itself. Nowhere else in the world is the rock so exfoliated, so glacier-polished, and so devoid of handholds. All of the climbing lines follow vertical crack systems. Every piton crack, every handhold is a vertical one. Special techniques and equipment have evolved through absolute necessity."

The essay went on to document the notoriously unwelcoming attitudes of the local climbers, including Chouinard himself. It was a cliquey, standoffish crowd that had little patience for newcomers or amateurs. "The native climbers are a proud bunch of individuals; they are proud of their valley and its climbs and standards," Chouinard wrote. "Climbers have left the Valley saying that they will never return because of the way they were treated by the native climbers."

With "Modern Yosemite Climbing," Chouinard was trying to reconcile his passions and his ideals, his business interests and his affection for nature. He was reinforcing his bona fides as one of the preeminent climbers of his day, establishing himself as one of the sport's most astute in-house chroniclers, and exploring his own conflicted relationship with the valley. "There have been times when I have felt ashamed to be a Yosemite climber, and there are times when I feel as if I truly hate the place," he wrote. "But then there are times when I should rather be there than anywhere else in the world. If at times I hate the place, it is probably because I love it so. It is a strange, passionate love that I feel for this Valley. More than just a climbing area, it is a way of life."

## "Oh My God, I Am a Businessman"

In between sessions hammering away at the anvil and weeks of climbing in Yosemite, Chouinard began spending more time in San Francisco with Doug Tompkins, who had started a company called The North Face. In the beginning, The North Face was little more than a small storefront with an eclectic assortment of outdoor gear and knickknacks. But Tompkins was tuned into the zeitgeist, and the outpost quickly became a sort of mecca for climbers, Beats, vagabonds, and hippies, the odd lot Jack Kerouac envisioned when he wrote about a "rucksack revolution" in *The Dharma Bums*.

The North Face was located in the North Beach neighborhood. Nearby was the Condor Club, a strip joint. Across the street was City Lights, the legendary bookstore founded by the poet Lawrence Ferlinghetti, which served as the nerve center for the Beat generation, publishing works by Allen Ginsberg and drawing the likes of Kerouac and Neal Cassady to its dusty shelves. The crackle of rebellion was in the air, with protests against the Vietnam War spilling into the streets, the Free Speech movement blossoming at nearby UC Berkeley, and the dirtbag climbers were swept up in the countercultural moment.

Inside The North Face, green carpet covered the floor, and the walls were clad in wood from old barns. The shelves were stocked with assorted outdoor gear including climbing ropes and tents, Chouinard's pitons and carabiners, reindeer skin rugs, fisherman's sweaters and bikinis, which Tompkins's wife, Susie Russell, sold to her friends. Chouinard stored boxes of his excess inventory in the basement, where he and Tompkins retreated to smoke the occasional joint. Ginsberg and other Beats hung around the store, gaping at the large photographs of Yosemite Valley that adorned the walls. Once, Janis Joplin picked Tompkins up in a yellow Porsche and sped off.

The apotheosis of The North Face social scene came on October 26, 1966, when Tompkins, just 23 years old at the time, threw a party at the store. The Grateful Dead, then an up-and-coming San Francisco band, played a set. Joan Baez roamed the crowd. The Hells Angels provided security. The party was notable enough to be mentioned in the local papers. "What a collection of people," read an article in the *San Francisco Examiner*. "There were nattily dressed individuals rubbing shoulders with bearded, long-haired and sandal-clad beatniks from the neighborhood."

Tompkins capitalized on the buzz generated by the party to expand The North Face, opening two more stores in the nearby cities of Berkeley and Palo Alto. He had a knack for business and seemed destined to succeed at just about whatever he set his mind to. "I've always considered Doug to be the most intelligent, street-smart person I've ever run across," said Dick Dorworth, a longtime friend. "You could throw Doug naked out in the desert with a stick, and within ten days, he'd have an empire going." But while a part of Tompkins was animated by visions of expanding the business and building an empire, he had already grown restless and came to believe that running a retail chain was an insufficiently large canvas for his swelling ambitions.

So, in 1967, Tompkins sold The North Face for just $40,000. In the years that followed, The North Face would go on to be a co-lossal hit, growing into a reputable outdoor apparel manufacturer and ultimately becoming part of the fashion behemoth VF Corporation. But Tompkins, who founded the brand, walked away with only a pittance. He put half his meager proceeds into his wife Susie's fledgling clothing business, Plain Jane. With the other half, he hoped to make an adventure film similar to *The Endless Summer*, the surf documentary that had just broken through to the mainstream with its sepia-toned depictions of halcyon beach days.

Chouinard, meanwhile, took a decidedly different tack with his company. In 1965, he moved his workshop out of the chicken coop in his parents' backyard and rented a shack nearby for $60 a month. But the commute from Burbank to the ocean, where he was chasing waves each day, was tedious, and the next year he moved the company to Ventura, a sleepy beachside community an hour's drive north of Los Angeles. Ventura was just right for Chouinard; it had a laid-back vibe and great waves in the winter, when all the best climbing spots were covered in snow. Chouinard rented a small cabin on the beach with thin walls but a perfect view of the swell. He set up the new offices of what was now an official company, Chouinard Equipment for Alpinists, at 235 West Santa Clara Street, in a rented tin shed.

The shed, next to a former slaughterhouse and near the railroad tracks, had once been used by a pair of pioneering surfboard makers, Karl Pope and Tom Morey, and soon became the nexus for Ventura's climbers and craftsmen. Their work spilled into the rutted driveway, and the ragtag band of craftsmen used salvaged driftwood and tree stumps for furniture, working shirtless in the sun, their tattered clothes held together with patches. Bottles of cheap Bohemia beer littered their workplace, and the smell of marijuana wafted through the ocean air. A cacophony of industrial noise—metal on metal, hammer strikes, roaring fires—drowned out the sounds of Simon and Garfunkel and the Beatles playing on a portable radio. Sparks flew, and the place hummed with industriousness. But the whole shop could be shuttered in minutes if the surf was up, the blacksmiths racing to the beach when the waves were good. Chouinard lived in the shop for a few months each year, camping out on the loading dock when the owners of his rental cabin came back for the summer. When he needed a break from all of it, he went to Tijuana, Mexico, and took in a few bullfights, or went on extended climbing trips in Yosemite and the Tetons.

As the company grew, Chouinard brought on a formal business partner: his climbing buddy Tom Frost. Consumer appetite for Chouinard Equipment's offerings was growing fast as climbing became more popular, and the gear was getting more complex. Before long, Chouinard could no longer keep up with demand while making everything by hand; he needed to automate the process, using sophisticated dies and new machines. That was where Frost, who also happened to be a Stanford-educated aeronautical engineer, came in. It was an ideal match, a partnership that moved seamlessly from the walls of Yosemite to the workshop in Ventura, at least at first. "Designing was as much fun as the climbing," Frost said. "Yvon was the idea man, and I was the engineer."

Chouinard and Frost expanded their operations, leaning on a loose-knit group of itinerant climbers for labor and assembling an ad hoc workforce that included Chouinard's nephew, Vincent Stanley, a few Mexican craftsmen, an Argentinian toolmaker, and a handful of Korean garment workers. Legendary alpinists like Don Whillans would swing by, earn some money, and move on. Jeff Chouinard, who once employed his younger brother as a guard for Howard Hughes, started working for the company as a production manager. And a pair of local siblings, Roger McDivitt and his younger sister, Kris, who lived a few doors down from the beachside cabin that Chouinard was renting, joined the fray. Kris, still in high school and usually barefoot, started as a packer for Chouinard Equipment, sorting pitons and shipping out climbing gear. Roger, with a degree in economics, started in the blacksmith shop but swiftly gained more responsibility after he returned from Vietnam with three Purple Hearts. Together, this motley assemblage made up Chouinard's first real workforce.

The first year, the business did a couple thousand dollars in sales. It then doubled annually for the next five years. But margins were slim. The best Chouinard ever managed in those early days was a profit of about 2.5 percent, hardly a lucrative business, especially in a relatively small market. Complicating matters was the fact that the designs were evolving quickly, meaning the company often had to discard tools and manufacturing equipment after just a year as they became obsolete.

The company's offerings expanded in tandem with Chouinard's quixotic pursuits. During a 1966 trip to Chamonix, France, he went ice climbing in the Alps, but came away from the expedition dissatisfied with his equipment. The ice axe he had been using was not particularly good at cutting away steps, nor did it serve as a sturdy enough anchor; when he put weight on the axe's straight pick, it popped out of the ice. Confident he could improve the design, Chouinard tracked down an axe factory in France and paid a steel forger to make him a curved pick that was 55 centimeters (about 22 inches) long. This served as the basis for what, after some improvements from Frost, Chouinard Equipment soon began marketing as its "piolet," the French word for an ice axe. With deep serrations in the blade, the ability to hold more weight, and a curved shape that followed the arc of the arm that swung it into the ice, it was a classic Chouinard bit of design, refining a utilitarian object to make it even better at doing the one thing it was designed to do. Despite the improvements, sales were slow at first. But after a few seasons of Chouinard and his pals using the hammers to scale frozen waterfalls, word got around the climbing community, and the orders began pouring in. Soon the Chouinard-Frost ice axe was being manufactured by an Italian cutlery firm, and the company was selling them for $60 apiece.

The ice axe was a breakthrough not only as a product but also as a model for how Chouinard would make his mark in the years ahead. He hadn't invented an entirely new tool. Rather, by identifying opportunities for improvements and focusing on design, he had turned an ordinary object into something extraordinary. And in doing that, he had made a profit. Helmed by the most unlikely entrepreneur and making the most obscure items, Chouinard Equipment was, against all odds, becoming a real company. No one was more surprised by this than its proprietor. Chouinard still considered businessmen to be "greaseballs." That is, until he woke up one day and realized he was one of them. He was going to have to learn an entirely new set of skills, and just as he had when he needed to understand falconry and blacksmithing, he went back to the library. This time, he checked out books that explained how to run a company.

## "Viva Los Fun Hogs"

With a chunk of cash burning a hole in his pocket after selling The North Face, Doug Tompkins was restless and bored. One day, he came across a mountaineering magazine that featured a photograph of a striking summit he had never before seen. It was Cerro

Fitz Roy, an arrowhead of granite lurching out of the Andes in Argentina, and Tompkins was instantly obsessed. Wider and more imposing than the surrounding peaks, it was named after Robert FitzRoy, the captain of Charles Darwin's ship, the HMS *Beagle*. Tompkins got on his motorcycle, raced from San Francisco to Ventura, and showed Chouinard the photograph. They should drop what they were doing, Tompkins insisted, drive to the tip of South America, to the land known as Patagonia, and scale that mountain.

Chouinard was familiar with the peak. Earlier that year, he had read an account of the first ascent of Fitz Roy by Lionel Terray, a French climber, who had described hellacious conditions and said Fitz Roy was the one mountain he never wanted to scale again. Others would have been scared off, but Chouinard took it as a challenge. He was also hankering for adventure. Patagonia, from what he had heard, was largely unexplored, the closest he might get to a real-life Shangri-la. Encompassing an enormous swath of Chile and Argentina, it was bisected by the Andes and marked by relatively dry grasslands and deserts to the East, with glacial fjords, turquoise rivers, and verdant rainforests on the coast, all of it undeveloped and sparsely inhabited.

Chouinard agreed to the adventure at once. Chouinard Equipment would be alright without him, he figured. Frost and his wife, Doreen, who helped with the books, could look after the company while he was away. Tompkins's departure was more complicated. His wife Susie had just given birth to their second child and was working to expand Plain Jane, which was showing early signs of success. Nevertheless, Tompkins told Susie that he was going to make his own version of *The Endless Summer* and won her reluctant blessing. Fueled by a maniacal drive to ascend the world's most treacherous mountains, Tompkins, and to a lesser degree Chouinard, were spiritual descendants of George Mallory, the

British climber who in 1923 was asked why he wanted to climb Mount Everest and replied, "Because it is there." (Mallory died the next year while climbing Everest.)

With Chouinard on board, Tompkins set about recruiting others for the journey. He roped in Lito Tejada-Flores, a Bolivian skier and climber he knew from skiing in California. A native Spanish speaker, Tejada-Flores was an adept photographer who Tompkins designated as the trip's documentarian, entrusting him with a hand-cranked 16-millimeter Bolex movie camera. He also enlisted Dick Dorworth, an accomplished downhill skier who had bonded with Tompkins the year before, when the men had dropped LSD and driven through the night from Sun Valley, Idaho, to Reno, Nevada. Dorworth had been to Chile before. In 1963, he set the world speed skiing record on a mountain there, going 106 miles per hour. But by 1968 he was pursuing more conventional aspirations and studying to become an English professor—that is, until he met Tompkins. The day after their acid-fueled drive, Dorworth went to the head of the English department and quit.

Tompkins got his hands on a well-used, white 1965 Ford Econoline van. Chouinard built shelves and a sleeping platform in the back. They crammed in as many skis, climbing ropes, carabiners, tents, wetsuits, fishing rods, and clothes as they could, and affixed four surfboards to the roof. Besides trying to make Tompkins's movie, the goal was to "hog fun," and Tompkins christened the trip "The 1968 California Fun Hogs Expedition to Patagonia." The phrase stuck, and Susie Tompkins sewed them a flag that they would fly from the Fitz Roy summit, if they made it. In black block letters on red fabric, it read: "VIVA LOS FUN HOGS. Patagonia '68." Then on July 24, they gathered in the parking lot outside the tin shed that housed Chouinard Equipment and started driving south.

A week later, they had made it to Mazatlán, Mexico, and were surfing perfect breaks on empty beaches. They passed through Mexico City, which was humming with energy as it prepared to host the Olympic Games. Along the way, Tejada-Flores did his best to capture footage that Tompkins could turn into a film. But with a faulty camera and an inexperienced crew, he struggled to make anything of professional quality.

From Mexico, they navigated endless dirt roads, aiming for Argentina. They were held at gunpoint by suspicious Guatemalan soldiers and waylaid in Costa Rica when a volcano erupted. They loaded the van, their gear, and themselves onto a freighter ship to get around the Darien Gap, which is impassable in a vehicle. After that, they hung around in Colombia, where Chouinard dove into a shallow river and hurt his neck, an injury that he would deal with for decades. They surfed in Ecuador, then sold their surfboards in Peru, and were joined by Chris Jones, one of England's best climbers. Along the way, they crammed in some skiing, trekking up Volcan Llaima, a 12,000-foot-tall active volcano at the tip of the continent. As Tejada-Flores filmed, Tompkins and Dorworth flew down the slopes, smoke from the crater rising behind them. Chouinard was tasked with carrying 40 pounds of equipment down from the summit to their base camp, at 5,000 feet. Strapped into skis for only the second time in his life and loaded up with gear, he tumbled most of the way down.

The trip was almost derailed at the Argentinian border. In order to drive into the country, new entrants had to have proof of their vehicle's deed. The Fun Hogs had no such paperwork. Tompkins suggested a solution: they went to an office supply store in Puerto Montt, Chile, bought a rubber stamp for $3, and made an official-looking document. It worked. They sailed through the border, then sold the van in Bariloche. They had been traveling for almost four months and had finally reached the heart of Patagonia.

Among the most remote places on Earth, Patagonia remained largely isolated from the rest of South America well into the 20th century and remains miraculous to this day. Glacier fields flow into lapis-blue lakes. Snowcapped peaks abound. Active volcanos belch smoke. Geothermal vents hiss steam. And an infinite network of clear rivers weaves through grasslands, ancient forests, and rocky, lunar landscapes. As the cone of the South American continent narrows and approaches Antarctica, the peaks become sharper, granite knives thrusting into the sky. And there, near the foot of the Andes, is Fitz Roy.

Before attempting their climb, Tompkins had business to attend to back in San Francisco. Plain Jane, which would later become Esprit, was having a breakout moment, and Susie needed help. One of the company's dresses had been featured in a department store ad in the *San Francisco Chronicle*, and sales were suddenly booming. The department store ordered hundreds of dresses, and Susie and her business partner, Jane Tise, were scrambling to ramp up production. Doug flew home, leaving Chouinard, Dorworth, Tejada-Flores, and Jones fidgety and annoyed, while he helped Susie find new partners for sourcing and sewing. Three weeks later, Tompkins returned to Bariloche, eager to complete the trip. The men made a final push south, traversing Route 40, a barren highway that flanks the eastern edge of the Andes, and finally reached their mountain.

Only two teams had made it to the top of Fitz Roy before the Fun Hogs showed up, and they soon understood why. The weather was relentlessly awful, with storms creating perennial squall. Their tents were too flimsy to withstand the winds, so the men dug an improvised shelter into a wall of ice. It was close enough to the summit that when the time came, they would be able to make their push. But it was deep in the wild, far from any trace of civilization.

They spent 31 days in the snow cave, brooding and bored, waiting for the weather to break so they could climb. Chouinard cut open his knee with an axe while trying to hack some ice to melt, and as a result lay mostly immobile for weeks. Cooking caused the ice cave to thaw, and the water soaked their sleeping bags. The team was hungry and cold, and Chouinard, on his 30th birthday, called it a low point in his life. To pass the time, he read *The Hero with a Thousand Faces* by Joseph Campbell and fiddled with his gear, adjusting his climbing equipment, stitching up clothes, and sharpening the spikes that helped his boots cling to the ice.

Food was sparse. To supplement their meager rations, they snuck onto nearby land owned by a gaucho, one of the only humans within a few hundred miles, and killed a few sheep. To snare their prey, the men worked as a team. Chouinard or Tompkins would hide behind a rock while the other four chased a ewe around the steppes below Fitz Roy. When the sheep got close enough, they would spring out from behind the boulder, tackle the animal, and slit its throat. "Doug and I were the only ones who would kill them," Chouinard said. "The other guys would eat it, but they wouldn't have anything to do with killing them." Having slaughtered the sheep, they stored the meat in the same ice cave where they slept.

The climbing equipment they had brought along was holding up, but their clothes were coming apart at the seams. Their jackets weren't waterproof, their socks took forever to dry, and the layers they wore weren't keeping them warm. Holed up in the ice cave, their boots disintegrating and the Patagonian wind knifing through their outerwear, crummy clothes came close to killing the Fun Hogs. Outdoor apparel wasn't made for such conditions at the time, and Chouinard was learning firsthand just how treacherous the wilderness could be without the right gear. He also began to understand that there might be a market in making clothes that could stand up to the elements.

Tompkins encouraged this thinking, pushing Chouinard during their conversations in the ice cave to consider expanding his business beyond climbing equipment and into apparel. The market for clothing was infinitely bigger than the market for pitons and carabiners, Tompkins noted. Just look at the breakout success Plain Jane was enjoying while they were trapped in an ice cave. A climber would only need to buy equipment every few years at most. People buy new clothes all the time. "Doug convinced him to go into clothing," Dorworth remembered. "Because unlike pitons, which last ten years, when it comes to shirts, you want a new one next year. That was the seeds of it." Chouinard was cool to the idea at first. Clothing was a commodity, and didn't require any real craftsmanship, he thought. What special value could he bring to the table? Besides, the last thing he cared about was fashion. But in the years ahead, Chouinard would come around, embracing this pivotal economic insight and becoming one of the most successful retail founders of his generation.

Chouinard and Tompkins also reprised some of their conversations from their days in the Bay Area, mulling all the ways in which humans were mucking up the planet. They knew they would be running companies when they got back from the trip and began to understand that if they had any chance of using their businesses to change the world, they would need to stay in control. Although they had no experience with investment bankers and shareholders, they knew enough to appreciate that outside investors almost certainly would not share their idealistic worldviews. These conversations would shape their careers for the next half century. If they were going to do well for themselves, they would have to do it by doing good.

After a full month in the cave, the weather finally broke and they had a window to try and summit Fitz Roy. Scaling some of the sheerest rock in South America, the Fun Hogs made their way up the granite. At times, they considered aborting the attempt. But on the evening of December 20, 1968, the five men completed the third successful ascent of the 11,020-foot spire. Standing at the pinnacle, they took a picture with the VIVA LOS FUN HOGS banner. "Well, now," Chouinard said at the top, "we have earned our freedom for a while."

## "Great Harm to the Rocks"

Chouinard's environmentalism started close to home. By 1970, Chouinard Equipment was the largest maker of climbing gear in the United States. With the mimeographed price lists getting handed around, a patchy network of dealers, and Chouinard himself still selling his gear out of the trunk of his car, the company managed to capture about 80 percent of the market and was grossing around $300,000 annually. Most of those revenues were still coming from the sale of pitons, which climbers would wedge into the granite walls of Yosemite and the Tetons, allowing them to secure their ropes and make their daring ascents. But while Chouinard's reusable pitons were a marked improvement from the softer metal ones that got deformed so easily and were often left behind, they were causing new problems.

With hundreds of dirtbags trying to replicate Chouinard's exploits by attempting the same routes that he had made famous, the rock was getting ruined. Piton by piton and pitch by pitch,

America's growing legion of climbers was chipping away at the granite. Ancient geological formations were being permanently scarred in a matter of years. "I always thought of rock climbing as a completely harmless sport—one that didn't hurt anyone," Chouinard said. "But I came to realize it could do great harm to the rocks." Chouinard felt responsible for the damage. After all, he had made most of the pitons that were desecrating the granite. So, without much second-guessing, Chouinard decided his company would look for an alternative.

It was a bold move. Pitons were still a huge part of Chouinard's business, and the ones he made were widely regarded as the best. Chouinard Equipment was finally making a profit. But he was un-daunted by the prospect of radical change. Once he realized his gear was damaging the walls, there was no question he needed to find an alternative. "I love this planet," he said. "My parents taught me that if you make a mess, you clean it up. So, I have a pretty good sense of responsibility, and I blamed myself for a lot of the stuff that happened."

Once Chouinard decided to phase out pitons, he had to figure out what to replace them with. Once again, the answer was at his fingertips. A few years earlier, Chouinard had begun experiment-ing with a piece of climbing gear known as the chock. A simple, perforated chunk of metal that a rope could be threaded through, chocks were wedged into a crevice rather than hammered into a seam. One advantage to this approach was that when the climber moved on, he could take his gear with him rather than leave pi-tons in the rocks. The first chocks Chouinard used were made of the aluminum nuts designed to hold airplanes together.

Chocks weren't new. As far back as 1926, climbers scaling the Clogwyn du'r Arddu, a set of sheer cliffs in Wales, were tying their ropes around small stones and wedging them into cracks in the wall. Even then, the Welsh climbers were attuned to the fact that had they hammered pitons or bolts into the wall, they would have been irreparably damaging the stone. "It was widely felt at the time (and indeed still is) that bolting this wall would be a terrible desecration of the crag, and represent a threat to the whole delicate basis of British free climbing," recalled one of the Welsh pioneers. By the 1940s, climbers had moved on from rocks and begun using large nuts that came loose from the tracks along the Snowdon Railway. Fast-forward to the early 1960s, and a British blacksmith, John Brailsford, was manufacturing metal wedges with eyeholes that could accommodate carabiners and be fitted into even slimmer cracks. Whether stones, nuts, or manufactured wedges, climbers called these objects chocks, short for chockstones, the small rocks that get stuck in vertical clefts.

With pitons on their way out, Chouinard got serious about chocks. He and Frost came up with new designs, and within a few years, they had unveiled a whole universe of chocks: 14 sizes of hexentrics, 16 variations of stoppers, tube chocks, and more, each one designed to fit into a particular type of nook or cranny. Yet again, Chouinard's instinct for tinkering was paying off. He hadn't invented a new product. Rather, he had fiddled with an existing one, using his experience in the field and his innate design sense to deliver something vastly improved.

And while it was true that Chouinard Equipment was undergoing a major change with the move from pitons to chocks, something much more fundamental was taking place as well. For the first time in his career, Chouinard was overhauling his company to avoid harming the environment. This was just what he and Tompkins had discussed in the ice cave: there was no point in running companies if they were messing up the planet. Now these ideas were being put into action, and Chouinard was shaking up the business in a bid to protect the natural world.

On the wall, too, Chouinard was pushing in new directions, adjusting his techniques as he learned to scale massive walls without pitons. It was a wholesale revolution in the sport, and one that called for some sort of organizing principle. Chouinard, who was developing a keen sense of marketing, landed upon a good bit of branding when he decided to call this new ethos "clean climbing."

Having homed in on the idea of clean climbing, Chouinard set about spreading the word. In 1972, Chouinard Equipment printed 10,000 copies of its first catalog. Far from a Sears, Roebuck & Co. compendium that simply displayed pictures of available offerings along with their prices, the Chouinard Equipment pamphlet was created in the spirit of the *Whole Earth Catalog*, the counterculture bible produced by Stewart Brand. The cover featured a 16th-century Chinese scroll painting depicting a towering rock formation that conjured up the grandeur of nature. In addition to listing the company's wares and their prices, the catalog featured quotes by Albert Einstein ("A perfection of means and a confusion of aims seems to be our main problem"), the Rolling Stones ("Lose your dreams and you'll lose your mind"), and Antoine de Saint-Exupéry, the author of *The Little Prince* ("In anything at all, perfection is finally attained not when there is no longer anything to add, but when there is no longer anything to take away, when a body has been stripped down to its nakedness").

The meat of the catalog was a 14-page essay by Doug Robinson, a mountaineer from California, that explained in minute detail the ethic and process of clean climbing. "There is a word for it, and the word is clean," it began. "Climbing with only nuts and runners for protection is clean climbing. Clean because the rock is left unaltered by the passing climber. Clean because nothing is hammered into the rock and then hammered back out, leaving the rock scarred and the next climber's experience less natural. Clean because the climber's protection leaves little trace of his ascension. Clean is climbing the rock without changing it; a step closer to organic climbing for the natural man."

But the heart and soul of the catalog was found in its opening pages, in an introduction written by Chouinard and Frost. Their brief essay was the clearest articulation to date of Chouinard's worldview. Imbued with a reverence for nature, it was at once self-critical and forward looking, a critique of modern society and a declaration of morality in the business world. Today it endures as an astonishingly prescient call to arms that rings even truer 50 years on. It was titled, simply, "A word . . ."

In the essay, Chouinard and Frost noted that while climbing was more popular than ever, it was coming at a cost. "The deterioration is twofold, involving the physical aspect of the mountains and the moral integrity of the climbers," they wrote. "No longer can we assume the earth's resources are limitless; that there are ranges of unclimbed peaks extending endlessly beyond the horizon. Mountains are finite, and despite their massive appearance, they are fragile."

Chouinard and Frost went on to assail other climbers—their own customers—for what they said was an erosion in character. "Equally serious is a moral deterioration," they wrote. "Armed with ever more advanced gadgetry and techniques the style of technical climbing is gradually becoming so degraded that elements vital to the climbing experience—adventure and appreciation of the mountain environment itself—are being submerged."

They argued that more important than reaching the top was a sort of Zen-like oneness with the mountain itself. "It is the style of the climb, not the attainment of the summit, which is the measure of personal success," they wrote. "Traditionally stated, each of us must consider whether the end is more important than the means. Given the vital importance of style we suggest that the keynote is simplicity. The fewer gadgets between the climber and the climb, the greater the chance to attain the desired communication with oneself—and nature."

In closing, they called on climbers to look into their own souls. "As we enter this new era of mountaineering, re-examine your motives for climbing," they wrote. "Employ restraint and good judgment in the use of Chouinard equipment. Remember the rock, the other climber—climb clean."

This manifesto didn't just articulate Chouinard and Frost's views on climbing, but their perspective on business as well. If they were going to sell chocks and other gear to the climbing community, they were going to do it with a point of view that might make some of their customers uncomfortable at times. They would be capitalists, yes, but before that, they would strive to be good stewards of nature and responsible citizens of planet Earth.

It was the dawn of a new era of American environmentalism, and in his own way, Chouinard was working to shift the public narrative. A decade earlier, Rachel Carson, a pioneering journalist, published *Silent Spring*, her investigation into the perils of the pesticide DDT, which had decimated the peregrine falcon population that Chouinard had played a small role in saving. Presidents John F. Kennedy, Lyndon Johnson, and Richard Nixon all made conservation and the protection of nature cornerstones of their administrations. In 1969, President Nixon's advisor, Daniel Patrick Moynihan, wrote a memo outlining the perilous consequences of global warming. The burning of fossil fuels like coal, oil, and gas were increasing the concentration of carbon dioxide in the atmosphere, creating "the effect of a pane of glass in a greenhouse." The result, Moynihan correctly predicted, would be a rapid increase in global temperatures. Looking a bit further out, he anticipated the melting of glaciers and a catastrophic rise in sea levels. "Goodbye New York," he wrote. "Goodbye Washington, for that matter. We have no data on Seattle."

It didn't take long for clean climbing to catch on. As the piton business tapered off, Chouinard and his team couldn't make enough chocks to keep up with demand. With the uptick in sales, the business itself matured. Chouinard outsourced manufacturing of its carabiners and crampons to Germany, and fabrication of the ice axe to Italy. In 1972, Chouinard Equipment was incorporated into a new entity, the Great Pacific Iron Works, a move designed to facilitate additional expansion. The business was growing up, and Chouinard would soon face a whole new set of challenges.

# CHAPTER 3

# Pushing the Limits

## "Our Own Way of Doing Business"

During one of his extended stays at Camp 4 in Yosemite, Chouinard witnessed an altercation between an unruly driver and a plucky young woman that would change his life. As a car passed through the camp, the driver tossed an empty beer can out the window. The woman chased down the car and told the driver to pick the can up. A passenger in the car offered a middle finger in return, prompting the now irate woman to rip off the car's license plate with her bare hands and turn it over to a park ranger.

Chouinard liked what he saw, and when the fracas was over, he went up and introduced himself. The woman's name was Ellen Malinda Pennoyer, and she was an art student at Fresno State College. During the weekends, she worked as a maid at nearby Yosemite Valley Lodge, sometimes hanging around with the climbers at Camp 4. The daughter of an Air Force pilot who flew in World War II and went on to fly for Pan Am, Malinda had spent her life on the road, living in Germany, all over the United States, and beyond. In 1959 alone, she moved six times. Her parents were adventurous. She once joined her father on a river trip from Chattanooga, Tennessee, to Birmingham, Alabama. And her family had been coming to Yosemite for years, instilling in her the same abiding love for the natural world that animated Chouinard.

As they began dating, Malinda was able to see past Chouinard's rougher edges. Visiting his house for the first time, she opened the refrigerator and was confronted with a furry hoof; Chouinard had poached a deer on public land and was eating it bit by bit. But the dirtbag lifestyle was part of the charm, and he leaned into it. "Been away from civilization for only a week and a half and already my crotch smells like a vulture's breath and my teeth have a film of yellow scale on them," he wrote her in a love letter not long after they met. "Been letting myself go I'm afraid. I'll be a real wild man after a month!" They married in 1970. Not long after the wedding, Malinda quit her job as a high school art teacher and started working for Chouinard Equipment.

Back in Ventura, the scaffolding of a more conventional life came into place. Chouinard Equipment bought the tin shed and some nearby buildings, establishing a permanent home base for the company. And while Chouinard and Malinda spent a few years sleeping in the basement of the office, the couple eventually bought a small house on Faria Beach in Ventura, a few miles to the north. With a perch right on the water, Chouinard could sit in his living room and assess the wind and the waves, the swell and the tide. The couple also had their first child, a son named Fletcher. As a toddler, the boy would ride in a backpack, strapped to Chouinard as he roamed around the office, the baby looking on as his father inspected carabiners and designed shirts. Once Fletcher could walk, Malinda had to put up a wooden gate on the back porch to prevent the boy from following Chouinard out to the ocean and into the surf.

A second child followed, a daughter named Claire, and the Chouinards built a second home, this one in Moose, Wyoming. A two-story log house at the edge of an unincorporated community, the structure occupied a plot of land that abutted the Snake River. Looking out from the living room, the Chouinards could watch herds of elk graze and behold the Tetons jutting into the sky. They furnished the property with surplus chairs and beds the National Park Service was auctioning off. Today, hardly anything inside the home has changed. The furniture is still a mishmash of hand-me-downs. The tableware is all from Goodwill. Chouinard fillets fish with a knife he bought 50 years ago. Books and board games are stacked to the ceiling. There is no television in sight. "Almost everything I have is old," Chouinard said. "I use everything until it completely falls apart." In the gravel driveway is an old Toyota hatchback with a bumper sticker that reads, "Every billionaire is a policy failure." The front door is never locked.

Despite the home's simplicity, this was exclusive property. The Forbes family had a compound nearby. Back in the 1920s, John D. Rockefeller Jr.—the son of the founder of Standard Oil—had bought up much of the surrounding land. Using a shell company to conceal his identity, Rockefeller amassed 33,000 acres, including some of North America's most iconic mountains, all with the aim of conserving the pristine wilderness in perpetuity. He made good on that promise in the 1930s, donating the land to the federal government and contributing an essential piece of what became Grand Teton National Park. Now Chouinard, another conservation-minded businessman, was living on that park's doorstep.

He was putting down roots, and the real world was catching up with him. No longer was he just a climber and a surfer and blacksmith. It was dawning on him that, like it or not, he was the leader of a company with an expanding set of responsibilities. He had payroll to make, people to look after, orders to fulfill. At the same time, he understood that he wasn't going to adhere to the normal rules of business. His employees would not wear suits and ties. The office would not be covered in drab gray carpet and carved into cubicles. He sneered at the "pasty-faced corpses" he saw shuffling through their days in corporate America. If he had to be a businessman, he was going to do it on his own terms.

In practice, that meant rethinking the workday. Doing one's job, Chouinard resolved, had to be fun. A sense of adventure was at the heart of the sports he loved and would have to be at the heart of his company, too. He wanted his employees to have a healthy sense of irreverence and not take themselves too seriously. Colleagues would ideally be friends. He also was clear about what he didn't care about—shoes were optional. Perhaps most importantly, employees needed to have the freedom to do the things that really mattered to them, like surf. "We just invented our own way of doing business," Chouinard said. "It was a bit unusual, but it worked."

As they settled in Ventura, Chouinard and Malinda started getting involved in local politics. On March 12, 1972, Malinda helped organize a 48.6-mile bicycle ride to raise funds that would support Proposition 9, a ballot initiative known as the Clean Environment Act. More than five hundred riders joined, and Malinda was quoted in the paper calling on the local government to step up efforts to protect the California coast, marking one of the company's first forays into environmental activism.

Not long after that, Chouinard went to a local theater to watch a surf movie. After the screening, one surfer got up and asked the crowd to attend an upcoming city council meeting and voice concerns over a plan to divert and develop the mouth of the Ventura River. That small river flowed just behind the Chouinard Equipment office and then into the Pacific Ocean, shaping one of the best surf breaks in California. If the plan went ahead, the break that drew Chouinard to Ventura in the first place could be gone. Beyond its importance to the local waves, Chouinard and his pals knew that as recently as the 1940s, the Ventura River had been a major spawning ground for thousands of steelhead trout and Chinook salmon. But over the years, the river had been dammed upstream, drying it up and killing the fish.

At the city council meeting, which was held at the Ventura High School auditorium to accommodate the unusually large crowd, a parade of experts on the city's payroll testified that further development wouldn't hurt the wildlife in the area because the river was already effectively dead. It looked as if the plans would proceed. Then a young environmental activist named Mark Capelli took the floor. Armed with a slide projector, he displayed photos of wildlife he had recently documented in the watershed, including muskrats, snakes, eels, and birds living in the willows. After Capelli displayed pictures of baby steelhead, the crowd cheered. There was life in the dead river, after all. His testimony swayed the debate, the development was halted, the river was protected, and the surf break was preserved.

After the meeting, Malinda called Capelli and asked if he would display some of his photos in the new company showroom. Capelli agreed and soon befriended Chouinard, who offered to let Capelli's nascent nonprofit organization, Friends of the Ventura River, have some free office space. Capelli wasn't a businessman and Chouinard wasn't an activist at this point, but the men shared an affinity for nature and a willingness to challenge authority. "We were both marching to our own drummer," Capelli said.

Not long after that, Capelli ran into Chouinard in the company parking lot. After chatting about the waves, he asked Chouinard for a donation. Friends of the Ventura River was suing to block a water use agreement between the Casitas Municipal Water District and the City of Ventura, arguing it would have decreased the flow in the river. He needed money for the legal fees.

"How much do you need?" Chouinard asked, without missing a beat.

Capelli said he was hoping for $3,000.

"Just go upstairs and have Clova write you a check," Chouinard said, referring to Patagonia's bookkeeper at the time.

Capelli hustled upstairs, but Clova was on her way out. "Can you come back tomorrow?" she said.

Capelli was back the next day, Clova cut the check, and the case succeeded in the end, beating back appeals that went all the way to the California Supreme Court. That cemented the partnership between Chouinard and Capelli, and soon, outside the office's front door, Chouinard affixed a placard reading, "Friends of the Ventura River."

The check for Capelli was the first environmental grant Chouinard ever made. One small donation had made a difference, and Chouinard understood for the first time that his money could have an impact. Chouinard continued to support Capelli and his organization for the next 50 years, underwriting his work at the University of California, Santa Barbara, which included teaching a course on endangered species management. And with time, the Ventura River began to heal. Some of the wildlife that had been crowded out by urbanization began to come back, and steelhead started spawning again.

With his move from pitons to chocks, Chouinard had overhauled his product lineup in order to take better care of the planet. Now he was using the power of his purse to support grassroots environmental activists, taking the first step on a philanthropic journey that would shape his career, and the world.

# "Software"

While climbing limestone cliffs in the Peak District of England in the mid-'60s, Chouinard spotted some locals wearing corduroy pants. The fabric was tough and didn't rip easily, and he figured it would make for durable climbing clothes. He tracked down the mill where the fabric made, in Lancashire, and introduced himself. In short order, the mill was turning out pants and shorts for Chouinard, who began selling them to his friends. A few years later, during a climbing trip to Scotland, Chouinard bought himself a local team's rugby shirt. If it was tough enough for rugby, he figured, it would be tough enough for climbing. With red and yellow stripes cutting across a blue base, it was startlingly colorful compared to most outdoor clothes, which at the time were mostly drab, neutral tones. Just like corduroy, the thick cotton didn't wear out on the rocks; even better, its collar protected his neck from the gear he often had slung over his shoulder. "Every time he went climbing, he would come back with new ideas," said Hall Stratton, who worked for Chouinard during this time. "He just knew there had to be a better way."

Back home, Chouinard wore the rugby shirt around Yosemite. It was an instant attention getter, and soon all the other climbers wanted one. Besides being durable, the pops of color brightened the mood on the mountain. Chouinard joked that spending months in monochromatic tents could leave climbers feeling like they were in an Ingmar Bergman movie, and that without some color in their lives, the climbers would drink themselves to death with Aquavit. A bit of unsolicited market research further convinced Chouinard he was on to something: one day he got a piece of mail from a customer asking him to make clothes in a "non-ugly color."

Figuring that it might be an easy way to garner some quick profits, Chouinard began importing rugby shirts from England. He started by ordering them direct from Umbro, the English sportswear company, and reselling them at a markup. They were a hit and started moving faster than he could bring them across the border. But even after he began importing additional rugby shirts from Argentina and New Zealand, Chouinard couldn't keep up with demand.

From that point on, the company started carrying more clothing, which it called "software," as opposed to the metal chocks and carabiners it made, which were "hardware." Soon Chouinard Equipment was selling rain slickers imported from Scotland, mittens and gloves from Austria, reversible hats from Colorado, and French-made shoes designed by Chouinard's friend, Royal Robbins. Then one day, as Chouinard sorted boxes with Malinda and friends in the tin shed, he wondered aloud why the hell he was selling so much stuff that he didn't make. Except for the climbing equipment, everything else was manufactured by other companies. Davey Agnew, a Scottish climbing friend who was with Chouinard at the time, remembers watching a signature insight take shape in real time. "That epiphany made it very clear to him," Agnew said. "He needed to have his own clothing brand." Chouinard was coming to realize that Tompkins had been right during his ramblings in the ice cave; he could sell a lot more shirts and pants than chocks and carabiners.

For the first product of his own design, Chouinard dreamed up a pair of shorts he wanted for climbing. They would feature a double layer of fabric on the bottom for extra toughness, and huge pockets to store gear. After disassembling a pair of shorts and studying how they were made, he created the patterns himself and cut the shapes out of a thick canvas used for lawn furniture. When sewn together, the shorts were so stiff that they could hold their shape standing upright on a table. They were dubbed Stand Up Shorts, and they soon became one of the company's best-selling items. Chouinard may have been new to designing clothes, but he was able to correctly intuit what customers wanted.

A growing team of seamstresses was soon producing tops, bottoms, outerwear, and more. As the software business took off, Chouinard decided to separate it from the hardware business and create a stand-alone clothing company. But what to call it? The Chouinard Equipment name was well known in the climbing community, and he considered porting his surname to the apparel line. But he wanted to differentiate the clothes from the gear and was hoping for a more memorable brand, perhaps a name that evoked far-off places, like Timbuktu or Shangri-la, and was easy to pronounce. From his Fun Hogs trip, Chouinard knew that he was trying to make clothes that could withstand a harsh environment like Fitz Roy, which had put him and his friends to the test. And so, in 1973, as the clothing company came into being, Chouinard chose the name Patagonia.

It was an opportune moment to start a new company. American consumers were flush with cash and looking for new ways to stay active. By the 1960s, there were at least 100,000 customers for climbing equipment, *The Wall Street Journal* reported. Interest in rock climbing was surging, chain stores including REI and Eastern Mountain Sports were proliferating, and Chouinard was at the center of it all. With sales booming, the Patagonia team set up a sewing shop on the second floor of a nearby building, not far from the tin shed. Val Franco, a young woman with dark, flowing hair who rode her motorcycle to work, started churning out Stand Up Shorts and backpacks. And when it came to the clothes that Patagonia wasn't making itself, Chouinard and company began striking out ever more ambitious relationships with suppliers around the globe—sometimes too ambitious.

By 1974, demand for the rugby shirts was so robust that Chouinard and his team made a bold decision. Rather than continue to import them from England, they would contract with a garment factory in Asia to produce their own. To find a supplier, Chouinard turned to Tompkins, whose own company, Plain Jane, was doing a brisk business selling colorful skirts and tops at department stores like Bloomingdale's and Saks Fifth Avenue. Tompkins recommended a factory in Hong Kong, and Chouinard placed an order for 3,000 rugby shirts a month, in eight different designs.

From the outset, it was a mess. Craftsmanship that might have worked for simple women's wear was unacceptable when it came to technical mountaineering garb. The quality of the shirts was horrible, the fabric wasn't durable, the sizes were unpredictable, and deliveries were late. Chouinard canceled the contract as fast as he could but not soon enough. The order had depleted Patagonia's cash reserves, the shirts weren't selling, money was getting tight, and the whole company was suddenly in jeopardy because of one bad decision.

Chouinard was getting an early lesson in the difficulty of managing a global supply chain. It was one thing to make climbing gear by hand, inspect each piece, and manage some limited inventory. The clothing business was far more complex. Suppliers were in distant countries, quality varied widely, lead times were months out, and it was hard to know in advance whether new garments would shrink or fade.

As the cash crunch intensified, Chouinard and Malinda started meeting with bankers, looking to shore up the company's finances. But most of the local banks weren't interested in doing business with Patagonia, believing the company was too disorganized to be trusted. A friend of the Chouinards introduced them to a Mafia associate, who offered a loan with an interest rate of 28 percent. They declined. Eventually, the Chouinards were able to secure a more affordable and less dubious line of credit from a local bank that allowed them to stabilize the business.

With its finances in order, Patagonia began expanding its offerings. An early product, the Foamback jacket, was an improvement on the rain jackets of the day, which tended to collect condensation on the inside of the shell. Chouinard and his team added a layer of foam to the interior of the shell, making the jacket warmer and drier. From there, Chouinard looked to develop new pieces that would be durable and warm enough for tough expeditions into the mountains. Searching for inspiration, the team hit upon the idea of designing a synthetic pile sweater. Chouinard had seen a bolt of acrylic fabric at a textile dealer in Canada that was ugly and odorous but, promisingly, water repellent. But in the mid-'70s, such material wasn't in ready supply, and the team knew they would have to get creative when it came to sourcing.

One day in 1976, Malinda drove to the merchandise mart in the heart of Los Angeles's fashion district and began hunting for something that could work. After going from stall to stall, she found the right material, but it wasn't being produced for clothing. Rather, the light-blue, synthetic pile was for bathroom floor mats and toilet seat covers. Malinda had a few bolts of the bushy fabric sent to Ventura, and it sat there for a while until Chouinard happened upon it and brought it to the sewing room. After inspecting it, he thought it might be the material he'd been looking for. "We knew the pile would capture dead air space and you'd stay warm from that," said Franco, the seamstress. "It was lighter than wool. It dried fast and didn't freeze if you were in the cold."

The obvious move would have been to make a design with the

puffy pile facing inward, toward the body. That's how most jackets with similar material were made at the time. But as the Patagonia team quickly discovered, when the flat side faced out, the smooth fabric pilled easily and quickly looked ratty. Chouinard decided to reverse it. Drawing inspiration from sheep, he had the jackets sewn with the bushy pile facing out. "Animals have the fur on the outside," he said. "This should, too." It was a stroke of inspiration that would influence fashion for decades to come.

Franco stitched together a few sweaters of Chouinard's design. The pattern was simple as could be. They had a zip front, no pockets, and looked unusual with the pile on the outside. Then Chouinard took them up to the mountains to see how they performed. They turned out to be marvels. They were warm, they didn't hold water, they dried quickly, and they were incredibly durable. Patagonia wanted to buy the fabric in bulk, but couldn't place a big enough order to get the manufacturer to produce a custom color. So, it bought up the existing stock, which came in just two colors: a bland tan and a light blue. Soon, Patagonia was selling its first synthetic pile jackets. They weren't perfect. The exterior pilled after repeated wear, they tended to hold body odor in the armpits after a few weeks in the backcountry, plus they were ugly. But they kept people warm on the mountain and quickly became one of the company's most popular products. They also represented an inflection point in materials: Patagonia was now making apparel not with organic substances like cotton or wool, but with synthetics. That is, it was making clothes with plastic.

A warm outer layer now in hand, Chouinard turned his attention to the next problem: his underwear. A quick-drying jacket was useless if it was worn over cotton underwear that held moisture and froze. Impressed with the performance of the pile jackets, Chouinard looked to synthetics again. Polypropylene fiber was buoyant, didn't absorb water, and was used to make things like fishing nets and ropes for boats. A couple other companies had already tried experimenting with polypropylene as a fabric, but Patagonia was the first to make it thick enough to provide a layer of insulation. In a matter of years, the polypropylene long underwear was selling briskly.

With the base layer in place, as well as the pile jacket, Patagonia began extolling the virtues of layering, a new approach to staying warm and dry in the elements. A base layer wicked sweat, a midlayer provided warmth, and an outer shell kept out wind, rain, and snow. It was a significant innovation that transformed how people dressed for the outdoors. Before long, the layering system was being replicated by dozens of other companies jockeying for a share of the growing outdoor apparel market.

The pivot to clothing was going full steam. Chouinard Equipment was still there, still making its carabiners and hexes and stoppers. But it was becoming clear that the real money was going to be made in clothes. With new fabrics, innovative designs, and bold color choices, Chouinard was pushing outdoor apparel in new directions. In a matter of years, Patagonia's sales skyrocketed from roughly $250,000 annually to more than $2 million. But there was a dark side to all that success. Although it wasn't fully understood at the time, the embrace of synthetic fabrics helped usher in a new era of environmentally destructive apparel. As Patagonia and other companies used fewer natural materials like cotton and wool, they accelerated a transformation that reshaped the apparel industry at large. Today, some 60 percent of new clothes in the world are made of synthetic fabrics like polyester, nylon, acrylic, and polypropylene—all of which are made with fossil fuels.

## "A Box Full of Misfit Toys"

The cash crunch provoked by the crappy shirts from Hong Kong set in motion a series of events that would profoundly reshape the company. For one, it ratcheted up stress levels. Malinda Chouinard and Tom Frost never got along. Malinda, freewheeling and leading with her heart, constantly clashed with Frost, the meticulous engineer. Amid the financial stress, they found themselves locking horns even more frequently. Relations didn't improve when Frost, who was a Mormon, implored Chouinard to hire a fellow member of his church, Ray Heagle. Besides being a bishop in the Church of Jesus Christ of Latter-day Saints, Heagle ran an electrical services company, and Frost figured he could bring some much-needed discipline to the business. Chouinard resisted at first, fearing that an outsider wouldn't mesh with the unruly culture he had cultivated. But he ultimately relented, and Heagle came on to lead a company he knew nothing about.

It didn't take long for Chouinard's worst fears to be proved right. The culture clash between the rigid Mormon executive and the laid-back climbers and surfers was glaring from the get-go. Heagle discouraged employees from bringing their surfboards to work and taking breaks when the waves were going off, instantly drawing the staff's ire. Once, Heagle asked Stanley to have a new price list printed on bright yellow paper so it would catch people's attention. But the yellow paper was out of stock, and Stanley decided to have it printed on blue paper instead.

When the price lists arrived at headquarters, Heagle came raging into Stanley's office. "How dare you countermand my orders?" he bellowed.

Stanley just laughed at an outburst that was so out of proportion with the purported offense. Chouinard was on the same page. "I can't work with this guy," he told Stanley. "Nobody can."

Chouinard soon ousted Heagle, and the company paid him to go away. It was an early lesson in human resources for the young company. This wasn't the kind of place where an off-the-shelf middle manager could come in and succeed. And yet even after Heagle was gone, the tensions between the Chouinards and Frost increased. There were competing visions about how to run the company and what its culture should be like, and when relations finally reached a breaking point in 1975, Chouinard bought out Frost. He and Malinda now owned the company outright.

With the Frosts' departure, Patagonia was more than ever a family affair, for better and worse. Stanley was there, Malinda was helping out, and Kris and Roger McDivitt were getting more involved. That close-knit crew enjoyed a sense of community and a high degree of trust. But none of them had Tom Frost's manufacturing and engineering expertise, or Doreen Frost's organizational chops, leaving Chouinard exposed. "He had relied on Tom and Doreen to handle a lot of how the business was structured, to pay the bills, to keep things going when he was gone," Stanley said. "Now he was on his own as a businessperson."

Still, the company kept humming along. By 1977, Chouinard had redesigned practically every piece of climbing equipment there was, and the staff had grown to 16 full-time employees. The Ventura headquarters had evolved into an unlikely scene, part corporate campus and part cultural mecca. The original tin shed was still there, home to a team that hammered out the pieces of hardware still being made domestically. More complex climbing gear was fashioned in a nearby machine shop. The old slaughterhouse was refurbished and turned into offices, a shipping area, and a sewing shop.

On a wall in the office, a quote attributed to Henry David Thoreau provided inspiration: "Simplification of means and elevation of ends is the goal." A key to the office was hidden under a rock, allowing workers to come and go as they pleased, with some eccentric craftsmen hammering away in the middle of the night if they chose. A couple black Labs were always lurking around. Climbers would drop by, sometimes earning a bit of money packing boxes or helping sort inventory. The parking lot was still a party. The place still cleared out when the waves got going. "The people working with him were a box full of misfit toys," said Hall Stratton, who worked in the shop.

Was it fun? Yes. Was it organized? No. With Frost gone and Chouinard still taking monthslong breaks to go climbing, Patagonia needed a new leader. Chouinard knew as much. He also knew that bringing in another suit from the outside wouldn't work. He needed to choose someone from within his own ranks, and in 1979 he made an inspired, if unlikely, choice, tapping Kris McDivitt to be the company's general manager. Her title wasn't chief executive officer, as might have been common in other companies, but there was no mistaking it: Kris was now in charge.

McDivitt had grown up in the area as a child. Her family owned a farm in nearby Santa Paula, but when she was a child, her father took a job as a petroleum engineer in Venezuela, and the family moved abroad. Roger was sent to boarding school in Barbados. Kris was younger and joined her parents in the South American bush, enrolling in a one-room schoolhouse. But after just a couple years in Venezuela, her father died. Polio was raging, and he had failed to take the vaccine developed by Jonas Salk. McDivitt and her family moved back to Southern California, and it wasn't long before she and her brother were hanging out with Chouinard.

At first, Chouinard enlisted McDivitt and her brother for simple jobs. Roger was tasked with cobbling together a little retail area, creating something that passed for a small store for the climbers who dropped by. Customers were sparse, so Roger helped organize the wholesale accounts, too, creating a system to pay suppliers and expand the mail-order business. Kris was still a teenager and started as a part-timer packing boxes, then went off to spend a few years at the College of Idaho, earning a double major in sociology and psychology. While there, she got serious about downhill skiing and became an accomplished racer. But her competitive career ended when she crashed, resulting in a spiral fracture in one leg and torn ligaments.

Back in Ventura after college with a new degree and a bum knee, Kris went to work for Chouinard in 1973. She started with odd jobs, packing boxes, doing chores, delivering goods, and taking orders. And while Roger was older and had more experience with the business, it was Kris who displayed intuition and leadership at just the right moments. She and Chouinard grew close, and he began trusting her with more of the company's critical operations. As Roger focused more on the wholesale business, Kris took on more and more responsibilities, becoming a sort of translator for Chouinard, turning his often mercurial ambitions into practical directives the staff could follow. She knew when to take him seriously and when to ignore his whims. She won Malinda's trust and the respect of the growing workforce. And finally, in 1979, she won the top job. Chouinard was burned out and tired of keeping the place running. As ever, he was more interested in being outside than in the office. "Here's Patagonia," he told her one day. "Here's Chouinard Equipment. Do with them what you will. I'm going climbing."

It was one thing to serve as Chouinard's deputy. But now Mc-

Divitt had been handed stewardship of Chouinard's companies and was responsible for not only keeping the lights on but also growing the business. She had no idea how to scale up a clothing company, so she went looking for advice and called the president of Manufacturers Bank in Los Angeles, which was the main lender to fashion companies. Once she got him on the line, she pleaded for help. "I've been given this responsibility to start this clothing company with a very small team of people, and I have no idea what to do," she told him. "I don't know what a letter of credit is, sir. I don't know anything. I have to learn, and I want to go to the best and get it right from the get-go and not make it up."

The banker was impressed with her pluck and surprised she had the gall to call him up, so he unspooled his managerial wisdom. After giving her an overview of the financial side of the apparel business, he insisted she work with an accountant he trusted. McDivitt obliged and went straight to the accountant's office, signing on the firm to handle Patagonia's books.

A cross-country sales trip quickly made it clear that McDivitt had a knack for business development, too. Early in her days as general manager, she traveled to Maine and pitched L.L.Bean, which was then one of the country's largest clothing catalogs. Patagonia had sold some clothes through L.L.Bean before, but this time, McDivitt returned to Ventura with an order for thousands of pairs of shorts. Her tenure was off to a charmed start.

Then came the incident with the time card machines. With a growing staff coming and going as they pleased, and most employees still being paid hourly, it was impossible to keep track of who was working when. McDivitt took what she thought was the reasonable step of putting in time card machines, so workers could punch in and punch out. It was hardly a radical development, but Patagonia's staff reacted as if they had been put in a prison camp. They were furious and turned on their new leader. For years, McDivitt had been one of the gang, part of the ragtag bunch that, improbably, made the company work. Now she was the boss, and she had already lost the team's trust.

She didn't second-guess her decision, though. The time card machines were a necessary step at this juncture, and McDivitt stuck to her guns. "I could see there was an inherent weakness," she said. "We needed to professionalize ourselves without losing who we were. But how do you do that while maintaining culture, taking care of growth, and maintaining trust?" Employees vented their frustrations at all-staff meetings for a while. Then, as often happens with office microdramas, the fracas fizzled out. The boss wouldn't budge, and no other company in town would hire this lot, so it was back to work. The episode was an early test for McDivitt, exposing her to the often competing impulses animating Patagonia and giving her a new appreciation of the enigma that she had been tapped to lead. "We're as complicated as any person," she said. "Full of flaws and contradictions."

## "Making It Up As We Went Along"

After the Fun Hogs trip, Tompkins returned to San Francisco ambitious and directionless at the same time. He thought about opening a restaurant or maybe starting up another version of The North Face to capitalize on the growing interest in climbing. At the end of the day, he wound up helping Susie build on her success at Plain Jane. The clothes were soon in New York's trendiest department stores, and the product line swiftly expanded beyond dresses to include brightly colored T-shirts, blouses, bell-bottoms, and skirts. Tompkins was suddenly flush with cash. Whereas Chouinard was in no hurry to grow Patagonia's sales, Tompkins was moving as fast as he could. By 1972, Plain Jane sales had topped $8 million. Tompkins, never one to deny himself the finer things, bought a red Ferrari. Then he bought a plane. As the business grew, Tompkins tried to come up with an overarching brand name that could encompass Plain Jane and his other budding business ventures. It was one of the Fun Hogs, Lito Tejada-Flores, who came up with "Esprit de Corps"—the spirit of the people. That became Esprit.

Despite a name with democratic undertones, Esprit was firmly in Tompkins's control. He was a fastidious micromanager who decided which stores could sell the company's clothes, what the marketing looked like, and how the office was designed. He came up with a list of 10 principles that would guide the business ("Know who we are and stick to it . . . Create demand rather than supply demand . . . Quality before quantity.") And he singlehandedly set up a bigger global supply chain, traveling to Hong Kong and finding factories that would meet his exacting standards.

But Tompkins's embrace of offshoring backfired in 1974. That was when a group of Esprit's unionized Chinese American garment workers in San Francisco learned that he was considering moving their jobs to India. The local workers marched over to the company's offices and picketed in the street. At first, Tompkins said the move was necessary to achieve higher quality; then he slipped up and acknowledged it was so he could save money on wages. Because the workers were part of a union, that would have fallen afoul of the National Labor Relations Board. The demonstrations grew, Tompkins locked the workers out, and San Francisco police arrested some protestors as the picket line turned violent.

A judge ordered the workers reinstated the next year and required Tompkins to pay a hefty fine. But the turmoil didn't end there. On the last day of January 1976, which also happened to be the first day of the Chinese New Year, an arsonist set the Esprit offices on fire. The roof collapsed, and it took 70 firefighters to combat the blaze. Miraculously, Esprit's most essential files—which were stored on magnetic IBM tapes—survived. Had they burned, Tompkins said he would have likely closed up shop.

A couple hundred miles south, Patagonia was also experiencing growing pains. Bringing a measure of discipline to an anarchic workforce was never going to be easy. But for the first many years of Patagonia's existence, it was sometimes a miracle that business got done at all. Once, Chouinard returned to the office after weeks on a climbing trip. Wandering over to his own desk, he noticed some paper crumpled up in the wastebasket. He took it out to see what had been thrown away and discovered it was an order for thousands of dollars' worth of gear. Chouinard brought the paper over to the associate who was responsible for fulfilling dealer orders and asked what had happened. "Oh man," the employee said. "This order came in while you were away, and it was so big that there was no way we were ever going to fill it, so I just threw it away."

Another time, a group of mountaineers placed a major order for equipment and clothing as they prepared for an expedition to the Ural Mountains in Russia. Months went by, and the team leader began badgering the company for the order. When they reached Roger McDivitt on the phone, he just laughed and told them the team would try to get it done, but as the first mimeographed price sheet made clear, timeliness was not one of the qualities that distinguished the company's approach to customer service. (The order was eventually filled.)

Beyond Ventura, Patagonia was beginning to make a name for

itself thanks to the efforts of a handful of traveling salesmen: Billy Kulczycki, Henry Barber, Dale Day, Howard Sloan, Denny Mays, Paul Marsh, and Tex Bossier. These men fanned out across the country, each one covering a different region. Crisscrossing the interstates with climbing gear, Stand Up Shorts, and rugby shirts stored in the trunks of their cars, they hustled to get outdoor shops to carry Patagonia clothes, reprising Chouinard's glory days as an itinerant blacksmith with a car full of pitons.

It was slow going at first. Patagonia was still an unknown brand, and the products were sometimes subpar. Marsh's first task was to offload a few thousand unsightly black-and-orange rugby shirts that had been sitting on a warehouse shelf for more than a year. Selling thick cotton shirts in Alabama wasn't so easy, and the sales reps initially struggled. During his first year, Barber made $6,000 in commissions and spent $9,000 on his own expenses, netting himself a hefty loss. Price sheets were written in pencil, and the home office was often uncommunicative. "Nobody knew what they were doing," Kulczycki said. "We were making it up as we went along." Sales improved within a few years, however, and the reps were soon making more money from their commissions than the executives back in Ventura drew in salary.

During her first years as general manager, McDivitt also made a series of critical organizational moves. The machine shop and the quality-control operation were established into a new legal entity, Rincon Iron Works. Patagonia was legally incorporated as well, formally separating it from Chouinard Equipment. And as excess Patagonia products began to pile up in Ventura, Chouinard and his brother Jeff opened a retail outlet, Real Cheap Sports, where they sold overruns, samples, and outdated merchandise. Patagonia was starting to resemble a real company, with an org chart, sales reps, and a sophisticated distribution network.

And as the business started to pick up, the company made some seemingly counterintuitive moves. Following McDivitt's initial success with L.L.Bean, the Maine retailer became one of Patagonia's best customers, moving large volumes of sportswear through its mail-order catalog. One year, as L.L.Bean put together its spring catalog, it told Patagonia that it wanted to buy 3,000 pairs of Stand Up Shorts. It was a huge number, the kind of order that could make or break a quarter or even a year. But L.L.Bean had a catch: it wanted to sell them at a small discount, just a few dollars less than Patagonia's suggested retail price. Back in Ventura, the leadership team agonized over the dilemma. Patagonia wouldn't have made any less money; L.L.Bean was still willing to pay the full wholesale price. The Maine retailer simply wanted to offer them to its customers at a discount. Patagonia had every interest in accommodating one of its biggest partners. Other retailers did this sort of thing all the time. But in the end, the decision was unanimous: there would be no discounting. Patagonia's whole ethos was built around quality, and allowing L.L.Bean to undercut its suggested retail price would have undermined that message. The company refused the order.

## CHAPTER 4

# Patagoniacs

## "Real People Doing Real Things"

As a blacksmith, Chouinard had developed an elegant touchmark—the small design element, often engraved in a metal object, that identified its craftsman. It was a simple diamond with the letter *C* inside. That touchmark appeared on most Chouinard Equipment products, and a version of it is still in use today, as the logo for Black Diamond. But by the early '70s, Chouinard needed another distinctive visual flourish, in this case, a logo for Patagonia.

Chouinard asked two local freelance artists to come up with dueling versions of a design. Jocelyn Slack was one of those who got the assignment. Looking for inspiration, she leafed through a guidebook that described climbing in the region and came across an image of Fitz Roy, which the Fun Hogs had summitted eight years earlier. Studying the routes, Slack used a pencil to rough out a silhouette of the peaks. Eventually, going back and forth with Chouinard, she added some color to her simple mountain range. The company's name was set in lowercase letters below the mountains, and the company had its logo.

Next, Patagonia needed its own catalog. Until 1980, hardware and software were marketed together, even as the clothing business grew exponentially larger than the climbing business. And while the clothes were improving, the way the company marketed them was not. For the 1980 catalog, Rick Ridgeway, a climber and friend of Chouinard's who helped out with odd jobs, had simply taken some employees from the machine shop down to the Ventura River, dressed them with the latest offerings, and had them stand in the sun, staring at the camera with their hands on their hips. When he showed Chouinard and McDivitt the catalog, there was no mistaking how they felt about his work.

Chouinard shuffled his feet and refused to make eye contact.

McDivitt was more direct. "The photographs really suck, pal," she told Ridgeway.

A week or so later, while surfing with Ridgeway, Chouinard had an insight about how to solve the problem. As the pair bobbed in the waves, Chouinard said: "Hey, Rick, you know that catalog you made?"

Ridgeway cringed and braced himself for what was coming next.

"It's kind of hokey," Chouinard said. "But I think I've got an idea how to fix it."

Chouinard went on to explain his new vision: actual customers, wearing the clothes and using the gear, out in the field. No staged models looking at the camera. No studios and fake backgrounds. Just humans in the wild, enjoying nature. All the better if some of the clothes were ripped or dirty. "Real people doing real things," he said. It was a simple vision and an authentic representation of the brand.

Chouinard soon found a creative partner who could realize his vision in Ridgeway's wife, Jennifer, who had recently joined Patagonia as the head of the art department. Jennifer and Ridgeway had met at the bar of the Hotel Yak & Yeti in Kathmandu, Nepal, a few years earlier. Ridgeway was there doing a story for *National Geographic*, and Jennifer, then a fashion executive on a work trip to Thailand to look at silks for Calvin Klein, had missed a connecting flight in New Delhi and made an impromptu trip to see the Himalayas. Ridgeway, immediately smitten, invited Jennifer to join him on a three-week trek to the Mount Everest base camp. Jennifer retorted that the farthest she had ever walked was from the door of a cab to the front door of Bergdorf Goodman on 5th Avenue and declined.

Although Jennifer didn't join Ridgeway on the hike, she agreed to visit him a few months later in Santa Barbara. When she showed up at the airport wearing pearls and heels, she wondered what she had gotten herself into. Ridgeway was waiting there along with Chouinard, who had driven his dumpy 1969 Datsun. Assessing her escorts, she concluded that she was being hosted by "drunk dwarves." Yet the allure of the dirtbags proved irresistible, and Jennifer soon traded her heels for flip-flops and moved to Ventura.

Jennifer was universally beloved and would become dear friends with Malinda and McDivitt. But when McDivitt first met her, she was thinking like a recruiter. Here was a bona fide fashion executive, a confident woman who knew the apparel business, and even more importantly, someone who could tolerate Chouinard and his friends. McDivitt immediately offered Jennifer a job.

"But I don't know anything about advertising," Jennifer protested.

"Neither does anyone else around here," McDivitt shot back.

Soon, Jennifer, McDivitt, and Chouinard were working together on Patagonia's catalog, and introducing a whole new level of authenticity to advertising in the process. Gone were studio shots and the stiff models looking awkwardly into the camera. Instead, the pages were filled with athletes and families enjoying life in their Patagonia gear. At first, they used their friends and colleagues as models. One iconic shot featured the children of Peter Metcalf, a senior employee at Chouinard Equipment. His infant was in an unattended stroller, rolling down a hill while an older child ran behind, trying to catch up. There were also pictures of Chouinard, bare-chested and hammering at the anvil, covered in mud in the middle of some adventure, clinging to the wall on a perilous climb.

Then Patagonia turned to its customers for contributions. The company put out the request to "Capture a Patagoniac," inviting its fans to send in photos of themselves and their friends in the wild using the gear. Thousands of pictures began arriving at the office, piling up in cardboard boxes. Jennifer and another colleague, Jane Sievert, went through them one by one, selecting the choicest examples to be included in future catalogs. It was a savvy move that helped forge even stronger ties between the company and its customers. It also represented the dawn of an entirely new field of marketing: user-generated content. In the years that followed, other brands would follow Patagonia's lead, paving the way for a new generation of brand ambassadors and social media influencers.

With pictures from Patagoniacs pouring in, the catalogs soon featured images of everyday people testing their own limits: oily mechanics working under filthy cars, ropeless climbers holding on to a ledge with just a few fingers, sea kayakers squinting into the sun, backpackers riding atop trains in Ecuador, and bike campers soaked as they forded wild rivers. In one famous shot, a climber wearing blue shorts and a neon green jacket hangs by one hand from a giant statue of a Tyrannosaurus rex. Perhaps the most iconic image is simply known as "The Flying Baby." Amid a copper-toned boulder field at Joshua Tree National Park, a mother, wearing a red Patagonia fleece, tosses her 6-month-old daughter, clad in a purple Patagonia onesie, across a chasm to the outstretched arms of her father. Decades later, with the rise of social media, the image went viral—photoshopped, shared, captioned, and turned into a meme.

With contributions from customers and an authentic aesthetic, the Patagonia catalogs were doing much more than just advertising. They served as visual testimonials, tributes from other dirtbags that spoke to the quality, functionality, and coolness of Patagonia products. The pictures were also a call to action. With image after image of badass climbers, kayakers, hikers, and skiers, each catalog implored anyone who picked it up to get off their butt and get outside.

Crucially for Chouinard, the catalogs were also a way for him to maintain control of Patagonia's identity. He couldn't tell retailers how to display the clothes, and he was loath to pay for advertising. Patagonia would never convince the world it made the best gear with billboards and magazine ads, he reckoned. Instead, the company had to prove it. And there was no better way to do that than with a catalog full of real people doing real things.

## "It's Me or the Baby!"

Carissa Ridgeway was a wailer. The daughter of Jennifer and Rick Ridgeway, Carissa started coming to the office with her mother in 1982. Colicky and irritable, she cried loudly throughout the workday. It didn't help her temperament that Jennifer's office was in a windowless room called "the box," where temperatures sometimes reached 110 degrees Fahrenheit. All day long, Carissa's cries pierced the Patagonia office, making it impossible for others to have a phone call or conduct a meeting.

Carissa wasn't the first infant to appear on the Ventura campus. Tom and Doreen Frost brought their newborn to work in 1974, and years later, the Chouinards were toting around their infant son, Fletcher. As more employees had children, infants were getting stashed in bassinets under desks and brought along to meetings. Babies began springing up "like tiny fireflies appearing at night," remembered McDivitt.

It was all charming enough, but disruptions were inevitable. With the business growing and a certain degree of professionalism required even at a company like Patagonia, it became increasingly difficult to have children alongside their parents during the workday. During one especially busy week, Malinda turned to the classified ads in the newspaper and hired a transient camper to look after Fletcher. Shortly after that, some of the new mothers at the company who were going through divorces found themselves struggling to meet childcare needs while also keeping up with their responsibilities at work. McDivitt would sometimes hold someone else's baby during a meeting. Once, while nursing Fletcher, Malinda inadvertently exposed herself to a customer at the company store. Not long after that, the manager, when confronted with a dirty diaper in the showroom, issued an ultimatum: "It's me or the baby!"

But it was Carissa's piercing cry that forced the issue. At the time she was born, the State of California didn't require companies to provide maternity leave, so most mothers came back to work after just three weeks. Daycare options in Ventura were mediocre at best. Jennifer would sometimes nurse Carissa in the car, but this proved to be an uncomfortable experience; a local group of Hells Angels had a nearby clubhouse and would interrupt her breastfeeding with their roaring bikes. Rick Ridgeway was gone for months at a time on expeditions, and Jennifer was short on options. So, Malinda, who exerted a powerful influence on the company's trajectory while remaining largely behind the scenes, made a unilateral decision: she would open a childcare center.

From her days working as a maid in Yosemite, Malinda had developed a deep empathy for the working class. Most people, she knew, needed some measure of help—help paying the bills, help getting through the day, help with the kids. As Patagonia took off, it became clear to her that she had the opportunity to help those in need at her own company, particularly working mothers. As a first step, Malinda procured a trailer in January of 1983 and had it placed in the parking lot. Jennifer's mother came and lived in the trailer, looking after Carissa and some other tots during the day. Word about the ad hoc daycare center got around, and before long Ventura County officials showed up and informed Patagonia that if it was operating a childcare facility, it would need to be licensed.

Requisite permits were soon obtained, and not long after that, as a new building took shape on the company's burgeoning campus, Malinda took it upon herself to give Patagonia's childcare program a permanent home. Spotting some architects working with blueprints of the new building, she marched over, grabbed the drawings, produced a pencil, and drew a square in a corner of the first floor, making her intentions clear by writing the words: "day care center." Oh, she told the architect, the space needed to include small sinks, and toilets, too.

Not everyone was sold on the idea. "Why?" asked McDivitt, when informed about Malinda's ambitious daycare plans. "I mean, what are we talking about?" It was hard enough running a company, McDivitt thought. How was she supposed to run a school, too? No matter. A few months later, with the new building complete, the company had a proper childcare center, plumbing and all. Touring the new space, Chouinard and Tompkins squatted on the toddler-size toilets and posed for a picture. In 1985, the company inaugurated the formal childcare facility and bestowed it with a grand title that echoed the Great Pacific Iron Works; the children would be cared for at the Great Pacific Child Development Center.

Malinda kept improvising as needed. After a parent forgot to pick up their child at the end of a workday, she bought a van that functioned as a makeshift school bus, burying the expense in the shipping department's budget. From that point on, Patagonia provided transportation for children through third grade. And very quickly, the program evolved from a mission of mere caretaking to a more expansive goal, aspiring to forge curious, generous, resilient, active children. Drawing on the educational philosophies developed by Maria Montessori and Rudolf Steiner, who shaped the Waldorf curriculum, Patagonia's caretakers emphasized the virtues of self-directed play, time in the outdoors, and independence. The program, Malinda would explain to the local paper at the time, had lofty ambitions: it aspired to reduce "wasted childhoods" which she believed "was the norm for the American child today." Children should learn but not be taught. They should use their imaginations but not be entertained. Having toys was not the same thing as playing. And perhaps most importantly, it was important for children to see their parents doing work they loved.

The kids in the childcare center took this last part of the message to heart. One day, Chouinard walked in and addressed some of the 4- and 5-year-olds: "Hi, kids! How's school?"

"We're not in school," one boy retorted. "We're at work. My mother works over there, and I work here."

As more children enrolled and the childcare program needed to expand, Malinda distributed its facilities around Patagonia's campus—a classroom on one side of the office, a sandbox on the other side. It was a deliberate effort to fan the kids out, rather than isolate them, to weave family life into the fabric of the company and make the peals of young laughter inescapable. The move had surprising consequences. "No matter where you were, you were close to kids," Ridgeway said. "We all started to observe that when you were in a meeting and the windows were open and you heard kids playing, people were nicer to each other. They were more collaborative. The men were less aggressive. It calms everybody down, and it provides a sense of unity that you belong to an extended family. That influences the culture of the company and influences the way people treat each other. How can you put a dollar value on that?" As McDivitt explained, "Language changes in the presence of babies. . . . We are our best and most loving selves in the presence of babies and toddlers, and there is some invisible lasso that ties all of us more firmly together as our work lives dovetail with our personal lives."

At times, the rougher edges of American life intruded on Patagonia's idyllic oasis. In one dark chapter, vandals broke onto campus in the middle of the night, slashing car tires, breaking sprinklers, and bludgeoning to death two of the program's pet guinea pigs and two of its rabbits, leaving the bloodied carcasses for the children to find the next morning. More recently, with homelessness and drugs common on the streets of Ventura, vagrants have occasionally wandered around the office and used the outdoor showers. This prompted the company to erect a tall, black, steel fence around the main campus, sealing it off from the outside world. And still, within the company's walls, the program is regarded as an integral part of the culture.

Childcare at Patagonia was born from necessity. The Chouinards and many of their friends who worked at the company were having children, and they needed someone to look after them. But for Malinda, the issue quickly became a defining passion. The United States is virtually alone among industrialized countries in not offering federally mandated paid maternity leave. To Malinda, who is quick to home in on injustices and tenacious in her pursuit of solutions, it was just the kind of lopsided fight she relished. Large swaths of society might not grasp the importance of child-care, but at least one scrappy company could show the rest of the world the right path.

Beyond being a cause that she believed in, Malinda quickly realized that offering childcare on site would help the company, allowing women to stay in the workforce without sacrificing their careers. Virtually every mother at Patagonia returns to her job after maternity leave, compared with about 70 percent at most companies. Employee engagement also significantly improved thanks to the childcare program. And Patagonia has for years had an unusually large number of women in senior leadership roles.

More than 40 years after it started, the childcare program is still going strong. Wander on to campus on any given day, and you might see dozens of children participating in Mexican heritage activities, climbing trees, or making up their own games, their Patagonia clothes covered in mud, their laughter echoing through the cubicles. There are three childcare facilities across the company's offices, with 17 classrooms, more than 200 students, and 70 teachers, a remarkable 3-to-1 ratio. Some two thousand kids have gone through its program, "and not one of them has ended up in jail," Chouinard said. When women who work at the company are nursing and need to travel for work, the company pays for them to travel with a nanny, an arrangement known as the "child and companion program." And breastfeeding women are no longer relegated to the parking lot; instead, it is routine for them to nurse their newborns during meetings—even board meetings. "When you value families, when you value women, when you value breastfeeding at work, when you do ridiculous benefits, you don't just have childcare for the people in the corporate office," said Dean Carter, the former head of human resources. "You care about it so much you have it in the distribution center. That's what a value is."

## "Management by Absence"

Even as Patagonia turned into a fully fledged business with millions of dollars in sales and a growing staff, Chouinard continued to spend months on the road, climbing, fishing, and at times pioneering new extreme sports. He helped popularize ice climbing—a treacherous feat that involves using crampons and a specialized pickaxe to scale frozen waterfalls and icy rock walls—writing a book on the topic and mentoring younger climbers in the craft. He did the same with surfing and whitewater kayaking, using the Patagonia catalogs to champion his favorite outdoor activities. Tompkins brought Chouinard into the fold with a handful of other hardcore adventurers, and together they began calling themselves the "Do Boys." It was a riff on the Japanese term for "active sports," or "doing sports." It was also a shorthand way to indicate that they weren't wasting their lives as couch potatoes. They were out in the world, doing things, not sitting on their asses like so many lazy Americans.

On one early trip, Chouinard and the Do Boys went whitewater kayaking in Northern California. Chouinard had never done much kayaking, but they told him he would be fine. Before he knew it, he was hurtling down a Class 5 stretch of the Tuolumne River. Chouinard's boat careened off a drop, flipped upside down, and he landed on his head. His spine compressed, and he emerged from the 12-day trip with 15 stitches. A few months later, his right elbow gave out, requiring surgery. Forty-three years of adventures were finally catching up with him.

These travels would often take him away from the office for months at a time, and he took to calling the sojourns his MBA. Not a master's of business administration, the graduate degree bestowed on aspiring titans by business schools. Rather, this was his own kind of MBA: "management by absence." And yet Chouinard's expeditions served an important purpose for the company, or at least that's what he told himself, Malinda, and his colleagues. It was only by going out and testing gear in the wild that he could be sure it worked well and come up with the ideas that would lead to the incremental improvements that made Patagonia's products some of the best in the world.

Still, his extended absences occasionally led to turmoil back home. After being away for a few months, Chouinard would return to the office brimming with ideas and impatient for results. In the weeks before his impending return, employees would get nervous, girding themselves for the mayhem that would inevitably ensue. "We would be running around like a chicken with our head cut off, trying to plug the holes," said Mary Ellen Smith, a quality tester. "He caused a lot of chaos that he didn't need to." Projects Chouinard had greenlit just months ago were no longer adequate; marketing plans months in the making needed to be redone; new lines of business needed to be opened immediately. "He was not a great communicator," Smith said. "If you worked for him, you were kind of at his mercy." When Chouinard would set off again, bound for another adventure on the other side of the world, the staff would breathe a sigh of relief.

Certain trips expanded his mind in more profound ways. In

1980, Chouinard went to Alaska to summit Denali, the highest peak in North America. He was joined by Ridgeway, a seasoned mountaineer who was a member of the first American team to summit K2, and it was among the coldest climbs Chouinard had ever attempted. The air was minus 40 degrees Fahrenheit, so frigid that the plastic water bottles they carried shattered. Following a successful ascent, the pair spent a few days hanging out in Anchorage, staying with their friend Peter Hackett and sleeping on the floor. One afternoon, Hackett suggested they go down to Bishop's Beach in nearby Homer. It was low tide, and if they were lucky, they could dig up some razor clams. Before they left, Hackett pulled out a few buttons of mescaline that had been sitting in his dresser drawer for months. Figuring that the drugs were expired, the trio ate the whole batch.

Down at the beach, the mescaline kicked in hard, the Yukon scenery turned psychedelic, and they dug in the wet sand like feral animals, laughing madly as they tried to secure some of the elusive mollusks. Families with toddlers splashing in the surf regarded the apparent lunatics with trepidation and ushered their children away. Miraculously, the psychedelics didn't completely impair their ability to gather seafood, and by sunset they had collected enough razor clams to make a meal, and roasted them over a bonfire on the beach. As the day wound down, Hackett snapped a photo of Chouinard and Ridgeway, filthy and giggling, wearing matching red Patagonia sweaters and holding a bottle of Mondavi wine. The picture was included in one of Jennifer's catalogs with the caption: "Lucidly searching for clams."

On the way back from Denali, Chouinard got an invitation to join an expedition that would attempt to summit Minya Konka, a remote, 24,800-foot peak in the Himalayas, on the edge of the Tibetan Plateau. Al Read, who had acquired a permit for the climb from the People's Republic of China, also secured a deal with ABC to film the expedition for its long-running series *ABC's Wide World of Sports*. Ridgeway and his friend and climbing partner, Jonathan Wright, would be the producer and cameraman. Chouinard joined as an additional member of the team.

Minya Konka had only been summited twice before, by an American team in 1932 and a Chinese team in 1957. No one had reached the top in more than two decades. With no reliable maps, and in an age well before GPS and satellite maps on smartphones, the team relied on a book that the first American expedition wrote called *Men Against the Clouds*. When they checked into their hotel in Chengdu at the start of the journey, Chouinard listed his occupation as "capitalist."

On October 13, the team was establishing its route when disaster struck. They had set up Camp I on a ledge of snow at 18,000 feet. Chouinard, Ridgeway, Wright, and another climber, Kim Schmitz, decided to ferry some packs up another 2,000 feet, to where they planned to place Camp II. Having deposited their gear, the team was clambering down the mountain on soft snow. After an arduous trek up, the descent was a breeze. It was afternoon, and the sun had warmed up the mountain since the morning. They were sliding down sections, laughing as they glided on their butts. Chouinard was in the lead. They could see the yellow tents of Camp I below. Suddenly, a slab of packed snow broke just above the group and enveloped them, most likely triggered by Chouinard and Ridgeway, who were in the lead. Avalanche. The men were swept over a 30-foot cliff, tumbling in a wave of snow until they came to rest more than a quarter mile away. Then the mountain began moving again, this time pushing them toward a 300-foot cliff. "We knew we were dead," Chouinard said. "And we accepted the idea that we're dead. We're gonna die."

When the snow finally stopped moving for good, Ridgeway, bruised and bleeding, took charge. Chouinard was down the slope, half buried, blood leaking from his mouth, ribs broken, and disoriented but conscious. Concussed, he didn't know where he was, asking Ridgeway what had happened, which mountain they were on. Schmitz was screaming in agony, his back broken, rope cinched around his body, unable to catch his breath. Ridgeway managed to free Schmitz from the rope, and Chouinard eventually dug himself out. Wright, with a broken neck, was in the worst shape of all. As Ridgeway held him in his arms, the last life slipped out of him.

The next day, the team buried Wright under a pile of stones, just steps from where he passed, marking the gravesite with two bamboo poles and a string of Tibetan prayer flags. As they hiked out, Chouinard turned to Ridgeway and cursed the Himalayas. "Fuck these mountains," he said.

The avalanche weighed on Chouinard for years. He had almost gotten himself killed plenty of times, but this was different. "I've had a lot of close calls, near-death experiences, but always afterwards you go around sniffing the flowers and be really happy to be alive and everything," Chouinard said. "But after that, all of us were deeply depressed for several months." With time, however, the experience changed Chouinard's outlook on life. "It's taught me that there's nothing to fear about death itself," he said. "When my time comes, I'm gonna go out pretty peacefully."

In addition to a new appreciation for his own mortality, Chouinard's time in the wild gave him a visceral understanding of the damage being done to the planet. Over and over again on his many expeditions, he saw pristine landscapes spoiled by development, pollution, and mismanagement. In Africa, grasslands and forests surrendered to cities and slums. In Patagonia, glaciers that hadn't moved in millennia were melting in a matter of decades as the burning of fossil fuels heated the planet. Kayaking in Russia, he saw vast swaths of the landscape deforested and denuded by the Soviet Union's efforts to keep pace with the United States. And at home in California, the coastline was cluttered with new homes, the Central Valley was filling up with subdivisions, and animals and insects began to disappear. The avalanche changed his perspective on overdevelopment, too. "When I came out of it, I had lost all fear of dying," he said. "And it's helped me to cope with my feeling that mankind as a species has ended its days. That thought used to really get me down. Now I think, hey, we're all gonna die. Maybe all at once, and so be it. We're an incredibly damaging species, and we're pulling all these other beautiful species down with us, and maybe we ought to just get out of here. You do what you can. Then—even if you're burning gasoline to get there—you just have to say fuck it, let's go surfing."

Chouinard knew he was part of the problem. With two houses of his own, an aggressive travel schedule, and a growing business next to the Ventura River, he was hardly an ascetic. "There are a million holes in my philosophy," he said. "It's kind of like being a sinner. You go to confession, do your penance, then you go out and sin again. It's a process." And yet even though he was living large in some ways, he was keenly aware of the growing threats to the natural world.

Nowhere was the sting of new development more painful to Chouinard than in Fitz Roy, the site of the Fun Hogs climb that formed the spiritual foundation for his career. Chouinard returned to Fitz Roy in 1986 and found its landscape transformed. What was unspoiled land less than two decades before was now in the throes of development. Gone were the grazing Rojo sheep and the grassy fields. Instead, there were new buildings and a grid of orange tape demarcating where new streets, hotels, and restaurants were to be built. A new city, Chaltén, was under construction. Where there was once just Patagonian scrub, a wild river, and an intimidating steppe approaching one of the fiercest peaks in the world, there were now the makings of a suburban development and strip malls. What was worse, it was hard to escape the conclusion that Chouinard's own career contributed to this mess in some way. The legends of his exploits, the Patagonia logo—all of it had served as an unofficial advertisement for Fitz Roy, and here were the unsavory results. Chouinard was horrified and has not been back since then. "I don't want to see it," he said.

## "The Kleenex of Fleece"

Chouinard was never satisfied. Yes, the quality of Patagonia gear was improving, and the product line was diversifying. The company was selling the first long underwear made of polypropylene, which helped adventurers stay warm in the backcountry. It introduced Baggies, lightweight multisport shorts that Chouinard insisted had pockets spacious enough to accommodate two tennis balls. And yes, business was booming. But when it came time for Chouinard to do his most ambitious expeditions in the backcountry, his own clothes kept failing him. Wool was slow drying, stinky, and a favorite meal for moths. The early synthetic pile, known as bunting, helped with warmth but still trapped moisture. He needed something new, and he found it in Malden, Massachusetts.

Back in 1906, a Hungarian immigrant named Henry Feuerstein was struggling to break through in the apparel business. He had lost a good chunk of an early fortune and figured he would spend the rest of what he had on one last shot: a textile factory. His new company, which he called Malden Mills, started making bathing suits and wool sweaters for outdoor workers. The gamble paid off, and soon Feuerstein's company had distinguished itself as one of the finest fabric makers in the country. In the decades that followed, Malden Mills developed sophisticated research and development operations and innovative manufacturing practices.

As it expanded, Malden Mills remained vertically integrated, doing the spinning, dyeing, printing, and finishing of fabrics in-house. That technical edge and consolidated production made the company a preferred vendor of the US Army, which turned to the company to make the wool knits that kept soldiers warm during World Wars I and II. By the middle of the 20th century, Malden Mills was experimenting with synthetic fabrics. Nylon was hitting the market, spandex was on the horizon, and it was clear the company needed to move beyond wool. But with cheaper manufacturing from Asia starting to chip away at America's edge, innovation stalled, the US textile business went into decline, and in the 1970s Malden Mills found itself in crisis.

By this time, Feuerstein's grandson, Aaron, was running the business, and he made a gamble of his own. Malden Mills, he decided, would become the world leader in fake fur. Animal rights activists were on the march, and the younger Feuerstein figured women would pay up for a noncontroversial alternative to mink. Malden Mills also began making toilet seat covers and bathmats. Indeed, it was the company that made the material that Malinda found at the merchandise mart in Los Angeles and that was used for Chouinard's original synthetic pile sweaters. But fake fur and toilet seat covers weren't enough to pay the bills, and by the early '80s, Malden Mills was on the verge of bankruptcy once again.

In search of a lifeline, Feuerstein pushed his team to tap into its history of R&D and find the company another new material. The fabric whizzes delivered. It turned out that polyester, when spun into superfine yarn, created a remarkable texture that was a good alternative to wool. Soft but voluminous, light but warm, this new fleece not only functioned well as insulation but it also wicked moisture away. When Malden Mills showed it to Patagonia, Chouinard was delighted. It was exactly what he had been looking for. Working together, Patagonia and Malden Mills refined the material until it was as good as they could get it at the time. It was warm, light, and sturdy. Unlike the pile toilet seat covers, it was fuzzy on both sides. Just as crucially, it didn't pill. And it was incredibly soft, almost like the fur of a chinchilla, the cute, furry rodents native to the Patagonia region in South America. With that realization, they had their name for the new material. It was "synthetic chinchilla," or Synchilla. Soon, Patagonia introduced its first item made with the new material, the Synchilla Snap-T, which would become one of the company's best-selling products.

Synthetic fleece was the foundation for a new era of tinkering and innovation at Patagonia. The company would go on to launch the Retro Pile fleece jacket, an updated version of the original pile piece Chouinard had sewn out of toilet seat cover material. And the Snap-T underwent myriad little improvements, including a signature pocket design that was both functional and distinctive. The original Synchilla fleeces had a square pocket on the left breast. But Bob Kettenhofen, a Patagonia employee who designed the brand's first sailing line, was bothered by it. When he was on a boat and the wind kicked up and he had to quickly remove his sunglasses and stash them in that front pocket, they would inevitably slide toward his armpit, an uncomfortable inconvenience. The solution: angle the inside of the pocket away from the armpit. That design became the norm in Snap-Ts and was echoed in the pocket flap's unusual angular design.

With the Snap-T in hand, Chouinard had a better insulation

layer. But he still had a serious problem: his underwear was getting wet, and during long trips into the backcountry, they stank. "If you wear the same underwear for 70 days, you think a lot about it," he said. "And you think of ways to make it better." The polypropylene versions Patagonia had introduced back in the '70s were an improvement over cotton and wool. But when he was deep in the backcountry and days away from a shower, let alone a washing machine, it didn't matter what he did, he couldn't get his base layers to stay dry. "I can't make it through a month in the mountains," he told his fabric designers. "It just doesn't work because it gets wet and it stays wet and there's no way to dry." There was another problem. "It smells terrible," he said. Now that Patagonia's insulation layer had been improved with Synchilla, it was time to improve the base layer, and Chouinard told the team to figure it out.

Chouinard had a hunch about what might work. In 1984, he had been wandering the floor at the Chicago sporting goods show and saw a demonstration that caught his eye. A vendor was showing off football jerseys that were easy to clean, with even grass stains coming right off. The jerseys were made with polyester, and the company that made the fabric, Milliken, had found a way to make the material easy to clean. The Patagonia team went to Milliken and explained Chouinard's demands. They replied that indeed, polyester would likely do the trick. It was cheap. It was easy to clean. It wicked moisture away from the body. And it had a higher melting point than polypropylene, allowing it to endure the rigors of a clothes dryer. Working with Patagonia's design team, Milliken developed three different weights of a custom polyester and gave it some texture that allowed it to hold heat and more effectively wick moisture. Soon they had an entirely new material: Capilene.

Going all in on polyester was a risk. At the time, 70 percent of

Patagonia's sales came from items made from polypropylene and bunting fleece. But Chouinard wasn't afraid to turn his back on a successful product. Years earlier, he had phased out pitons when they made up the lion's share of his business. Now he was doing the same thing, reinventing his go-to insulation layers and introducing Synchilla and Capilene.

Though the legendary management professor Clay Christensen hadn't coined the term yet, Chouinard was wrestling with the "innovator's dilemma." Christensen noted that when companies have a hit, they're not incentivized to innovate and come up with an even better alternative that might replace their primary breadwinner. As a result, successful companies often lose their edge and fall behind upstart competitors. At Patagonia, the safe bet would have been to keep on using polypropylene. After all, consumers didn't know what they were missing, and there were no rival companies stealing Patagonia's market share with newer technologies.

Chouinard was taking a risk by rushing headlong toward these new materials, but he did it anyway. Then, with the decision made, he had to get retailers and customers on board. A crucial test in this campaign came during a meeting in Las Vegas, when Patagonia's sales reps gathered with executives ahead of a trade show for the outdoor industry. Without much notice, the executives from Ventura sprung the new products on the sales reps. The old synthetic pile, known as bunting, was out; Synchilla was in. And the old polypropylene long underwear were gone; now they had Capilene.

The pivot was happening no matter what, but Chouinard wanted buy-in from his sales reps before the trade show began. It was just as big a gamble for the sales reps as it was for management. If the reps couldn't sell this stuff in bulk, their commissions were in jeopardy. But once they had seen the new gear, the reps were sold. "We didn't need to hedge our bets," said Henry Barber, one of the company's top salesmen. "Chouinard had given us something better, and we were ready to go full on into the new thing."

In the days following that meeting at the Bali Hai Hotel, the reps worked the convention room floor. "We've got good news and bad news," they told the retailers. "The bad news is that we've dropped polypropylene and bunting." Barber and the other reps would watch as the retailers' jaws hit the floor. "The good news is we've come out with something that is completely better in every respect. It wicks better in the case of Capilene. In the case of Synchilla, it doesn't pill, it's warmer, and it sheds water faster."

The retailers were convinced, too, and in the years that followed, Capilene and Synchilla pushed Patagonia's sales and profits to new heights. Capilene remains among the company's best sellers to this day. Synchilla was popular enough to more or less save Malden Mills; Patagonia soon was ordering huge volumes of it, and the Massachusetts fabric maker would go on to sell similar textiles to many other companies, too. The new material became so popular that for many years, it became synonymous with fleece. "For many, many years," said Rob Bondurant, vice president of marketing at Patagonia, "Synchilla was the Kleenex of fleece."

Chouinard was never the most methodical leader. He didn't lay out a grand strategy and diligently execute it with precision. Forethought was never Chouinard's forte. Instead, his genius came in bursts of spontaneity, a dynamic that calls to mind his performance on the rock walls he scaled as a climber. Just as he would have to make split-second decisions while hanging hundreds of feet above the Yosemite Valley floor, leaping for the next crag and holding on with his fingertips, so too would he redirect Patagonia in an instant when he sensed something was off. And as was the case when he was a climber, he usually made the right move.

# CHAPTER 5

# Winning Back the Wild

## "Tithing"

A lightning strike pierced the sky above Yellowstone National Park on June 14, 1988, sparking the Storm Creek Fire, which began smoldering in the backcountry. Nine days later, another bolt of lightning lit the Shoshone Fire in the park, and two days after that, the Fan Fire started raging. Yellowstone rangers let the blazes burn, recognizing that forests need fire to regenerate and trusting nature to find its own balance. But that "let it burn" approach was a relatively new policy. For much of the 20th century, fires had been suppressed. As a result, decades of combustible underbrush had built up on the Yellowstone floor.

By July, the fires had multiplied and exploded in size. Campers accidentally ignited new blazes, the usual summer rains didn't come, and a firestorm spread throughout the park. Old Faithful was under threat, flames swept into picturesque canyons, and tourists were evacuated. Millions of 100-foot-tall lodgepole pines exploded, each one booming with the concussive force of munitions. When Yellowstone officials finally decided they would fight the fires, it was too late. Crews dug fire lines, set controlled burns, and dumped retardant from the air, but nothing could stop the inferno. Yellowstone became a national news story, commanding the attention of President Reagan. Wyoming was covered in smoke. The sky darkened, and ash coated the Tetons. On a single day in August, which came to be known as Black Saturday, more than 150,000 acres were lost. In total, some 248 fires ravaged the greater Yellowstone area that summer. More than one third of the park was charred. Hundreds of elk perished, along with moose, bison, and mule deer. The fires raged for nearly two months until, in a remarkable act of natural intervention, snow came early, on September 11, blanketing Yellowstone in powder and snuffing out the fires.

Chouinard could smell the smoke from his house in Moose. Watching Yellowstone burn, he grew more convinced than ever that the natural world was in peril. He had seen pristine landscapes ruined by human development on his many travels, from Russia to Africa to Argentina; now that large-scale degradation was happening in his own backyard. The fires stirred up a new sense of responsibility in Chouinard. He now had money to spare; shouldn't he be spending it to protect nature?

As the fires burned in Yellowstone, an unusual congressional hearing took place in Washington, DC. Just days after the first blaze began, Dr. James E. Hansen, then a scientist at NASA, addressed the United States Senate and reported that man-made global warming had begun. The burning of fossil fuels had changed the composition of Earth's atmosphere, and the whole world was heating up. "It is time to stop waffling so much and say that the evidence is pretty strong that the greenhouse effect is here," Hansen said. A story about the hearing ran on the front page of *The New York Times*. The public wasn't much aware of global warming at that point, and news of Hansen's testimony didn't cross Chouinard's radar at the time. But he didn't need to hear it from Hansen. Chouinard knew the planet was in trouble.

Years before the Yellowstone fires, Chouinard had begun giving away some of Patagonia's earnings to nonprofit organizations working to protect wild places. In 1984 alone, recipients of his largesse included the Sierra Club Legal Defense Fund, the Audubon Society, the Environmental Defense Fund, Greenpeace USA, the Salvation Army, and Habitat for Humanity. The next year, Chouinard formalized his giving program. Each year, he decided, Patagonia would donate 10 percent of its annual profits to groups working to restore and protect the natural environment.

As sales increased and there was more money to go around, Chouinard tapped Paul Tebbel, a worker from the retail store who had a passion for conservation, to help manage the program. Chouinard would tell Tebbel the kinds of things he was interested in, and Tebbel would then go to research organizations working on those issues, bringing back suggestions on where to donate. They called it the "tithing" program, borrowing a term from Christianity that describes when congregants give 10 percent of their income to the church.

With more money going out the door to support activism, Patagonia workers sometimes grumbled that they weren't paid more. The company wasn't offering large salaries at the time, and now a major chunk of the profits was going to charity. But this was Chouinard's company, and he set the rules. The planet was his religion, and he was going to use his winnings to support environmental causes. "People realized that if you weren't on board with what Chouinard was all about, you might as well go somewhere else," Tebbel said. "We did all sorts of stuff that other companies considered crazy."

As Chouinard ramped up his philanthropic giving, he found himself wrestling with a central tension: yes, he was an environmentalist; but he was also running a business that was exacting an increasingly severe toll on the planet. It was a paradox that every executive at Patagonia pondered. McDivitt described it as "creative tension" and used it as inspiration. Patagonia needed to be a successful business; it would also try to preserve wilderness. If those goals were sometimes at odds, McDivitt figured, that would only force the company to be better, to work smarter. But the tension was more personal for Chouinard and Malinda. As owners of the company, it was really up to them how big this thing got and what kind of an impact it made on the world. And in 1987, as they wrestled with how exactly they should wield their newfound influence, the Chouinards went looking for outside help.

Kevin Sweeney was waiting tables at a San Francisco restaurant called Lily's Cafe, decompressing and figuring out what to do next. Months earlier, his career had flamed out through no fault of his own. He had been the press secretary for Gary Hart, then a prominent senator from Colorado and a frontrunner to secure the nomination to be the Democratic candidate for president. Then Hart's campaign imploded in scandal after revelations about an extramarital affair, and Sweeney abruptly left Washington.

Sweeney's journey, from the Capitol to the kitchen, was noteworthy, and just a few days after he started at Lily's, the ABC program *Nightline* did a feature on him. Among those watching was Malinda Chouinard. Intrigued by Sweeney, who came off as a savvy communicator who wasn't afraid to eschew conventional notions of success, Malinda sent him a FedEx package with some Patagonia catalogs and a letter. She explained that the Chouinards had been giving away money to environmental and political groups for four years but had no idea how to talk about it and no overarching strategy. Would Sweeney come to help?

Sweeney arrived in Ventura expecting to have a chat about philanthropy. Instead, Chouinard bent his ear about quality. How could Patagonia make the best products? How could they communicate to their consumers that their gear was durable and better than the rest? The same concerns that had preoccupied Chouinard since he started making pitons were still gnawing at him decades later. When the conversation finally turned to Patagonia's grant making, Sweeney was stunned to learn that Patagonia had been quietly giving away 10 percent of its pretax profits for years. Most of that money had been in the form of small grants to environmental groups, with a bit going to some of the more prominent environmental organizations. (At Malinda's insistence, the company also contributed to Planned Parenthood, which, she argued, was an environmental group since it was helping keep the human population down.)

Sweeney stopped serving pots of Darjeeling tea at Lily's and joined Patagonia as its director of public relations, a role that had him working on both media and marketing as well as the Chouinards' approach to philanthropy. As he got to know the family, it became clear that their commitment to supporting grassroots activists was about more than just charity. It wasn't even just about making themselves feel better about running a company that was taking a toll on the environment. At the end of the day, Sweeney teased out of the Chouinards a deeper and different motivation for their philanthropic work: they wanted to influence other businesses. If other companies saw that Patagonia could prosper even as it tried to clean up its act and gave away its winnings to causes it believed in, maybe they would be inspired to do the same thing.

It was an audacious aspiration, and it wasn't going to happen on its own. If that's what Chouinard really cared about, he would have to make a concerted effort to reform the rest of the business world. A first step in this plan came when Patagonia cofounded a new group of like-minded companies called the Conservation

Alliance. Shortly after Sweeney was hired, Chouinard rallied three other outdoor gear companies, Kelty, REI, and The North Face, and began pooling money to protect wild places. Today, more than 270 companies are members, and the group has given away more than $36 million.

Patagonia also began ramping up its own environmental activism. It launched its first national environmental campaign with a series of ads protesting the implementation of a new development plan for Yosemite National Park that would have increased traffic and paved the way for new construction. Next, the company ran ads calling for the preservation of Antarctica, where commercial fishing was decimating the wildlife population and untreated sewage was being dumped into polar waters. The campaign lashed out at a recent decision by countries to approve mineral exploration on the continent and called for customers to support a proposal by then Senator Al Gore that would have introduced new protections to Antarctica. When pro-life activists from the Christian Action Council began picketing Patagonia stores over its support of Planned Parenthood, Chouinard announced that for every demonstrator his staff spotted, Patagonia would donate an additional $10 to the reproductive rights group. The picket line quickly petered out. It was a little bit of public relations jiujitsu, and it would serve as a model for other Patagonia PR crises in the years ahead.

Closer to home, Patagonia waded into local politics, helping elect three city council members who took a dim view of development in Ventura. Those relationships mattered when the California State University system tried to build a new campus in town. Bringing in a college would have fundamentally changed the character of Ventura, and Chouinard was adamantly opposed to the plan. His no-growth friends on the city council shared his concerns and quashed efforts to build the campus. That left many development-minded locals fuming. "Our politicians are running scared," Jim Salzer, a local businessman, said at the time. "They have all been hesitant to take a stand because of the seemingly awesome ability of one local business, Yvon Chouinard and Patagonia, to marshal support for antigrowth issues."

With grassroots activism, coalition building, and charitable giving, Patagonia was starting to make waves beyond its own office walls, and the rest of the world was taking note. But if Chouinard was really going to make good on his emerging vision of a more responsible business world, he would have to turn the mirror on himself. It wasn't enough to encourage other companies to be better; Patagonia needed to be its own harshest critic. An activist in the outside world, Chouinard needed to be an activist inside his own company, too.

## "Everything We Make Pollutes"

The cover of Patagonia's Spring 1991 catalog featured an earth-toned watercolor painting of El Capitan in Yosemite, the site of Chouinard's grueling 10-day ascent in 1964. The style and color palette of the image were reminiscent of the Chinese scroll painting that appeared on the very first Chouinard Equipment catalog from 1972. And the essay inside was almost as consequential as "A word . . . ," the first manifesto penned by Chouinard and Frost.

In that original treatise, Chouinard acknowledged that with climbing getting more popular, the granite walls that were the foundation of the sport were getting damaged, leading to his embrace of clean climbing. The 1991 essay, titled "Reality Check," was similarly introspective. The growing environmental footprint of Patagonia was undeniable, and Chouinard and the rest of the leadership team needed to address it head on. They spent months deliberating whether to do it publicly and precisely how to phrase it. Then they laid bare the fundamental contradiction at the heart of a clothing company with grand ambitions to help heal the planet.

"Everything we make pollutes," it began. "The production of every piece of clothing we make has a negative impact on the environment. Period. We envision ourselves wearing our gear while enjoying the benefits of nature or, better yet, while fighting environmental sinners. But it's a fact that our synthetic-fiber clothes start as petroleum, and the subsequent refining process pollutes." There were no easy solutions, the essay made clear. "Should we then look to natural fibers? Perhaps, but it's not that easy," it went on. "Cotton has its problems. More pesticides and fertilizers are used for cotton than for any other crop; preparing cotton fields for mechanical picking requires powerful and harmful defoliants. Formaldehyde is often used in the spinning process, and chemical finishes are applied. Wool garments—including some we make— often require dry cleaning. Sheep, the cute critters from which we shear our wool, are some of the most destructive grazers in the animal kingdom. There are organic, sustainable methods of producing both cotton and wool. But production is still small, and there are long-range doubts that there is sufficient land to produce enough cotton, wool, and food to support five or ten billion humans above the poverty level."

It was a grim self-assessment, not exactly the kind of messaging designed to inspire nature lovers to spend their money on a new fleece. But that was the point. Because at this critical juncture, now more than two decades into running a retail business, Chouinard had arrived at a deeply counterintuitive conclusion: he didn't want people buying more and more of his gear. Unlike just about every other business owner, he didn't fetishize endless growth or dream of constantly enlarging his market share. Instead, Chouinard fantasized about the very opposite: selling less. Or at least not selling that much more. If making Patagonia jackets and shorts and T-shirts was taking a toll on the planet—and it certainly was—then the surest way to reduce that harm, he figured, would be to reduce the number of goods Patagonia sold.

In the essay, Chouinard started to tease out this subversive line of thought. "As individuals, each of us has power as well," he wrote. "Unless we each begin to change our patterns of consumption, we can't expect the broader realities to change. Because the production of virtually all consumer items in the industrial world is polluting, the best way to reduce our impact is to demand less (to buy fewer items) and to demand better (to buy things that last)."

Patagonia wasn't the only retailer publicly questioning its role in the world. Yet again, Chouinard and Tompkins were on the same wavelength. A year earlier, Tompkins had placed an unusual ad for Esprit in *Utne Reader*, a magazine that catered to the far left. Titled "A Plea for Responsible Consumption," Tompkins used the ad to bemoan the growing environmental toll of Esprit's own operations and lament the rise of rampant consumerism. "We know this is heresy in a growth economy, but frankly, if this kind of thinking doesn't catch on quickly, we, like a plague of locusts, will devour all that's left of the planet," Tompkins wrote. "We could make the decision to reduce our consumption, or the decision will soon be made for us."

Tompkins was channeling the existential outrage that he and Chouinard had tapped into during their sojourns in the California hills, and it was no longer just idle talk. Esprit had just launched an "eco-collection" of women's clothing, using organic cotton and natural dyes. At a time when few brands were touting their ecological bona fides, it was a revolutionary bit of product marketing and an early preview of wider industry efforts to clean up the supply chain. But with the *Utne Reader* ad, Tompkins went even further, pleading with consumers to think twice before buying more stuff and suggesting that consumers could live a more righteous life if only they bought less. "By changing the things that make us happy and buying less stuff, we can reduce the horrendous impact we have been placing on the environment," it concluded. "We can buy for vital needs, not frivolous, ego-gratifying needs."

The Esprit ad made a minor splash when it was released, attracting some news coverage and putting Tompkins on the map as a heterodox thinker. Its biggest influence, however, would be felt two decades later, when Patagonia used it as inspiration for the most successful piece of marketing in the company's history, a 2011 ad titled "Don't Buy This Jacket."

With "A Plea for Responsible Consumption" and "Reality Check," Tompkins and Chouinard were starting a new kind of conversation with the shopping public. It wasn't enough to just buy quality goods or even patronize companies that supported worthy causes. Nor was it enough for businesses to make incremental changes in their supply chains and lean into some eco-conscious marketing. Instead, the two Fun Hogs—now middle-aged business leaders—were acknowledging that their companies were actively harming the planet and imploring consumers to question whether they even needed their products in the first place. "What we were doing with that catalog was admitting that 'Hey, we're a part of this mess,'" Sweeney said. "The next step was for us was to stop making a mess in the first place."

That was easier said than done. There was no obvious way to stop customers from buying more stuff, and neither company took any serious steps to limit their growth at the time. If anything, the *Utne Reader* ad led to more sales for Esprit. But if Chouinard couldn't stop people from buying his stuff, at least he would get Patagonia to clean up its act. Around this time, the company decided to formalize its "environmental review process," committing to a continuous self-audit of its operations. "We are deepening a lifestyle of environmental self-analysis that will become more and more a part of doing business," McDivitt wrote in memo. "In short, it will be ongoing and forever." On campus, the renewed commitment led to immediate changes: recycling began on a large scale; composting started in the cafeteria; the childcare program began using cloth diapers.

Further down the supply chain, Patagonia was also throwing its weight around. The company decided it would no longer do business with any factory if it wasn't allowed to visit and ensure quality standards and safe and healthy conditions for workers. It committed to undertake a life-cycle assessment of the four main fabrics it was using at the time: cotton, wool, nylon, and polyester. Understanding the complete environmental footprint of each of those materials would take time, but it would also give the company a sense of what more it needed to do to clean up its act. And Patagonia ramped up its efforts to use more eco-friendly materials, sometimes with disastrous results.

The same year "Reality Check" was published, Patagonia and Smith & Hawken, another American clothing company, agreed to buy 1 million buttons made from the tagua nut, a type of seed that grows on palm trees in the Ecuadorian rainforest. Polished tagua nuts resemble ivory and were a popular material for buttons before plastic became ubiquitous. Conservation International helped broker the deal, and Patagonia paid a premium for the nut buttons, accepting the extra cost as a worthwhile trade for using fewer petroleum products. The experiment lasted just a year. By

1992, the buttons were cracking, and Patagonia recalled the items that featured tagua. It turned out there was a reason plastic buttons had become the norm.

Another time, after a trip to Japan, Chouinard demanded that the company begin stocking a type of eco-friendly Japanese fishing shoe called Reef Walkers. McDivitt protested, arguing that they would never sell. Chouinard pulled rank and demanded that she place an order. McDivitt relented, but before doing so took out a black marker and wrote, in graffiti on the rafters above her desk, "My boss made me buy 20,000 pairs of Reef Walkers." Then she made Chouinard sign it. Chouinard got his way, and Patagonia ordered the Reef Walkers. But McDivitt was right: the shoes didn't sell. (The graffiti is still there.)

Other experiments with sustainable materials met similar fates. When Patagonia launched a line of rain shells that used an allegedly nontoxic water repellant, the project backfired. The fabric made an unusually loud noise when the sleeves brushed up against the body, and more to the point, it didn't keep the rain out. The shells were scrapped, and in the end, Patagonia had to accept that its effort had actually done more harm than good. Rather than giving customers a jacket they could use for a decade or more, Patagonia had made one that was destined for the landfill from day one. Worse, consumers who bought the faulty shells might well be scarred by the experience and think twice about buying Patagonia or any other brand touting its green bona fides, for that matter. "We were setting customers up to mistrust clothes with environmental claims," said Vincent Stanley, who by this time had assumed a newly invented role in the company that was one part continuing education and one part public relations: in-house philosopher.

In the end, the lesson was clear. If a product doesn't work and needs to be replaced right away, there's no way it can be considered good for the environment; if it doesn't last, there's no way it can be sustainable. "Durability and high quality are key elements to environmental responsibility," Stanley said. "The world doesn't need a lot more crappy products." But before Chouinard could double down on Patagonia's quality, he would have to let go of the business that got him started.

## "Sever Those Roots"

Chouinard was getting sued. With Patagonia enjoying more success in the late 1980s, Chouinard Equipment became a target for frivolous lawsuits filed by ambulance-chasing lawyers who mistakenly believed the hardware and software businesses were still part of the same company. One plaintiff broke his ankle playing tug-of-war with a Chouinard Equipment rope. In another case, a window washer was injured when he misused a Chouinard harness. "No equipment failed, and no equipment broke, but when people get hurt . . . they sue," Sweeney said in a response to news media inquiries at the time.

The lawyers suing Chouinard Equipment were never going to get a big payout. The climbing business had been carved out from the clothing company years earlier, with the entities separated into limited liability companies under a broader holding company. That insulated Patagonia from the legal and financial troubles, but it couldn't stop the headaches.

Following a first wave of lawsuits, Chouinard Equipment was hit with a wrongful death claim. A novice climber had improperly installed a Chouinard Equipment harness and fell to his death, and his family sued, seeking $10 million. Chouinard was livid and didn't hesitate to blame the victim. "I've taken a lot of pride in making the world's best climbing equipment and trying to do a good job at it, but times have changed," Chouinard said. "Nobody wants to take responsibility for their actions, to say, 'I screwed up, it's my fault, I didn't bother to learn how to use the gear.'"

Although the company maintained that the fault was with the man who misused the harness, the episode was laced with tragic irony. Designing products that would keep climbers alive had always been a priority for Chouinard. With each new design—of a carabiner, axe, and harness—Chouinard was optimizing for simplicity, and also safety. Now someone had died while using his equipment. The company was never found liable for the climber's death, yet it didn't take long for costs from the lawsuits to start adding up. Chouinard Equipment's insurance premiums jumped 2,000 percent in a year. Legal bills started mounting. And for Chouinard Equipment, which had just $6 million in annual sales, compared to more than $70 million at Patagonia, the litigation amounted to an existential threat.

Seeking to wash his hands of the mess and preoccupied with Patagonia, Chouinard decided to let the hardware company go. In 1989, Chouinard Equipment filed for Chapter 11 bankruptcy protection. That allowed a group of employees, led by the general manager, Peter Metcalf, to gather the funds they needed to buy the company, and it was spun out into its own independent corporation.

Chouinard purported to be unfazed by the sale, maintaining the sort of stoicism that allowed him to endure torturous ascents on granite walls and 30 days in the Fitz Roy ice cave. "I sold the climbing company, and I walked away," Chouinard said. But many longtime Chouinard Equipment employees were pained to see the founder go. "We thought we were doing them a favor by selling them the company," Malinda said. "But the employees felt abandoned by Yvon. Some people get a father figure complex with him."

Once the transaction was completed, Metcalf moved the operations to Salt Lake City, Utah, and decided to rename the company—it would now be known as Black Diamond. On the ski slopes, black diamond runs are for experts only, and with the name, a modified version of Chouinard's original diamond $C$ touchmark could still be used as a logo. More than 30 years later, Black Diamond is still one of the most successful manufacturers of climbing gear in the world. But at the time for Chouinard, letting go of his first business represented the end of an era. "The company's roots were in hardware," Sweeney said. "To sever those roots does cause sadness around here."

## "We Could Buy That"

On April 22, 1989, Earth Day, Chouinard hosted an activist named Rick Klein at the Patagonia offices in Ventura. Klein, a native Californian who had first visited Chile in the 1970s and fallen in love with the land, had come straight off the plane from South America, and he was there to ask Chouinard for money. He was running an organization called Ancient Forest International, working to preserve old-growth trees around the globe. In particular, he was trying to protect a 1,100-acre swath of forest in southern Chile that was home to ancient Araucaria, also known as monkey puzzle trees. Rumor had it that a New Zealand–based timber company wanted to buy the land, situated in the Cañi mountains, and clear-cut the trees to make paper for fax machines. Making his pitch, Klein described the land and unfurled a spread of nine photographs he had taped together, displaying a majestic vista of forests and lakes. It was a rare opportunity to preserve pristine land, he told Chouinard. Klein had already raised money from Alan Weeden, another philanthropist; would Chouinard help?

Chouinard didn't hesitate. He was in for $40,000. That was an enormous commitment and took even his family by surprise. "It wasn't a great time for us financially," Malinda said. "Is any time a good time to spend an unbudgeted $40,000?"

Chouinard told Klein that if he wanted to raise more money, he should go to San Francisco and hit up Doug Tompkins. Chouinard was sure his friend would match his contribution. He was right. When Klein arrived in San Francisco, Tompkins cut the activist a check on the spot. Klein now had most of the funds needed to save a unique stand of ancient forest.

Back in Ventura, Chouinard used the Patagonia catalog to spread the word about the conservation effort and solicit additional donations. "We ask our customers and friends—as concerned citizens of the earth—to speak with their wallets," read the copy, inside a catalog that featured pictures of old-growth trees shrouded in mist. "Winning back the wild is a long process; we'll keep you posted on our progress." Patagonia customers contributed, the funds were raised in short order, the trees were protected, and the Cañi Sanctuary became one of Chile's first great conservation success stories. It was the Fun Hogs' first foray into large-scale conservation and the beginning of a journey that would reshape land use across South America.

Not long after raising the funds to save the Cañi Sanctuary, Tompkins joined Klein on a trip to Chile and was reintroduced to a land that had played a formative role in his early days as an adventurer. The trip occurred at a pivotal moment for Tompkins. While Chouinard was a resolute dirtbag, eschewing materialism even as Patagonia afforded him the means to live lavishly, Tompkins had spent the '80s reveling in his newfound success. He flitted between Paris, Milan, and New York. His compound in San Francisco was a downtown oasis featuring a minimalist Japanese house replete with a small redwood grove; inside, the walls were decorated with a Francis Bacon triptych and paintings by Otto Dix and Fernando Botero. He tried to instill an appreciation of the fine arts on Esprit employees, too, reimbursing them for trips to the museum and tickets to the symphony.

But more than a decade of excess had left Tompkins disillusioned with the fashion business and disgusted with his own luxurious lifestyle. "By the mid-1980s I had slowly come to the realization that I was doing the wrong thing," Tompkins said. "I was in an apparel company making a lot of stuff that nobody needed. My main work was adding to the environmental crisis rather than helping revert it. I realized I had to do something else." It wasn't just that he was burned out by the spending, the travel, and the posturing, though that was a part of it. Rather, he had arrived at a more profound realization about his own role in a culture that revolved around consumption. "I found myself caught up in the marketing," he said. "I lost track of the larger picture. I was creating desires that weren't there. I was making products that nobody needed."

As part of his soul-searching, Tompkins became enthralled with the esoteric writings of Arne Næss, a Norwegian mountaineer who had pioneered a field of fundamentalist environmental philosophy known as deep ecology. Deep ecology removes humans as the central actors in world events and instead ascribes equal value to all living beings, regardless of their utility to modern civilization. Inherent in deep ecology is an understanding of the interconnectedness of all natural systems, from the climate to the plant world to the animal kingdom, and a recognition that when any part of this vast tapestry is harmed, the entire web of life suffers. It subjugates humanity to a supporting role in the story of life on Earth, and in doing so, it places renewed value on flora, fauna, and pristine landscapes. For Tompkins, who had spent more time in wild places than most, it amounted to a radical shift in perspective, and it reaffirmed his commitment to walk away from Esprit. "I left that world of making stuff that nobody really needed because I realized that all of this needless overconsumption is one of the driving forces of the extinction crisis, the mother of all crises," Tompkins said.

He decided he was done with Esprit. It would be a jarring transition, but it was made easier by the fact that Tompkins and Susie had grown apart. In 1989, they divorced, and the next year, Susie orchestrated a leveraged buyout of the company. It was a messy process, personally and professionally, but Tompkins came out ahead. As part of the proceedings, he sold his 50 percent stake in Esprit for about $150 million. He sold his interests in the company's international units for another $150 million. At the meeting where the paperwork was formalized, one of the bankers, wearing a suit and tie, asked Doug, "What are you going to do with all this money?"

Tompkins, casual in his trademark khakis, shot back, "Try to undo everything you guys are doing."

Disposing of his stake in Esprit was only the start of Tompkins's metamorphosis. He went on to auction off his impressive art collection, selling his paintings and sculptures for an additional $18 million, and disposing of his properties and cars. Newly freed from his responsibilities as a CEO, Tompkins was a jaded capitalist with a burgeoning environmental streak, a lust for adventure, and a fortune with which to remake his life. Yet instead of reveling in his success, he was stripping away all the trappings of his life as a successful entrepreneur. He was still wealthy, but in the absence of anything to do, he found himself wanting to reconnect with the wild, get back to his days in the backcountry with Chouinard, and return to his dirtbag roots.

One of his first orders of business was to start giving his money away. In a matter of months, Tompkins plowed nearly $50 million into the Foundation for Deep Ecology, a nonprofit organization he founded to champion his newest obsession. With grants ranging from $3,000 to $300,000, the foundation modeled its work on Chouinard's charitable giving, funding grassroots activists, conservationists, and environmentalists around the country who were seeking to slow development, preserve wild lands, and stymie the fossil fuel industry.

Sometimes, Tompkins enlisted Chouinard directly. Early in the '90s, the pair came to the aid of Dave Foreman, one of the founders of Earth First!, an environmental activist group that was being targeted by the FBI. Foreman had been arrested at gunpoint by a SWAT team at his home in New Mexico, falsely accused of sabotaging transmission lines that led to nuclear power plants. Chouinard and Tompkins footed the bill for Foreman's defense, subsidizing hotel rooms and airfare, and enlisting a legal team led by Gerry Spence, a legendary trial lawyer from Wyoming. Foreman was acquitted after it became clear the FBI was trying to frame him, a victory that would have been impossible without the support of Tompkins and Chouinard.

But Tompkins had much grander ambitions and soon was spending lavishly to achieve his goals. This time, though, he wasn't buying rare art or fancy cars. He was looking to buy nature itself. He and Chouinard had already helped preserve the Cañi Sanctuary. Now Tompkins went scouting for even bigger acquisitions. Instead of just buying a small tract of forest, he thought, what if he began gobbling up vast swaths of unspoiled land and protecting them from development?

In January 1991, Tompkins piloted his Cessna 206 from San Francisco to Argentina and began surveying the land, looking for large parcels he could buy. A close friend, Peter Buckley, joined Tompkins for some of the flights and recalled him scanning the horizon for cattle farms he might buy like "some sort of demented real estate guy."

Each time he flew over a pristine valley or a wild river, Tompkins remarked, "Look at that. Isn't that beautiful?"

Each time, Buckley concurred, awed by the untouched landscape. And each time, Tompkins bounced with excitement at the prospect of a new find.

"That's for sale," he said. "We could buy this. We could buy that."

Before long, Tompkins had purchased a 37,500-acre farm called Reñihué not far from an active volcano, where he built a house for himself. From there, he kept buying cattle ranches in Patagonia, accumulating nearly 800,000 acres altogether. He was spending his fortune attempting to make real the deep ecology vision articulated by Næss. The land would be left alone, free from human disturbances. It was an expensive gamble, but Tompkins was confident it was a bet worth taking. "You never know if you're doing the right thing," he said. "But the way I see it with land conservation is that the risk of something negative coming from this seems to be rather small compared with taking an exploitative approach."

Almost as soon as he sold his stake in Esprit, Tompkins began needling Chouinard to follow his lead. Sell Patagonia, take the money, and do something big, Tompkins would tell his old friend. With the money he would have, Tompkins told Chouinard, he could buy his own swaths of land, or go fund even more activists, or disappear into the backcountry and fish his life away. Now that Tompkins was liberated from the headaches of being a boss, it was unfathomable to him that a Fun Hog like Chouinard still wanted to spend his days sweating about a supply chain and distribution channels if he didn't absolutely have to.

There were times when Chouinard was tempted to take Tompkins's advice. Running a company was a hassle, and Chouinard was always happier when he was out in nature rather than in a board meeting. But he could never get there. "Chouinard's not financially driven," said Bill Bussiere, a former Patagonia CFO. "He just doesn't give a shit. He and Malinda could make millions if they went public, but they don't want to. Yvon feels he could be a better instrument of change if he keeps things in his own hands."

And while he didn't succumb to Tompkins's pressure campaign, Chouinard began to accept that there was a deeper purpose to what he was doing. In maintaining Patagonia as an outlier in the business world, he saw the potential to have an impact that went beyond mere acreage; he thought he could shape America's corporate culture. "There have been a few times when, frustrated with the business, I've thought about selling it, putting the money into a foundation, and using it to effect environmental change and protection," he said. "Each time, though, I've decided that the better strategy was to keep the company and use it as a model for responsible business."

## "All the Margin"

By 1990, annual sales had ballooned to $100 million, a fivefold jump in a matter of years. Sales reps like Henry Barber and Billy Kulczycki were making small fortunes in commissions, regularly netting more than the senior-most executives at the company. The disparity irked Chouinard, who made an abrupt decision to put the sales reps on salaries instead of letting them earn commissions, effectively slashing their earnings. To Barber, who considered Chouinard a close friend and had been on grueling climbs with his boss, the move felt like a betrayal. Patagonia had only gotten as big as it had thanks to his ground game; now Chouinard was effectively punishing him for his own success. "We really had a bond, and then he went and did something like that," Barber said. "He never really let a person get in the way of his decisions."

The chaotic staffing and rapidly shifting loyalties weren't an altogether uncommon phenomenon. Patagonia was largely run by managers who had grown up inside the company, not seasoned leaders who had been schooled in best-in-class human resources practices from other big companies. Employees could quickly fall in and out of favor with Chouinard. "There was a sense that the higher you went up the ladder, the more likely it was that you were a god one day, you were much less than that the next day," said Libby Ellis, who helped manage Patagonia's environmental efforts in the early days. It was but one indication that behind the laid-back façade there was a sometimes shrewd business, run by often unsentimental executives. "Things get idealized," said Lynda Grose, who worked as a designer at both Patagonia and Esprit. "You just have to navigate this territory between the activist and the capitalist."

From the moment Kulczycki joined Patagonia, he understood the demanding expectations. The Chouinards told him they expected the company to generate at least 10 percent annual EBITDA, or earnings before interest, tax, depreciation, and amortization, a common way of evaluating a company's financial performance. "It always had to be a successful business," he said. "Yvon was always very clear that if it's not making money, there's no point in doing this." At the same time, Chouinard maintained his disdain for the tawdry business of finance. "Yvon has no respect for accounting people—people who wear coats and ties," said Steve Peterson, who worked as chief financial officer for a spell. "It's almost a loathing. But that stuff is part of business. It's like hating your left arm."

As sales boomed in the late '80s, Patagonia's success started catching up with the company. For years, Chouinard deliberately kept the payroll at about 150 people. That was the number of people that Robin Dunbar, the British anthropologist, posited was the upper limit to the number of primary relationships a person could manage. Chouinard didn't want Patagonia to get any bigger, fearing that rapid growth would compromise the culture. He also figured it was an artificial way to limit the company's growth, and thereby its toll on the environment. But there was simply more work that needed to be done, more bodies required to fulfill the growing volume of orders that were coming in. Chouinard finally relented and very quickly, the company expanded in size.

It was an awkward time for an American apparel company to have a growth spurt. Across the industry, manufacturing was moving to Asia, and Patagonia followed suit. Up until that point, many of the company's clothes had been made domestically, at factories where a Patagonia employee was embedded on the factory floor, monitoring production, keeping an eye on quality, and even loading fabric into the cutting machines. "You kept track of how the factory ran," said Randy Harward, one of Chouinard's quality-control gurus. "You literally loaded the lines in each factory, so you knew what they could do, and if they were having trouble meeting their schedule." With the move to Asia, costs went down, but the company lost a measure of control. "We didn't really think about the implications at first," Harward said. "But pretty quickly it became clear that it was more distant, more removed. We didn't have people visiting the line every day. Instead, we had somebody visiting every month. There were language barriers and cultural barriers, and it became clear we were going to need to define our specifications much more carefully."

With the company growing and its supply chain expanding at a rapid clip, problems started to emerge. Buttons started falling off, snaps weren't staying shut, seams were coming undone. At one point, more than 10 percent of orders were being returned, a ludicrously high figure that revealed deep problems with the manufacturing process. This was maddening to Chouinard, who was obsessed with quality. Ever since he hammered his first piton, the notion that the things he made were the best in class had defined his work. He wanted to believe it was still true now, even as he outsourced manufacturing to contract factories halfway across the world. Chouinard even taught classes about quality to Patagonia employees. He would bring in bag of Peet's coffee beans, set it down on a table, and ask his students: "Is that a quality coffee bean?"

An awkward silence inevitably followed. Did the boss like Peet's? What was he getting at?

Then Chouinard would begin the lesson: "Quality is objective," he would say, arguing that the coffee beans either were or weren't excellent. There was no in between.

That would get folks going. "Quality is not objective," some would protest. "It's a matter of taste."

Chouinard would dig in his heels. "No," he would say. "It's about consistency. It's about a product fulfilling its function." He pressed his students, challenging them to define a perfect shirt. If someone suggested it was a custom-tailored, Italian dress shirt made from the finest cotton, Chouinard would scoff. How would that shirt hold up in a washing machine? How long would it last?

A delicate shirt couldn't be considered quality. These lessons divided the staff—designers who obsessed over every stitch appreciated Chouinard's unwavering stance, while executives who saw the world in units sold thought he was being too aspirational. But with the esoteric lessons, Chouinard was trying to transmit to his employees the same fixation on quality that had for so long animated him. Unless Patagonia's jackets and shorts and pants and fleeces worked perfectly, the company might as well not make them at all.

As the problems persisted, Chouinard tasked Harward with cleaning up the mess. Harward spent a year on the road, visiting factories, working with manufacturers to make sure they understood Patagonia's high standards, and at times, buying up old sewing machines. One of the most common complaints from customers was that buttons were falling off after the stitching holding them in place unraveled. Harward figured out that the problem was that the new factories were using chain-stitch button-sewing machines, rather than the lock-stitch machines that had been used in Patagonia factories in the United States. When the chain-stitch machines weren't adjusted correctly, the buttons were liable to come off. The solution was obvious to Harward: He would buy all the lock-stitch machines he could find and have his new factories in Asia use them. It didn't matter that the lock-stitch machines were cumbersome and a bit slower to use, or that it was necessary to change the bobbin every couple hundred buttons, or that they cost $6,000 apiece. If they sewed on buttons that didn't fall off, it was a worthwhile investment. Bit by bit, the imperfections became less commonplace, and return rates went from double digits down to 1 percent. "It was like shutting off a faucet," Harward said.

Between legal headaches and quality issues, a decade of rapid growth had left Chouinard in need of a break. By conventional metrics, he was more successful than ever. Patagonia was making $10 million a year in profits, virtually all of which was going to him and Malinda. They gave much of their winnings away, but they also had the means to live exceedingly comfortably, flying around the world for exotic adventures and maintaining their homes on the beach in Ventura and at the foot of the Tetons, in Moose. That disconnect—between his professed disdain for materialism and his increasingly lavish lifestyle—was not lost on him. Yet the bigger Patagonia got, the more Chouinard grew concerned about its influence on the natural world. He was consumed with dread about the destruction of wilderness and keenly aware that while he was making an effort to improve Patagonia's manufacturing processes, he was still a part of the problem. "We're sleazeballs," he would say. "We're doing just what all the other companies are doing."

McDivitt was also burned out after more than a decade running the company and told Chouinard she wanted to retire. She was one of the few executives to have fully gained his trust and was the only person besides Chouinard, Malinda, and their two children to ever own stock in Patagonia. (She eventually sold the stock back to Chouinard.) Hoping to prepare the company for its next chapter, Chouinard and McDivitt hired a handful of new leaders they believed could shepherd the company through the last decade of the 20th century. Bill Bussiere, a former accountant, became chief financial officer. And Pat O'Donnell, who had experience running ski resorts, was tapped to be the company's next CEO, despite having no experience in the apparel business. "I didn't know anything about making clothes," O'Donnell said. "But Yvon said he wanted to use Patagonia as a tool for social and environmental change."

It was a hasty bit of succession planning, and in a bid to instill in the new recruits a sense of purpose, Chouinard and McDivitt took them down to Patagonia. Along with a handful of other executives, they spent a week talking about the unusual philosophy behind the company and the creative tension between solving hard problems and making things worse. With a series of talks in the places that inspired him the most, Chouinard was trying to pass along the same spark that had animated him and McDivitt for the past two decades. He didn't expect them to have all the answers. After all, there were no tidy solutions to the big, thorny questions that Patagonia was grappling with. But that was the point. Chouinard wanted his team to grasp the profound enigma that was his life's work. He wanted them to strive for perfection while knowing it was impossible. He wanted them to accept that they would never get it all right and to resolve to keep trying their damnedest, anyway. "He wanted them to understand who we were," McDivitt said, "and what was important to us."

# CHAPTER 6

# A Critical Time

## "The End of It"

"What happens when you die?"

For decades, that was what Patagonia insiders would ask Chouinard in their moments of candor when conversation turned to the ultimate fate of this most unusual company. On the surface, the question had everything to do with Chouinard's singular role as the face of the brand. He was an icon, and Patagonia's identity was wrapped up in his exploits and ego. But the issue was as much about succession planning as it was about marketing. When Chouinard was gone, who would have the final say on big decisions? Who would make the hard choices that often flew in the face of conventional wisdom? Who would have the conviction to forgo profits in pursuit of some idealistic goal? And there was an even more fundamental question: Who would own Patagonia? As a privately held corporation controlled by Chouinard, some sort of transaction would have to happen when he died. Among the most likely scenarios were that it would be inherited by his children, sold to another corporation or a private equity firm, or taken public. Yet any one of those transactions would be enormously disruptive, fundamentally altering the peculiar balance of power that allowed Patagonia to be the strange company that it was and throwing into question what it would stand for when Chouinard was gone.

In search of some guidance on how to think about growth and succession planning, Chouinard and Malinda went to Florida to chat with Michael Kami, an eccentric management consultant who had helped revive Harley-Davidson and done strategic planning for IBM. They caught up with Kami on his yacht, where he was resplendent in a captain's hat and a military shirt left open to expose his bare chest. Kami began interrogating Chouinard and quickly homed in on the question of why he bothered running a company in the first place.

Chouinard replied somewhat disingenuously, quipping that he had always hoped to make enough money to disappear to the South Seas and go find the perfect spot to surf and hunt bonefish. He went on to tell Kami that while he could have done that a long time ago, he and Malinda were worried about the fate of the planet and hoped to use their resources to help in some small way. They had given away $1 million that year to 200 organizations and found deep satisfaction in this. "Our bottom-line reason for staying in the business was to make money we could give away," he said.

Kami didn't buy it. "I think that's bullshit," he said. "If you're really serious about giving money away, you'd sell the company for a hundred million or so, keep a couple million for yourselves, and put the rest in a foundation. That way you could invest the principal and give away six or eight million dollars every year. And, if you sold to the right buyer, they would probably continue your tithing program because it's good advertising." This was just what Tompkins had been telling Chouinard to do—maximize his influence by letting go of the company and plowing his proceeds into conservation efforts.

Chouinard replied that he was concerned about what would become of Patagonia if he sold. He had no faith that a new owner would continue to manage the company in a responsible way. "If I did sell the company, that would be the end of it," Chouinard said.

Kami listened and quickly understood a truth that Chouinard himself had started to articulate in recent years: Patagonia didn't exist as a means to make the family wealthy enough to retire in paradise. It didn't even exist solely as a font of philanthropic dollars that could fund his favored causes.

"You're kidding yourself about why you're in business," Kami said.

Instead, he told Chouinard that it seemed like he was running Patagonia the way he did—prioritizing environmental causes, interrogating his own supply chain, not losing sight of the people at the heart of the company—in order to show the rest of the business world that there was a different way to do things. The whole point of Patagonia was to demonstrate that capitalism didn't have to be so awful.

Chouinard left Florida with a new sense of clarity about the fate of Patagonia, at least in the short term. "We aren't going to sell the business," he said. "I think I can do more good by continuing to run the company in a responsible way and show other companies that you can do good and have a good business." And while there was no clear answer to the question of what would happen when Chouinard died, he began to take the question seriously. There was even an inkling of what was to come. "I really believe this is a movement, not a business," he said. "When Malinda and I are gone, I want Patagonia to become an environmental foundation."

Chouinard didn't have much time to dwell on the future, however. Shortly after he visited Kami, Patagonia was plunged into its most serious crisis to date.

# "Black Wednesday"

Patagonia was flying high as the '90s dawned. The company had added more wholesale accounts and was doing a brisk mail-order business. It had opened stores in Chamonix, France, and Tokyo, Japan, as well as many retail locations around the United States. For a stretch, sales were growing by an astronomical 50 percent a year. There was an equestrian line featuring Patagonia riding pants, which Chouinard came up with after meeting a woman who showed horses. There were three different sailing lines, for three different types of boats. The company was even producing a blazer. Planning for continued growth, Patagonia went on a hiring spree, adding more than one hundred employees to the payroll and blowing well past Dunbar's number. The finance and supply chain operations were told to anticipate annual growth of up to 40 percent in the coming years, and the idea was to build the capacity up front so as not to get caught flat-footed when the demand arrived. O'Donnell, the new CEO, tried to keep the momentum going. He took on new debt to finance the expansion plans, stocked up on inventory to prepare for the influx of business, and generally started running Patagonia like a normal company. Within months of the new team taking over, however, the wheels started coming off.

The Savings and Loan crisis had rattled the economy, a slump in the aerospace business was dragging down business in Southern California, and the troubles on Wall Street finally arrived in Ventura. High interest rates started to crimp consumer spending, the economy tilted toward recession, and banks grew more cautious with their lending. Losses started piling up. So did excess inventory. Wholesalers canceled orders. Overseas growth slowed down and the mail-order business started flagging. The company tried to triage, implementing a hiring freeze, cutting costs, slashing production, and trimming its offerings, but things kept getting worse. The S&L crisis led to the closure of hundreds of banks, and the cascading effects ultimately hit Security Pacific National Bank, Patagonia's primary lender at the time. Fighting for its own life, Security Pacific tightened the company's line of credit. Twice in a matter of months, the bank slashed the amount Patagonia could borrow to meet its basic operating needs. That forced the company to further reduce its spending, going so far as to close offices and showrooms in Vancouver, Munich, and London. Worse, Patagonia's revolving short-term loan from Security Pacific, which had been the company's main source of cash, was called in by the bank. In a matter of days, Patagonia was deeply in debt and on the verge of being unable to make payroll.

Chouinard and McDivitt were mostly checked out as the crisis spiraled in the first months of 1991, having entrusted day-to-day operations to O'Donnell and Bussiere. That hands-off approach ended when McDivitt got a call from the company's longtime financial advisor, Ron Jones, who relayed an urgent message: Patagonia was on the brink of failure. Debts were coming due, cash was running short, inventory had piled up, and merchandise wasn't moving. McDivitt got the next flight to Ventura, and with Chouinard's support, reclaimed control.

When she arrived, she was mystified to learn that O'Donnell had changed the company's banking relationship and had begun working with HSBC. The move made a certain amount of sense, given Security Pacific's tightening of Patagonia's credit line. But it also meant that the company was starting fresh with a new lender, one that had no history with the company and the Chouinards, and no understanding of the company's quirks. Despite having run Patagonia for most of the previous two decades, when McDivitt went to try to sort things out, executives at the new bank didn't know who she was. Nevertheless, she negotiated a six-month window with HSBC that would give her a chance to turn the company around.

It immediately became apparent to McDivitt that she would have to slash headcount. Even if she could stabilize the cash-flow situation, there was simply not enough money coming in to pay all of Patagonia's employees after the recent hiring spree. So, on Wednesday, July 31, 1991, Chouinard made one of the hardest decisions of his career. He laid off 20 percent of staff, 120 people. It was the first mass layoff in the company's history. In a workforce composed largely of friends and family members, it was a brutal bout of bloodletting. Malinda was particularly anguished about laying off working parents and was embarrassed when she ran into former employees around Ventura. Henceforth, Chouinard would refer to the layoffs as "Black Wednesday."

"That was rough," he said. "Some of the people we let go were good friends. But we had to do it to survive. We finally admitted that we were businessmen and decided that if we were going to be in business, it would be on our own terms. We had to stop the runaway growth and get ourselves to a place where we measured success not by profits but by how much good we'd done at the end of the year."

Layoffs alone wouldn't get Patagonia out of trouble, though. There was still work to be done stabilizing the company's finances. The obvious move would have been to sell some equity, bringing in new investors. That's what the capital markets are for, after all. But Chouinard was wary as ever of bringing in new partners, convinced that doing so would ultimately destroy the company. Alison May, who had replaced Bussiere as chief financial officer, counseled him to hold fast. "There's one thing I know," she told

Chouinard. "You don't give away equity unless you have to. People will always lend you money."

With the turnaround underway, HSBC called McDivitt and asked for a new condition: they didn't want the company making environmental grants while it was working to sort out its debts. McDivitt protested. The point of this process was to save Patagonia, not change it; the grants would keep flowing, she told the bank. HSBC called again a few days later. Now the bank wanted Patagonia to bring in outside capital. Again, McDivitt rebuffed the pressure. They had a deal, and she expected HSBC to stick with it.

In the midst of these negotiations, McDivitt called up Doug Tompkins, seeking his advice. He had dealt with his own financial turmoil while running Esprit. Having cashed out, he now had some perspective that might help. Tompkins was resolute: "Whatever you do, do not take money in from the outside," he told her.

"Easy for you to say," McDivitt shot back. "But I'm getting hammered down here."

Tompkins then presented a solution: he would offer Patagonia a onetime $5 million line of credit, to be tapped only in case of emergency.

McDivitt and Chouinard gratefully agreed to the help, and Tompkins's assistant had the paperwork done in a day.

"I'll never use a penny of it," McDivitt told him.

She never did.

## "What Are Our Values?"

In the wake of the layoffs, Chouinard did what he knew how to do best: he went to the mountains. With a dozen top managers in tow, he retreated to the Andes for a few weeks, trying to process

Black Wednesday and make sure something like that never happened again. He dubbed the offsite a "walkabout," a reference to the vision quests that gave the Aboriginals a sense of their place in the world, and together Chouinard and his executives traversed the rugged landscape and interrogated themselves, and one another, about what kind of company they wanted to run. Profits were important, yes, but so was product; so were people. Having high-performing employees mattered and so did creating a sense of work-life balance. It was critical, above all else, never to let the company get to a place where it would have to do mass layoffs again. In practice, that would likely mean deliberately restraining growth. And it would be necessary to preserve the company's independence at all costs. That would mean avoiding debt.

Processing all that had happened, Chouinard arrived at an unsettling conclusion: for all its high-mindedness, Patagonia didn't look all that different from any other company. Here it was, stretched too thin, strapped for cash, and unable to pay its employees. It was, he said, "a wake-up call that I was doing business just like everybody else." Pained as he was to admit it, "I was growing for the sake of growing and not thinking about what I was doing," he said. "That forced us to sit down, all of us in the company, and ask ourselves why are we in business . . . We'd sit down for three, four hours a day and talk about, 'OK, why are we in business? What are we trying to do? What are our values?'"

Upon returning to Ventura, Patagonia installed its first board of directors. It was a long-overdue step that introduced some basic corporate governance to the company. But the board Chouinard selected was anything but average. Among those asked to help oversee Patagonia was Jerry Mander, an author and environmental activist. Mander immediately began pressing the company to confront the ecological crisis more directly. At one of the first meetings of the new board, while the rest of the team was at lunch, Mander wandered off by himself and drafted a statement of values. When everyone returned, he presented it to them. It is a document that still informs Patagonia's work today. "We begin with the premise that all life on Earth is facing a critical time, during which survivability will be the issue that increasingly dominates public concern," it read. "Where survivability is not the issue, the quality of human experience of life may be, as well as the decline in health of the natural world as reflected in the loss of biodiversity, cultural diversity and the planet's life support systems."

Mander's statement of values codified some of the things that Chouinard had been feeling but was unable to articulate fully. He was becoming more aware of the degree to which modern capitalism was straining ecosystems, depleting natural resources, and exploiting underprivileged communities. Now he saw the same dynamics playing out in his own company. The financial crisis, and Patagonia's subsequent missteps, reflected a broader economy that had lost its way, Chouinard believed. Patagonia had gotten too big, expanding in an unsustainable way. Without quite realizing it, Chouinard had allowed Patagonia to become dependent on ever-growing demand—just the kind of shortsighted, extractive orientation that defined the worst of American business. It had put itself at the mercy of a global financial institution that didn't care about Patagonia but would do whatever it needed to preserve its own profits. And in the quest for growth, Patagonia had let itself become dependent on cash it didn't have. It was essentially living off its credit cards, hoping it could make its payments each month. "We were just going for growth, you know, not saying no," Chouinard said. "I mean, we were just opening more and more dealers. We were opening our own retail stores.

You know, nothing goes forever. And in fact, that's why the faster a business grows, the faster it dies also."

Chouinard also determined that the company had approached the limits of its natural niche, the specialty outdoor market. If it wanted to keep growing at this pace, it would almost certainly have to become a general market clothing retailer, selling everyday pants at department stores. That, Chouinard thought, would have compromised the whole endeavor, inevitably eroding Patagonia's quality and values. "Can a three-star French restaurant with ten tables retain its three stars while adding fifty tables?" he mused. "Can a village in Vermont encourage tourism (but hope tourists go home on Sunday evening), be pro-development, woo high-tech 'clean' companies (so the local children won't run off to jobs in New York), and still maintain its quality of life? Can you have it all? I don't think so."

Going forward, Chouinard resolved to limit Patagonia's growth. He wanted Patagonia to last for 100 years, and he would start making decisions with that in mind. That would mean intentionally depressing sales and saying no to potentially lucrative opportunities. It would mean eschewing advertising and learning to accept lumpier earnings; one year growth might be 3 percent, the next year it might be 30 percent—the company would have to adapt. But it would all be done with the aim of building a more resilient, nimble organization. "There's two kinds of growth," Chouinard said. "One, where you grow stronger and one, you grow fat."

As Chouinard looked to the future, Patagonia's messaging took a darker turn. His innate pessimism was never far away, and some of the company's marketing materials veered into Malthusian territory. One ad from the early '90s, featuring an image of a beach stuffed with sunbathers, challenged readers to consider "the essential dilemma of our times: Too many people, too few resources, too much waste, and not enough care. Life out of balance." The ad directed customers to support Planned Parenthood and another group called Zero Population Growth.

At the same time, Chouinard idealistically—and erroneously—predicted that a recession would lead to a revolution in human behavior. "We do not think spending will get us out of this one," he wrote in the fall 1992 catalog. "We don't see this as a temporary recession. Instead, it may presage a serious worldwide decline, possibly the end of economics based on consumerism. In the United States alone, it is clear that people are no longer interested in shopping as entertainment, no longer thrilled by spending for its own sake . . . Because of these obvious truths, we decided to make a radical change: we are limiting Patagonia's growth in the United States with the eventual goal of halting growth altogether. We dropped 30 percent of our clothing line. . . . Next season, more cuts will be made. The fewer styles we make, the more we can focus on quality. We think that the future of clothing will be less is more, a few good clothes that will last a long time. We have never wanted to be the largest outdoor clothing company in the world, we have only wanted to be the best."

And with Mander as an inspiration, Chouinard tried to codify the company's in-house values. With the aftershocks of the layoffs continuing to depress morale, product lines getting launched then scrapped, and more and more employees coming and going, Chouinard believed that Patagonia was losing its way. "I'm building this very successful company that I don't want to work for, that I don't want to be involved with because it doesn't reflect the values I care about in terms of the environment and also in terms of doing business," he said at the time.

In a bid to reconnect with his own staff, he began taking groups of employees off for small retreats not unlike the one he had done with O'Donnell and Bussiere in Patagonia, just before the layoffs. These trips were closer to home, but on each outing, Chouinard would gather with a couple dozen of his flock in the Marin Headlands or Yosemite and talk deeply about what it meant to operate a company. What was the purpose of Patagonia? What did success look like? After a few years of this, Chouinard came up with a set of principles which he would ultimately publish in a book, *Let My People Go Surfing*. Despite his lofty ambitions, however, many believed Patagonia's best days were behind it. Reflecting on the troubles in 1992, *Inc.* magazine wrote, "Yvon Chouinard touts his company as a model for the future, when, in fact, its time may already have passed."

## "A Pain in the Ass"

A few years before the layoffs rocked the company, Patagonia opened a store in Boston. But after only a few days of operation, workers at the store began complaining of headaches. When the symptoms persisted, Patagonia brought in a specialist to examine what was making the workers sick. It didn't take long for an air-conditioning technician to identify the culprit: the new clothes were off-gassing formaldehyde, and poor ventilation was preventing fresh air from circulating. The retail associates were breathing toxic fumes. Chouinard quickly arrived at a sobering conclusion: he was poisoning his own employees.

It was bad enough that people were getting sick. But with some upgraded air-conditioning, that problem was solved. The bigger issue was that new Patagonia clothes contained formaldehyde at all. Chouinard's high-quality products, it turned out, were toxic. "That was a wake-up call," he said. "That's when we decided to start asking a lot of questions about what we were doing."

The first question Chouinard needed to address was where, exactly, the toxins were coming from. The answer was cotton. As T-shirts and other garments were finished, they were treated with a wrinkle-resistant chemical that included formaldehyde. Patagonia had no idea this was the case until the Boston incident.

It wasn't immediately clear how to solve this problem. Patagonia was a relatively small buyer of cotton; most of its clothes were made from synthetic fabrics. That meant the company had little clout with its suppliers and no easy way to get them to phase out formaldehyde. But Chouinard had a hunch where he might find a solution. Years before, Doug Tompkins had started using organic cotton in some Esprit clothes. It cost more, and it was hard to source at scale. But as Tompkins went on his environmental journey, learning about deep ecology and growing more committed to becoming a good steward of planet Earth, he determined that going organic was worth the added expense and hassle. In the aftermath of the episode in Boston, Chouinard came to regard Tompkins's decision less as a novelty and more like necessity.

Before long, Patagonia had a team of employees digging into the details of the cotton supply chain. One of the first things they did was go on a field trip. On May 6, 1992, they showed up at the Holiday Inn in Bakersfield, California, in the San Joaquin Valley. Their guide for the day was Jo Ann Baumgartner, who worked for the Sustainable Cotton Project, a nonprofit organization that was both supporting cotton farmers in making the transition to organic and educating buyers about the problems with industrial agriculture. The mission for the day was simple: see with their own eyes the difference between conventional and organic cotton.

Crammed into a van, the Patagonia delegation started the day at conventional cotton farms. They could immediately tell that producing cotton the normal way was an environmental disaster. Outside the fields, ponds containing runoff festered in the heat. The water was so hazardous that regulatory agencies demanded farms install devices to discourage birds from landing in the ponds. On nearby backroads, piles of trash contained empty jugs that once held pesticides. The fields were lifeless save for the cotton bolls and branches—no bugs on the plants, no birds in the sky, no worms in the dirt. Crop dusters buzzed the skies, dropping more chemicals onto the fields. And the smell—a stench that burned the nostrils—hung over the whole valley. Conventional cotton, it turned out, was toxic in more ways than one. Beyond the formaldehyde that was used to treat the finished fabric, the chemicals used to kill any potentially intrusive insects were leaving fields barren. Cancer rates in the area were 10 times higher than normal.

After visiting a handful of these industrial growing sites, Baumgartner took the Patagonia employees to a small farm nearby that was growing organic cotton. The contrast was stark. There were no piles of industrial trash, no pools of hazardous water. Bugs and bees and birds flitted around the fields. The ground smelled like plants, not chemicals. Employees reached into the soil and dug up earthworms. "People would come back from those trips changed," said Vincent Stanley.

Beyond recognizing that conventional cotton was poisonous, the employees returned with a newfound conviction that they needed to transition Patagonia's supply chain to organic cotton. "They would come back and say, 'This is going to be a pain in the ass, but we're going to help make this happen,'" Stanley said. Groups of Patagonia employees went out on the tours over the next couple years, including, in 1993, Chouinard himself. (Malinda, not wanting to spend a day driving around the Central

Valley in a van, opted out.) As the lifelong outdoorsman walked through lifeless fields, witnessing the ecocide firsthand, he soured on conventional cotton for good. "I don't want to be in business if I've gotta use this stuff," he said. Returning from the tour, Chouinard gave Patagonia an ultimatum: It had 18 months to stop using conventional cotton. And if his team couldn't find enough organic cotton, Patagonia would stop making T-shirts and other casual clothes. "I'll get out of the sportswear business if you can't make it work," he told the team. "When we got Yvon out there, the light bulb went off," said Jill Dumain, Patagonia's environmental analysis director. "It was like, 'We can't do this anymore.'"

Walking away from conventional cotton wouldn't be easy. At the time, 25 percent of the company's products were made with cotton. Figuring out how to source that much organic material would be a Herculean task. It was also liable to cost a lot of money, an expense Patagonia would likely have to pass on to its customers. What's more, none of the company's customers seemed to think there was anything wrong with conventional cotton or were asking for organic cotton. Nevertheless, Dumain and her team made an inventory of organic cotton farmers and built up a supply chain. There were only a few cotton operations embracing organic methods, and few of them could deliver the kind of consistency needed for mass-market textiles. As Patagonia began making some items with this new, more eco-friendly stock, quality suffered. What was better for the planet wasn't good for the product, at least not yet.

A pullover sweater known as the Jumbo Pique made with organic cotton proved unable to hold its shape. "It became more jumbo the longer you wore it," Dumain said. Other attempts to recreate inventory with organic materials also failed. In a bid to use nontoxic dyes as well as nontoxic fabric, Patagonia started using inferior dyes that didn't bind to the cotton. When executives realized how poor the quality was, they stopped using the nontoxic dyes and kept using the conventional ones. It was a tacit acknowledgment that the company couldn't do everything at once, and that if it sold customers organic cotton shirts that didn't hold their color, consumers would quickly lose faith in organic anything.

After these false starts, Patagonia executives concluded that instead of buying from the ad hoc network of existing organic farms, they would need to convince conventional growers to embrace organic practices. That presented a whole new set of challenges. Some of the farmers Patagonia tried to convince going organic refused to make the switch. It was too onerous, too expensive, too unfamiliar. The cotton ginners, which separated the seed from the flower, needed to learn how to clean their gins before the organic material passed through, another added expense that Patagonia had to subsidize. But none of the problems was as complicated as what the spinners faced.

The spinners, who turned raw cotton into fabric ready to be made into T-shirts, told Patagonia that they hated working with organic cotton. Because it hadn't been treated with pesticides, there were still aphids, other bugs, seeds, stems, and other stuff mixed in with the bolls. All that junk made the cotton sticky and gummed up their machines. "It's a little bit like trying to comb your hair with bubble gum in it," Dumain said. "It's gooey. It's messy. You can't get through it." And yet some spinners rose to the challenge.

In Thailand, the head of a spinning mill named Johnny Yeung went out of his way to make it work. He told Dumain that he was a closet environmentalist and wanted to make a difference. If he went to his board and asked them to donate a bunch of money, they'd laugh him out of the room. But if the change was happening on the factory floor, he could bend his operations to support Patagonia's mission. The sticky cotton was still a problem, but Yeung figured out a solution. He turned up the air-conditioning in the factory full tilt, causing the sticky matter to crystalize and allowing the organic cotton to run though the machinery without a hitch. "As we went on, we knew we were going to have problems," Dumain said. "But we also gained the confidence that we were going to know how to solve them."

With Patagonia working out the kinks in its supply chain, it transitioned more and more of its line to organic cotton. Then, during a heated discussion at a management meeting in the summer of 1994, Chouinard made the call. "If we continue to make clothes with conventionally grown cotton, knowing what we know now, we're toast," he said. "Let's do it. Let's go organic." If that wasn't possible, Chouinard was prepared to make good on his threat and stop selling sportswear. In a news release making it official, the company said that it would be transitioning to 100 percent organic cotton, and that the decision was a permanent one. "We have realized for years that every product we make involves some level of pollution," Chouinard said. "There is no going back on this decision, regardless of its impact on the company's sales or profits."

Over the next year and a half, Patagonia made the switch. It involved slashing its sportswear line from 166 items down to 91, a drastic move that resulted in a sharp drop in sales. As the company spent more to help its farmers, ginners, and spinners convert to organic, it also saw its profit margin shrink. But executives viewed the expenditure as a worthy investment. "When the sales came back and the margin came back, we were in a stronger position with our customers," Stanley said. And there was never any doubt about it: the products needed to be profitable. Just as Chouinard resolved not to make sportswear if he couldn't do it with organic cotton, he also wouldn't do it unless he could make money. "Our mission statement at the time was to inspire solutions for the environmental crisis," Dumain said. "And I kept telling people: 'If you're not profitable, you're not inspirational.'"

The job of making organic cotton profitable fell to Dave Olsen, who joined as CEO in the mid-'90s as Patagonia went all in with the switch. The additional expenses associated with organic cotton were substantial, and passing the entire cost on to the consumer would have resulted in a sharp jump in prices that would have likely caused sales to crater. For the first year, Olsen decided Patagonia would pass on half the additional costs and absorb the rest as losses. "I was prepared to lose $10 million on the fall season when we first introduced it," he said. "But we were pretty confident this was the right thing to do."

The gamble quickly paid off. Customers bought into the environmental messaging, and within a few months, Patagonia was able to raise the prices of the organic garments to cover all its additional costs. One of Chouinard's core beliefs—that consumers would pay for quality—had been validated at the very moment it mattered most. And in doing so, Patagonia had made a statement to the industry: conventional cotton, despite being cheap and easy to procure, was a poisonous fabric that could be abandoned without imperiling the business. "The difference between an organic cotton field and a conventional cotton field is night and day, life and death," Olsen said.

Once Patagonia had its organic cotton operation up and running, it did something almost unheard of in the business world: it shared its newly acquired understanding of this supply chain with any competitor who wanted it. The only way to make organic cotton more popular—and cheaper—was to get more companies using the stuff, and in the absence of an industrywide marketing campaign, Patagonia assumed the role of pro bono evangelist. Dumain would spend time with other companies, explaining to them step by step, farm by farm, how Patagonia had weaned itself off conventional cotton. "It let a lot of companies leapfrog into a better spot," she said. "And it also instilled a lot of trust with our vendors that they weren't doing this just for one customer."

For Chouinard, abandoning conventional cotton was a victory. It was also, he realized, just a first step. He may have cleaned up one small part of his business, but what about synthetic materials? What about plastics? What about the dyes? What about the fuel and packaging and labor? "I started going deeper and deeper and asking questions and educating ourselves, so that we can try to do the maximum amount of good," he said. "Because at the end of the day, using organically grown cotton doesn't do the world any good. It just does less harm."

## "The Quality of Life on Earth"

Chouinard knew that interrogating his own supply chain would reveal some difficult truths. During a meeting with senior executives years before his trip to the cotton fields, Tebbel, the environmental grants manager, suggested to Chouinard that the company do a deep environmental analysis of the main fabrics it used. At the time, Chouinard brushed aside the idea.

"Why would I want to do that?" he said. "Then I'm going to be an environmental martyr. That'll kill my business."

Tebbel and the other execs took note: the boss didn't have an appetite for that kind of self-inquiry at this moment. But on the way out of the meeting, Kevin Sweeney, the communications executive, leaned over to Tebbel. "Just wait," he said. "You planted the seed. It can't be your idea. But just wait."

Now that time had come. Chouinard was ready to start cleaning up the supply chain. But leading an examined life was fraught with inconveniences. Phasing out conventional cotton and going organic was one relatively small part of an increasingly complex network of suppliers and manufacturing partners. If the company was serious about minimizing its impact on the planet, Chouinard and his team would need to go well beyond upgrading the fabrics they used; they needed to look at their dyes, transportation infrastructure, and labor practices, too.

Hoping to get their arms around the magnitude of the problem, Chouinard gave the green light to the project he had rejected all those years ago. Tebbel conducted an analysis of Patagonia's main fabrics, including cotton, polyester, and wool. Everywhere the team looked, it found new problems. At one of the factories in Portugal that made the dyes for its clothes, toxic outflow was spewing into the Douro River. Patagonia employees went to visit some of the factories in Hong Kong and found medieval conditions and children at work. Each new revelation led to a series of frustrating to-do lists.

It was arduous work, but bit by bit, Patagonia overhauled the ingredients it used to cook up its clothes. Olsen, the new CEO, pushed chemical companies to figure out if there was a less awful way to make the things Patagonia needed. Nylon was created by boiling sulfuric acid. Was there a better alternative? The black dyes used to color jackets and pants and bags used hexavalent chromium, a known carcinogen. Billions of gallons of water used to make those dyes were being contaminated. Olsen went to 10 chemical companies and tried to get them to make a vegetable-based dye, but the early versions wouldn't hold color as long as the toxic version.

Once again, Patagonia had to make a choice between protecting the planet and maintaining the functionality of its products. And once again, it favored the product, at least in the short term. Customers expected Patagonia's offerings to work as advertised, and the quickest way to lose them forever was by selling them substandard gear. "We did research to try and understand if our customers would hang with us while we figured it out, and the answer was 'No,'" Olsen said. "Our customers weren't willing to cut us any slack to do the right thing environmentally." Patagonia could be as idealistic as it wanted. But if the clothes weren't first-rate, it would lose its base.

Fleece was another puzzle the company had to solve. The Synchilla pullovers and pile jackets had become cash cows for Patagonia, among the most popular items Chouinard had ever dreamed up. But as executives interrogated the supply chain, it became clear that the polyester used to make them was almost as problematic as conventional cotton. Polyester was made of petroleum, a fossil fuel that the public was beginning to understand was responsible for the lion's share of global warming. True, it had been polyester that had provided the breakthrough when Chouinard needed to update his original wool sweater so it didn't hold water and didn't stink. But now, with the company's dawning environmental awareness, it was clear that what was once a solution was now a liability.

There was no easy replacement for polyester. Still, the Patagonia team began exploring if they could make their fleece not with brand-new plastic but with recycled products. It soon homed in a potentially limitless source of raw material: used soda bottles. In a flash, an alternative supply chain was getting stood up. Wellman, a New Jersey plastics recycling company, collected the bottles and turned them into plastic pellets. Then Dyersburg Fabrics, in Tennessee, spun the pellets into yarn. At first, the companies couldn't figure out how to create a neutral base that would hold different colored dyes. As a result, all of Patagonia's first recycled fleeces were the color of green 7-UP bottles. But those kinks were quickly ironed out, and within a couple years, Patagonia was selling more than 30 items made with post-consumer recycled plastic. Per usual, Patagonia didn't try to keep other companies from using recycled bottles; instead, it encouraged them to copy its methods. Soon, competitors like L.L.Bean were using plastic bottles, too—depriving Patagonia of its edge in marketing but allowing a more virtuous method of making fleece to proliferate.

Other fabrics were similarly problematic and required equally creative fixes. Cotton, as the company had discovered, was fraught with complications, leading to the investment in organic. But even wool had its issues—sheep denude fragile ecosystems and can wreck pristine stretches of wilderness. Looking for an alternative, Patagonia started buying recycled wool from the Calamai family in Prato, Italy, which had been gathering used wool clothes since 1878. It then started blending that recycled wool with its recycled fleece, creating a new hybrid fabric it called Woolyester.

A few years later, the company decided to stop using anti-odor technologies in its clothing. Anti-odor fabrics were popular at the time, a sort of built-in deodorant for activewear. But the more the Patagonia team learned about what was in the anti-odor chemicals, the worse it all smelled. The treatments contained several toxins and carcinogens. Years later, when the company began using the technology again, the anti-odor chemicals were natural, this time made from crushed crab shells.

Patagonia's efforts to remake its supply chain in a more environmentally friendly manner culminated in 1997, when the company hosted its first-ever conference for suppliers in Ventura. Flying in farmers, spinners, ginners, dyers, and stitchers from around the globe, the company spent days schooling its network of commercial partners on its unorthodox philosophy and drilling into them the idea that for Patagonia, preserving the natural world was a core value. That alone was a revolutionary assertion. For most suppliers, their primary value was profits—they were in business to get paid; not much more, not much less. Inasmuch as any of them thought of an end customer, it was perhaps Patagonia the company or maybe Patagonia's customers. None of them thought it was the planet.

For days, Patagonia executives challenged the company's suppliers, pressing them to think more expansively about their role. Between surf breaks and barbecues, suppliers were presented with detailed assessments of how their individual industries were polluting the environment and then sorted into breakout groups to brainstorm ways they might improve their processes. "We've spent the last ten or fifteen years with all of you talking about quality," Sweeney, who was instrumental in organizing the event, told the suppliers. "We now need to talk about the quality of life on Earth."

# CHAPTER 7

# Leaps of Faith

## "A World-Famous Sandbagger"

Kris McDivitt was ready for a reset. Having brought Patagonia back from the brink, instituted its first mass layoffs, and postponed her much-needed break, she was also suffering from the early stages of a mild identity crisis. Yes, she was successful. Yes, she had rescued the company, doing, by her own estimation, the best work of her career. With everything on the line, she had made the right decisions and saved Patagonia. But this couldn't be all there was. It was a big world, and she felt like she had a bigger role to play in it. How, though? She had no clue what to do next.

Burned out from running the business and eager to retreat from an increasingly materialistic world, she found a kindred spirit in Doug Tompkins. McDivitt and Tompkins had known each other from afar for years. Her previous husband, Dennis Hennek, had climbed with Tompkins in the Himalayas, she was familiar with Esprit, and Tompkins turned up now and then to make mischief with Chouinard. She also knew Tompkins was brash, arrogant, and a playboy, and she had been warned to keep her distance.

Then in 1990, during the Patagonia management retreat down in Argentina, McDivitt and Tompkins connected for real. On the last day of that trip, Tompkins caught up with the Patagonia execs over lunch. Sauntering into the restaurant, he sat down next to McDivitt, patted her on the back, and said, "Hey kiddo, how you doing?" An hour of relentless flirting culminated in Tompkins offering to fly her back to the United States on his private plane. McDivitt rejected his advances and flew home commercial.

Yet in the ensuing months, even as McDivitt was drawn back into work and consumed with the task of saving Patagonia, Tompkins kept pursuing her. Finally, with the business stabilized and McDivitt headed to Paris, on her way to climb Mont Blanc in the French Alps, Tompkins caught up with her again. And although she was engaged to another man at the time, McDivitt agreed to join him for a night on the town.

Tompkins's idea of a romantic evening was taking his date to an anti-globalization workshop. But after the workshop came dinner, and after dinner, McDivitt and Tompkins walked the streets until 3 a.m. A bit before dawn, he invited her to join him in Chile, where he had bought a farm and was making plans to embark on an epic campaign of land conservation.

"Absolutely not," she said. "You're a world-famous sandbagger."

Tompkins stopped and looked down, then back up at McDivitt and said, "I will never let anything happen to you."

She felt the ground shift beneath her feet. "It was one of those moments that you see somebody transform, even in their own mind," she said. "I thought to myself, that's the man I was supposed to marry. It was chemistry, like when you get hit by lightning."

After scaling Mont Blanc, McDivitt took Tompkins up on his offer and joined him in Chile, intending to stay 12 days. In the rustic cabin, deep in the heart of Patagonia, the modern world fell away, and she felt herself reconnecting with nature and bonding with this man she had been warned about. She stayed five weeks.

Soon, her previous engagement was over, and she was all in with Tompkins.

Chouinard and Malinda initially disapproved. But in 1994, McDivitt and Tompkins married at San Francisco City Hall. McDivitt then left her operational role at Patagonia for good, sold her house in California, and joined her new husband at Reñihué, his Chilean estate. Kris McDivitt was now Kris McDivitt Tompkins. "It was scandalous," she said. "I just blew up my personal life. And it was a big leap of faith. I mean it could easily have gone either way. This was insane what we were doing. But it turned out to be the greatest thing."

With McDivitt gone and no professional manager around running Patagonia, Chouinard needed to take his own leap of faith. His initial attempt to hand control of the company over to an outsider had failed. O'Donnell was genial and outdoorsy but had jeopardized the future of the company with his mismanagement. In need of a replacement, Chouinard turned to Alison May, the chief financial officer. May was initially reluctant to take the big job. She was content looking after the books and didn't harbor aspirations to run a company. But with McDivitt gone, the Chouinards implored her to step up, and she eventually consented. There was a catch, however. Chouinard didn't want to make her CEO. Instead, he gave her the title of "general manager," the same role McDivitt had assumed back in the late '70s when she took over as boss. May perceived the move as a slight. There was no other, more senior executive running daily operations. She was reporting directly to Chouinard and the board. But Chouinard wouldn't give her the validation of calling her CEO. "It really hurt my feelings," May said. "It pissed me off."

May and the Chouinards also clashed over fundamentally different visions of how Patagonia should be controlled, and who should benefit from its success. May was a longtime admirer of employee stock ownership plans. ESOPs, as they are known, are ways to reward workers when companies do well over the long term. Companies with ESOPs will grant employees shares, allowing them to accumulate stock over time. Then a company-controlled trust will buy the stock from employees, providing them with liquidity and returning the shares to the company. Doing so allows employees to participate in the success of the business without diluting ownership of the company or allowing outside investors to gain control. May pushed the Chouinards to consider creating an ESOP. They resisted. She encouraged them to find other ways to reward employees with ownership in the company—perhaps a profit-sharing plan or an initial public offering that would allow workers to buy stock. It was always a nonstarter. In the wake of Black Wednesday, the Chouinards were not entertaining any scenarios that would reduce their control.

May didn't agree with them, but she couldn't help but appreciate the consistency of their logic. "Their objective is to save as many species as possible before the human race destroys them all," she said. "That doesn't mean ownership for employees and things like that. That is not their objective. The projects that they think are important do not include people." May didn't stick around for long. After a couple years, she went on to become the chief operating officer of Esprit. After that, she joined the board of King Arthur Flour; and in that role, she helped the company create an ESOP.

With May's departure, Chouinard had to conduct yet another CEO search. This would be the fourth leadership change in a half dozen years, revealing a worrying level of instability at the top of the company. The job posting was classic Patagonia—at once irreverent, aspirational, and honest about the company's shortcomings. "Woman or man wanted for hazardous journey," it read.

"Explore frontiers of corporate and environmental responsibility. No equity, frequent navigation by board and founders, intense scrutiny from true believers, safe return doubtful. Honor and recognition in case of success."

As the process began, Chouinard entertained all comers, including the receptionist. Chipper Bro Bell had joined Patagonia a few years earlier. Having grown up in Southern California, Bell became a professional Frisbee player, winning an international competition for Frisbee tricks, touring with rock guitarist Stevie Ray Vaughan, and getting sponsored by Budweiser. When he applied at Patagonia, his resume said "Frisbee Player. Surfer. Gardener." He was hired instantly. His job: answering the phones. "I didn't know how to spell 'apparel,' let alone 'textile,'" he said. Bell became the company's gatekeeper, greeting guests and taking calls. Once, when a customer called and explained that a cat had peed on her new Synchilla jacket and asked for a replacement, Bell replied: "Absolutely, ma'am. What kind of cat would you like?"

When he heard the top job was open, he threw his hat in the ring. "I knew what it took to be the world champion, so why not?" he said. "I know what it's like at the top." He made it through an initial round of interviews with human resources. Then he got a call from Chouinard, who asked Bell to join him for some free diving. Bell had been waiting for this moment; he and Chouinard had talked about catching waves together for some time, but it had never happened. Now Chouinard was going to put him through the paces out in the wild to see what he was made of, as he had with so many other senior executives he had hired over the years.

They met at Hollister Ranch, an exclusive stretch of beach north of Santa Barbara where Chouinard had a property. Donning weight belts and flippers, they set out into the waves brandishing spear guns. About 300 yards offshore, Chouinard began diving down toward some rocks, hunting for sheepshead and sea bass. Bell tried to keep up, following his boss down 15 feet, then coming up for air, then down 18 feet, then coming up for air, then down 20 feet. Having practiced holding his breath since grade school, Chouinard could stay underwater for nearly two minutes. Bell grew fatigued after a while and stayed near the surface, watching. Then he saw Chouinard disappear into a small cave, watched as a puff of sand erupted from the opening, and finally saw his boss emerge with a 3½-foot sheepshead on the tip of his spear. As Chouinard swam toward Bell, who was ready with a net, he suddenly thrust his left hand into another outcropping and grabbed a lobster for good measure. Back onshore, Chouinard told Bell, "You can say you got the lobster."

Chouinard was flexing on his receptionist, demonstrating to his underling that his reputation as an elite outdoorsman was no accident. But Bell intuited a more profound meaning as well. By going deeper underwater, staying down longer, and emerging with the goods, Chouinard was showing Bell what it actually took to be a leader. "At that high level, he was telling me he didn't think I could take the pressure," Bell said. In the end, Chouinard didn't go with the receptionist. And while the next CEO could spell "textile," he was yet another apparel industry outsider.

## "Wake This Company Up"

Dave Olsen was out of work when the headhunter called. Olsen had spent his career stringing together odd jobs, interrelated interests, and some modest successes. He tried to pioneer a new business school that was sympathetic to organized labor and promoted the idea of worker representation on boards. He was a pioneer in the socially responsible investing movement that would come to encompass trillions of dollars in assets. And well before renewable energy was a mainstream industry, Olsen was working on wind, solar, and battery systems, growing familiar with the rigorous reliability and quality standards necessary for the electrical transmission industry. He had been running a small geothermal power generation company when the search firm called and asked him if he was interested in a job running Patagonia.

Olsen had the environmental credentials that Chouinard was looking for and experience working inside real companies that knew how to make money. To make sure he was a good fit, however, Chouinard needed to see how he fared in the wild. So, one morning, the two men set out for the Sespe Wilderness, a scrubby patch of rolling hills in the Topatopa Mountains near Ventura. Olsen was into water sports and was a competent white-water canoer and ocean kayaker; climbing was not his thing. Chouinard knew as much and wanted to see how the potential hire performed out of his element. The test: scaling a 400-foot vertical sandstone wall. Olsen showed up wildly unprepared, wearing hiking boots, not climbing shoes. But Chouinard kept him safe, both men survived the climb, and Olsen got the job as CEO.

Entrusted with the task of running Patagonia, Chouinard gave Olsen four words of instruction: "Wake this company up!" Sales had plateaued at $150 million a year for years under May. On the one hand, that wasn't such a bad thing; Chouinard had a fraught relationship with the idea of endless growth. But at this juncture, it had resulted in a sense of stagnation. There were no breakthrough products on the horizon, no new markets being pursued. Meantime, new competitors were taking an ever greater share of the specialty outdoor apparel market that Patagonia had once had largely to itself. "Yvon's perception was that people had gone to sleep," Olsen said. "They were resting on their laurels. There was no innovation."

Olsen was unfamiliar with the apparel industry, but he understood enough about market dynamics to see that Chouinard was right. "We were getting our lunch eaten," he said. "Nobody in Ventura headquarters was really paying attention to that." Working with a handful of other senior new hires, Olsen put together a presentation laying out the innovation that was happening at other companies, the growing number of competitors in the space, and the fact that other outdoor brands were growing while Patagonia sales were flat. Speaking to groups of about 25 employees at a time, he walked through the presentation dozens of times, trying to instill a sense of urgency in the rank and file. It didn't work. "Nobody responded," he said.

Olsen decided to shake the company up. In late 1996, he made every employee reapply for their jobs. He also opened up the process, allowing anyone at the company to apply for anyone else's job. "That got their attention," Olsen said. A huge reshuffling ensued, as some employees moved from the design studio to the back office, and others moved from the executive suite to the fabrication shop. Some people wanted to make more money and sought out more prominent roles; others wanted to chill out and took lower-profile jobs that paid less. As the reorganization unfolded, Olsen also created a new structure for the company, grouping the product lines into units that focused on individual sports, such as climbing, skiing, and fishing. This allowed smaller teams of employees who were passionate about specific sports to focus on the design and quality for those areas, which in turn led to a new spurt of innovation.

As the company's structure evolved, Olsen took steps to fortify its financial foundation, negotiating additional lines of credit with two banks. The extra cash offered Patagonia a newfound sense of security, virtually ensuring that it would never again find itself unable to meet payroll. It also gave the company additional flexibility to expand production, inventory, and sales, while at the same time expanding its technology operations.

Another pivotal development came on Olsen's watch: the opening of a new distribution center in Reno. At a cost of $19 million, it was Patagonia's largest-ever capital expenditure. The 171,000-square-foot facility was built with reclaimed materials, featured a high-efficiency heating system, included a major recycling operation, sported solar panels, and used ultra-efficient lights, but the expense was worth it. The distribution center turbocharged the mail-order business, and Patagonia began selling its clothes online for the first time. Alongside the wholesale business, the retail stores, and the mail-order catalog, the launch of Patagonia.com added a fourth distribution stream.

At first, there was concern that selling online would cannibalize the other sales channels. Retailers who did a brisk business selling Patagonia gear complained to the company, as did some of Patagonia's own store managers, fearing their business would slip. Instead, the launch of the online store was a good thing for all involved. The early web presence amplified the visibility of the brand, wholesalers who carried Patagonia gear caught some of the momentum, and the new products—driven by the sports-focused teams—started to take off. Sales picked up again, and within a few years, had jumped nearly 50 percent from the earlier plateau, touching the $220 million mark as the new millennium approached.

Olsen succeeded in turning the business around, but all that growth took a toll on him. An environmentalist at heart, he never grew entirely comfortable with the inherent tension at the heart of

Patagonia—how was it that a company making consumer goods could claim to be working in the service of the planet? It was the same dilemma Chouinard had been wrestling with for decades, the same creative tension that gnawed at McDivitt.

"Yvon and I were pretty much on the same page, but we resolved the conflict differently," Olsen said. "Yvon sees the ecological damage very, very clearly. He was determined to find ways to mitigate the damage as much as possible. I couldn't do that. It wasn't just the tension between increased resource use and increased environmental impact." But Olsen could never fully resolve the contradiction. "I felt that by driving sales higher, we were reinforcing a materialistic culture, and I got increasingly uncomfortable selling expensive clothes to a very elite demographic. It just didn't fit with who I am. It was almost a spiritual thing."

Olsen also said he grew disillusioned with some elements of the company's culture. He tried to reorganize senior management to distribute decision-making, changes that could have diminished Chouinard's influence. Those efforts were shut down. "Patagonia is all about Yvon," he said. "It's very difficult to get away from that idea of the founder and chairman as hero."

Then there were the issues around Chouinard and money. When Olsen joined Patagonia in 1996, he said Chouinard was considering whether or not to sell the company, and for a while, whether to try to buy back Black Diamond, which had started as Chouinard Equipment. He regretted letting go of the climbing gear business, and with the liability lawsuits finished and Patagonia in need of growth, he thought that bringing hardware back into the fold might be a masterstroke. But Peter Metcalf, who owned most of Black Diamond at this point, wanted no part in that talk, and the deal never materialized.

Around the same time, several major corporations expressed

interest in acquiring Patagonia. Nautica was interested. So was Ralph Lauren, which had just gone public and needed to demonstrate growth to impatient Wall Street analysts. Negotiations never got to the point of an actual term sheet, but Olsen spent significant time working on potential deals, hosting Ralph Lauren executives in Ventura and traveling to New York to learn about their operations. There was even talk about taking money from a private equity firm. But none of those plans came to fruition, either. Patagonia never took on additional investors, never accepted outside capital, and was never sold to a larger competitor.

One reason the talks never progressed very far: price. It was typical at the time to value clothing companies at one times annual sales. That would have put a price tag of about $150 million to $220 million on Patagonia. To Chouinard, that was a lowball. "No fucking way," Olsen recalls him saying. "I'm not selling this company for that."

More than his issues with Chouinard's management style or his relationship with money, what bothered Olsen most about Patagonia was what he perceived to be the family's low-grade disdain for their own employees. "Yvon and Malinda don't trust the people that work for them," Olsen said. "They never have." Chipper Bro Bell remembered Chouinard offering a similar reflection while they were spearfishing in Hollister. "I think I have the best workers in the world," Chouinard told Bell on the beach. "I think they do the best work. But not one of you inspires me."

It is a refrain shared by many longtime employees who know the Chouinards well. Despite all of Patagonia's success, despite their professed commitment to creating a company people want to work for, the family at the center of it all sometimes created the impression that it believed its own workers were slackers. The irony was impossible to miss: while the boss espoused the virtues of surf breaks and went on his own monthslong climbing trips, he grumbled that everyone was always goofing off. Chouinard was hardly the first founder to resent his own workforce. Many penny-pinching business owners come to believe that no one is working hard enough, that everyone on the payroll is somehow taking advantage of the company and mooching off the owner. It's an attitude that can breed resentment, and in the case of the Chouinards, it was a perspective that informed their refusal to share equity with employees.

Like May, Olsen believed that the Chouinards should have—and easily could have—found ways to allow employees to participate in the financial success of Patagonia. But the family wanted no part of it. "They said that if they shared stock ownership with employees, that the employees would act in their short-term interest to increase stock price and would stop investing in the long-term R&D," Olsen said. "But that's really disingenuous because there are many, many ways that they could have allowed some employee stock ownership."

And at times, Chouinard displayed irrational flashes of anger at his employees. One morning during Olsen's tenure, he was hanging out in the cafeteria when things came to a boil. The chef at the time had concocted a delicious recipe for cinnamon rolls, and the breakfast line was buzzing with employees stoked to begin their day with a sticky treat. Chouinard, stormy with rage over something unrelated, observed the scene and blew up at Olsen. "These people are eating me out of my business," Olsen remembers him howling. "Why should I provide breakfast for them?"

Later that day, Olsen went to the chef with a message: no more cinnamon rolls.

Looking back, Olsen said that while he had profound admiration for Chouinard, he was never able to reconcile the huge contradiction that is Patagonia: a consumer goods company trying to save the planet; a business that celebrated its people led by a founder who was never satisfied.

"I had wanted to find out the limits of how responsible a company could be, and Patagonia was the perfect test case: privately held, none of the Wall Street stuff, a sympathetic audience," he said. "I got a close-up look at that, and what I concluded is that it was not responsible enough. No business can truly be sustainable. Because no matter how much you mitigate, you will always cause more damage than you can repair."

Olsen was not the most beloved CEO among the rank and file. Many longtime Patagonians saw him as little more than a corporate tool. He could be stiff and didn't exude the innate Southern California cool that graced Chouinard and McDivitt. Once, after Olsen sent a companywide email reprimanding an employee for quitting after taking advantage of Patagonia's tuition reimbursement program, he faced a withering backlash during a town hall meeting. Staff chastised him for losing touch with the culture of the company and suggested that despite what the org chart said, it was actually he who worked for them.

It was the kind of internecine strife that animated the company, for better and worse. While Patagonia was in so many ways an extraordinary company—independent, idealistic, successful, generous—it was still fraught with fundamentally irresolvable tensions. Chouinard wanted his workers to be happy but also hard charging. He wanted to be generous but also stay in control. He wanted Patagonia to be lean but also abundant. He wanted the company to be profitable but also charitable. He wanted a small business with a big impact. In trying to run a responsible company, Chouinard had created an unsolvable paradox.

## "We Were Part of the Problem"

Several dozen grassroots activists had assembled at the Chico Hot Springs resort in Pray, Montana. They were there, on the outskirts of Yellowstone National Park, to share tactics, to draw inspiration from one another, and to plot their next moves. Patagonia was hosting its first Tools conference, bringing together environmental rabble-rousers from around the country for a few days of knowledge sharing and revelry, and their host, benefactor, and cheerleader in chief was Yvon Chouinard.

During one of the plenary sessions, the featured speaker was Dave Foreman, the founder of one of the edgiest groups out there, Earth First! Chouinard and Tompkins had footed the bill for Foreman's legal fees following the FBI's attempt to frame him, and Foreman was now repaying the favor by speaking at the Tools conference. Undaunted by his recent brush with the law, he called on the activists in the room to consider radical, even violent actions to achieve their aims. If the survival of planet Earth wasn't worth fighting for, what was? If it meant some prison time, might that not be worth it in the grand scheme of things? As a start, Foreman said, the assembled troublemakers ought to consider blowing up the Glen Canyon Dam, a concrete wall that spans the Colorado River outside Page, Arizona. Blow it up!

From the audience, Chouinard cheered.

A public relations executive in the room winced. So did Malinda. It was one thing to play host to a bunch of scrappy environmental activists. But it wasn't a good look for the owner of a name-brand company to encourage eco-terrorism.

For Chouinard, however, hanging out with Foreman and his ilk was an opportunity to reconnect with his dirtbag roots. In the activists, he sensed the same disdain for authority and willing-ness to exist on the margins of society that had animated his days at Camp 4 in Yosemite, his time living in the abandoned incin-erator in Wyoming. "Those are the people Yvon is really drawn to," said John Sterling, who worked on Patagonia's environmental programs and was at the Tools conference. "He feels a real kinship with those dirtbag activists who are trying to save the world."

As Patagonia grew and Chouinard had more money at his dis-posal, he began spending more and more of his resources sup-porting activists. At the Tools conference, he brought in Patagonia executives to teach the grassroots groups about communications strategy and marketing, hoping that some of the company's pixie dust might rub off on small groups working to clean up a river in Appalachia or block the construction of another dam in the West. And with the company's grants program, Chouinard began funneling ever more money to frontline actions. By the late '90s, he was giving away well over $1 million a year, insisting that the grants go to general operating funds rather than specific projects. This sort of so-called unrestricted giving is relatively rare in phil-anthropic circles, but it's just what most nonprofits need. For a financially strapped organization, having money to keep the lights on and buy toilet paper is just as important as funding protests on the front lines.

The strategy had its risks. If activists backed by Patagonia broke the law, the blowback could be swift. Sweeney cautioned Choui-nard about this. "You're going to get terrible press," he warned the boss at one point.

"No, I won't," Chouinard replied. "I'm going to get press. And the people who appreciate what we're doing are going to love us more than ever."

Those who didn't appreciate what Patagonia was doing also

took note. Shortly before it hosted the Tools conference, the company was selling a book called *Clearcut: The Tragedy of Industrial Forestry*, and donating all the proceeds to the Foundation for Deep Ecology. That prompted a pro-logging group called the Wyoming Resource Providers to organize a boycott of Patagonia. The group urged people to call Patagonia's office and inform the company it was losing business because of its stance on logging.

When company leaders learned of the plan, they decided to use the logging industry's tactics to their advantage. In a reprise of the response to the Planned Parenthood protests, they decided that for every call that came in, Patagonia would donate $10 to a Wyoming group that worked to prevent clear-cutting. More than 100 calls later, Patagonia had donated $1,340 to a nonprofit doing just that, Friends of the Bow. Patagonia didn't back down in the face of protests; it doubled down. But there was no communications playbook to follow when, for the first time, several Patagonia employees were arrested.

It happened in the redwood forests of Northern California on a late summer day. For more than a century, a company called Pacific Lumber had run logging and sawmill operations in Humboldt County. Locally owned and operated by the same family for generations, Pacific Lumber aimed to manage forests for the long term and mostly succeeded. One of the company's parcels was a particularly sensitive area, the Headwaters Forest, and included the largest privately held ancient redwood stand in California. Then Pacific Lumber was acquired through a hostile takeover by a Texas company called Maxxam, an industrial conglomerate with a reputation for ruthlessly clear-cutting old-growth forests.

The Maxxam CEO, Charles Hurwitz, financed the $874 million leveraged buyout with junk bonds, and as soon as he had control of Pacific Lumber, he abandoned the sustainable forest management practices. In order to pay down the debt Maxxam had assumed to buy Pacific Lumber, Hurwitz ordered the company to begin harvesting ancient redwoods, maximizing profits with no mind for the future. "They more than doubled and really nearly tripled the cut virtually overnight and were taking out so much more old growth," said Karen Pickett, one of the activists who protested Maxxam. "All of these practices were so very, very different than the way that Pacific Lumber had been operating the previous 100 years."

Sterling, who had recently joined Patagonia to work on the environmental programs, took to educating his new colleagues about the situation. Pressure to save the Headwaters Forest had been growing. The actor Woody Harrelson was arrested after scaling the Golden Gate Bridge with other activists to hang a banner calling attention to the cause. Then in September of 1996, Sterling convinced a few coworkers to join him at a Maxxam protest near Eureka. He had attended a similar protest before and found it cathartic engaging in direct action. Bringing along colleagues, Sterling figured, would give them firsthand exposure to the kind of activism that the company funded with its grants.

The night before the big protest, Sterling and the other employees camped in a nearby redwood grove with more than a thousand other activists. Bonnie Raitt and Glen Frey of the Eagles sang for the crowd. A cacophony of drum circles echoed through the forest. The next morning, September 16, a throng of protestors gathered outside the Headwaters Forest and began walking, slowly, methodically, toward the Maxxam property. The company was ready, as were the police. As each protester crossed the property line, deputies took them into custody and cinched their hands with zip ties. As Sterling stepped across, a cop said to him: "You know you're trespassing?"

"Yes," Sterling replied.

"If you don't leave, I'm going to arrest you," the cop said.

"I'm not going to leave," Sterling said.

The cop then zip tied Sterling's hands and led him to waiting buses, where he joined hundreds of others who had been arrested, including Raitt. The protesters were released later that day, and the charges were dropped. But when Sterling and his colleagues got back to Ventura, news of their action created a buzz on the Patagonia campus. Chouinard was thrilled when he heard about it and invited the Ruckus Society, a group of former Earth First! activists, down to campus to offer nonviolent civil disobedience training to employees. That training came with a new commitment from Chouinard. "Anyone who goes to that training and then gets arrested in some sort of protest that's consistent with our values, we'll bail them out," he said.

The year after Sterling and his colleagues were arrested, members of the Patagonia board joined the protest at Maxxam (though they stopped short of getting arrested). And soon after that, all the agitation paid off. Under a deal brokered by President Clinton, Hurwitz agreed to sell 7,472 acres of land—including the Headwaters Forest—to the federal government for $380 million.

Yet at the same time Chouinard was funding activists working to protect old-growth forests, the company was using up virgin hardwood. A major new office building on campus was designed with the exposed wood and laid-back aesthetics befitting a company headquartered near the beach. But the construction process was anything but sustainable. Throughout the building, there were giant beams of virgin Douglas fir, the very kind of old-growth trees that Patagonia was working so hard to save. "As we went deeper into that environmental world, we learned more and more how one hand was doing one thing, and the other hand was doing another," said Paul Tebbel, who ran the environmental grants program. "We were part of the problem."

Patagonia, meanwhile, was attracting more attention than ever. In 1996, Chouinard appeared alongside President Clinton in Washington at an event called the Corporate Citizenship Conference at Georgetown University, part of a White House effort to promote new fair labor standards. Wearing a suit and a tie for one of the few times in his life and seated next to other CEOs, including Starbucks's Howard Schultz, Chouinard tried to play the part of a normal business leader who did this sort of thing regularly.

As the roundtable discussion began, Clinton introduced Chouinard and asked him to tell the story of Patagonia's childcare program.

"I'd feel a lot more comfortable on top of a mountain than here right now," Chouinard said.

"Pretend that's where you are," Clinton said.

Although the president had asked him for a pithy response about childcare, Chouinard went on a tangent about his favorite topic: quality. "I don't think it's possible to make a great quality product without having a great quality work environment," he said. "So, it's linked—quality product, quality customer service, quality workplace, quality of life for your employees, even quality of life for all living things on this planet. If you miss any one piece, there's a good chance you'll miss it all. A family-friendly business tries to blur that distinction between work and family and work and play."

Clinton then enthused about his love for Patagonia. "I don't know how many of you have ever been in one of their stores, but every time I go into one, I feel like I'm in an evangelical mission because of all the young people there," he said. "You can't get out of the store, it doesn't matter if you don't even buy anything—you get the line, you know, that the company is really sort of environmentally responsible and you should be, too."

A week later, Chouinard was a world away from Washington, camping with friends and his daughter, Claire, on the Hawaiian island of Moloka'i. After paddling around the island in an inflatable kayak, Chouinard was back at the campsite and decided to free climb on a cliff forged by lava flows. As the rest of the group prepared dinner, Chouinard was about 15 feet up the wall when the rock he was clinging to broke. He crashed to the ground, badly injuring his elbow. Claire used two sarongs to make a sling and worked to stabilize his arm. "He had lost the cap to his front tooth and hadn't shaved in six days," she remembered. "His face was shiny with sweat, and he cried out twice as we slowly helped him up through the rocks to the camp." Chouinard began to go into shock, and a rescue helicopter arrived. "His usually dark face looked like skim milk with a tint of blue under his eyes and on his lips," Claire remembered. "I didn't know this look. I didn't know those soft spots around his eyes."

Chouinard was airlifted to The Queen's Medical Center in Honolulu but was without his wallet or insurance card. A doctor on duty cleaned his wound and set his arm in a sling. At 2 a.m., he was discharged with no place to go. A security officer directed him to the medical school, where he was able to crash in a guest apartment. As he waited for the sun to rise, he turned on CNN and saw footage from the Corporate Citizenship Conference the week before. There he was on TV with President Clinton.

Once recovered, Chouinard returned his attention to matters in Washington. This time, he was at odds with the White House. In a letter to the president, Chouinard unleashed a screed against the North American Free Trade Agreement, a multilateral pact between the United States, Mexico, and Canada that increased cross-border trade and made cheap goods more abundant but ultimately had the effect of hollowing out the middle class and weakening labor unions. "There seems to be a disconnect—because I don't believe you're applying to politics the practices you respect in business," he wrote. "The free trade accords have done nothing to help bring more security. Rather, they lead people to feel like we have less control over our own destinies because some faceless organization has say over our own laws and regulations. Equally important, these accords support the growing trend toward globalization. Security lies in small, healthy local economies and communities, not massive big business."

Chouinard was similarly irreverent when, around the same time, Yale University presented him with an honorary doctor of humane letters degree, lauding his "contribution to the protection of the environment" and holding up Patagonia as "a model of social responsibility." When he got the letter announcing the award, he said he was confused: "I thought, 'Humane letters? Shit. I don't even like humans. I like trees.' But Yale has a school of forestry, so I figured what the hell."

## "Bras Don't Kill People"

Tucked away in the high Sierras, just south of Lake Tahoe, is the US Marine Corps Mountain Warfare Training Center. At 6,800 feet above sea level, the installation has played host to generations of special operators, serving as a backdrop for exercises on high-altitude combat and mountain warfare. It is also where, in the 1970s, the US military started testing Patagonia's gear.

It began with the ice axe. As Chouinard pushed the boundaries of ice climbing, demonstrating new ways to scale frozen mountains, the military bought his axes and taught soldiers how to emulate his tactics. That got Chouinard Equipment in the door with the Pentagon. As an approved domestic supplier, the company was invited to bid on specialized projects, such as manufacturing thousands of oval aluminum carabiners. When Chouinard and his team began introducing innovative new fabrics like Capilene and Synchilla, the federal government took note. By the 1980s, enlisted personnel working in cold climates were being issued Patagonia base layers and fleeces. The army's 3rd Infantry Division was soon handing out full kits of Patagonia's off-the-shelf long underwear and dark blue pile suits to its long-range surveillance teams to ward off the cold. Not long after that, unbranded Patagonia gear was being included in the army's Extended Cold Weather Clothing System.

Patagonia was one of the few domestic companies that was developing new fabrics, and the generals responsible for keeping troops well equipped wanted to stay informed about the latest R&D not only in weaponry but in apparel, too. With a few discreet projects, the company began helping the military develop a custom cold-weather layering system for soldiers. The relationship deepened over the years, and Patagonia eventually began making military sports bras and knee pads.

On the face of it, a collaboration between Patagonia and the armed forces could seem discordant. What business did a bunch of hippies have designing gear that was meant to be used in combat? How could a bunch of dirtbags who prided themselves on sticking it to the man collaborate with the Pentagon and still sleep at night? But at first, the volumes were so small and the relationship with the military so financially insignificant that few inside the company spent much time worrying about it.

The military work continued at a slow burn for decades until

Michael Crooke showed up. Crooke was brought in by Chouinard to replace Olsen as CEO. It was another one of Chouinard's
erratic executive changes; this time inspired in part by an appetite
to grow the business and possibly ready it for a sale.

Crooke was a former Navy SEAL who was running Pearl Izumi,
the cycling apparel company, when Chouinard met him. In style
and substance, Crooke was an outsider to the Patagonia culture.
While he had the athletic chops, an evident tolerance for pain,
and some highly relevant professional experience, he did not pos-
sess the requisite vibes to thrive at a company full of surf bums.
A belligerent alpha male, he arrived in Ventura with a drill ser-
geant's intensity and a leadership style that was light on collaboration and heavy on intimidation. Each morning, before stepping
foot into the office, some employees remember Crooke doing 100
push-ups at the front door, a performative display of testoster-
one meant to intimidate the other workers. He also started getting copies of *The Wall Street Journal* delivered, a development
that elicited derisive chuckles from the staff, who knew that a real
Patagonian would rather be reading *Surfer* magazine or *Mother
Jones* and wouldn't be caught dead reading the *Journal*.

When Crooke learned about Patagonia's military sales, he saw
an opportunity to bring together his two worlds. Following the
terrorist attacks of September 11, 2001, the US armed forces put a
new emphasis on the needs of special operators working in areas
like the mountains of Afghanistan. Soon Patagonia was creating
specialized kits for the country's most elite fighting units including the Navy SEALs, Delta Force, and the Army Rangers. Over the
years, the company assumed the lead role in designing a special-
operations "combat uniform." At an event in El Paso, Texas, where
the company modeled the kit, soldiers suited up in the gear with
a full complement of tactical vests, assault rifles, and ammuni-

tion clips, and practiced combat maneuvers in the Patagonia garments. The uniform was a hit, and Patagonia went on to make it in a variety of camouflage patterns.

With sales picking up, the military business got its own identity, with a name derived from the famous Lost Arrow pinnacle in Yosemite: inside Patagonia, government work was henceforth known as the Lost Arrow Project. From there, a whole catalog's worth of Patagonia gear designed for deadly combat proliferated. There were basic garments like boxer briefs and T-shirts, and also versions of stalwart Patagonia items like the Nano-Air hoody in olive and camouflage. Deeper into the catalog were items like the Patagonia Level 9 Combat Pants, featuring belt loops that accommodate gun holsters, cargo pockets designed to fit medical kits, and knee pads. Also available was the Patagonia Level 9 Combat Shirt, designed to be worn under bulletproof armor.

Unlike most Patagonia clothes, the Lost Arrow gear was not made in southeast Asia. Instead, to adhere to the Berry Amendment, a rule requiring the Department of Defense to buy American-made goods whenever possible, it was produced by Peckham Vocational Industries, a nonprofit manufacturer in Lansing, Michigan, that employs workers with physical and mental disabilities. The Lost Arrow Project was never particularly lucrative. The most Patagonia ever sold to the government in one year was about $6 million worth of gear. Yet as the military work became more prominent, it sometimes roiled the employee base. "Not everyone at the company was okay with selling to the military," said Dean Carter, the human resources head. The fact that the unit's sales were so small made the decision to keep the Lost Arrow Project going all the more baffling. If it was materially insignificant to the overall business, employees wondered, why bother with the hassle at all? External critics also had a hard time reconciling Patagonia's image and its military work. "If you make clothes for killing people, sooner or later your logo is going to show up on the chests of some of the worst people in the world," wrote James Stout, an antiwar activist and critic of the program. "War has human and environmental costs that can't be offset by using recycled materials or giving money to charity."

The complaints didn't bother Chouinard. The company wasn't making weapons or ammunition, he reasoned. It was simply making clothing. "Bras don't kill people," Chouinard said. "People kill people." Besides, he was a veteran himself, having served in Korea. He could sympathize with the plight of the grunt who already had to endure the petty indignities and grueling monotony of army life. That was bad enough; why not at least make him comfortable? As a seasoned mountaineer, he also knew how important it was to have the right kind of clothes in foul weather environments. And while he had grown up speaking French, he was a lifelong American and a patriot, grateful to have the freedom to be an outsider—and a successful one at that—in a country where even a blacksmith without a college degree could make a fortune. "I had no qualms about any of that," he said. "I want our troops to be comfortable, and we make the most comfortable clothing for hot and cold conditions. So that was it."

Besides kick-starting the military business, Crooke is mostly remembered at Patagonia for not fitting in. "He always seemed very slick," said Elissa Foster, a longtime employee. "I didn't get a very genuine vibe from him." The early reputation he developed as a competitive, aggressive, hierarchical leader stuck, and he never won the affection of the rank and file, or for that matter, the family. Chouinard said that Crooke, more than any other CEO, probably took the job not to make a difference but to make a buck. "Michael Crooke was the only one who was really hoping we would sell the company, and he would come out ahead in some way or another," he said. Crooke left the company after less than six years on the job.

With Crooke's departure, Patagonia was facing yet another leadership change. Between Crooke, Olsen, May, O'Donnell, Tompkins, and a farmer named Eve Jursch who Chouinard tapped to manage the company for just one year, Patagonia had run through half a dozen leaders in a decade. "We've rushed through a lot of CEOs and management teams that didn't understand what we are about," Chouinard said of Crooke's departure. "The values here are so deep . . . it is hard to find a CEO that will grow with the company." Longtime employees saw the turnover as an expression of both Chouinard's genius, and his fickleness. "Once Kris stepped down, any CEO they hired would last between four to seven years," said Kulczycki, the longtime sales rep. "It was Yvon's philosophy of just changing things up."

That only partly explained the carousel of CEOs, however. It was also true that Chouinard was constantly changing his mind and would make rash decisions based on his own whims. "They'd bring in somebody and they'd be very excited by him at first," Kulczycki said. "And then the bloom wears off and then they decide that's not the right person."

# CHAPTER 8

# Leadership

## "Way Beyond My Comprehension"

It was just the four of them. Yvon and Malinda Chouinard. Doug and Kris Tompkins. As the calendar flipped from '03 to '04, they roamed the Chacabuco Valley in the Chilean backcountry, piloting a four-wheel drive truck through alien terrain marked by geothermal springs, red rivers, and black lakes. This was land that the Tompkinses were angling to buy. A 173,000-acre parcel virtually untouched by humans was on the market, and they knew that securing it could help fulfill what had become their overarching dream: creating a national park that would protect one of the greatest landscapes in South America.

As they closed in on a purchase, the Tompkinses invited Chouinard and Malinda down to experience the land. The main purpose of the trip was adventure for adventure's sake, a toned-down version of a Fun Hogs trip. More car camping and stories by the fire, less alpine climbing and starving in ice caves. But Doug and Kris Tompkins had a secondary motivation as well. The purchase would stretch their finances. To realize their most ambitious conservation plans, they knew they would need partners. After a week of road tripping, however, the money issue still hadn't come up. Finally, as they were driving to the airport to send the Chouinards back home, McDivitt Tompkins blurted it out.

"I've got to find $2.5 million," she said. "Would you be willing to partner on this?"

"Of course," Chouinard said.

The Chouinards helped the Tompkinses make that initial purchase in the Chacabuco Valley, acquiring the core of what is now Patagonia National Park. In an effort to keep the spotlight off Doug Tompkins, the Chouinards also bought an adjoining parcel on their own that they would fold into the property.

Downplaying the role of Doug Tompkins was an operational necessity by this point. Over the previous decade, he had spent much of his fortune buying up land in Chile and Argentina. And while he was committed to conservation and routinely stated publicly that his intention was to turn his landholdings over to the government, many locals turned against him. Some simply didn't believe the story he was telling, thinking there was no way that a wealthy American would spend millions on property just to give it all away. Environmentalists didn't trust Tompkins for a different reason, believing he would eventually develop the lands or sell them to industry. Local businessmen also objected to his plans, but they protested because he was getting in the way of economic development. Government officials worried that Tompkins was buying so much land in some narrow stretches of Chile, there was a risk that he could split the country in two, threatening national security. The Catholic Church even got involved, coming out in opposition to the Foundation for Deep Ecology, which it said was encouraging population control.

Tompkins was vilified in the local media, and protestors took to the streets to decry his work. He was called before Chile's congress, threatened with deportation, and received death threats.

"In Latin America there's no history of philanthropy," Chouinard said. "So here comes this wacko American, goes down there and he says, I'm going to buy up all this land in Chile, and I'm going to make parks and I'm going to give it back to the people, and they're going, 'Come on. Nobody does that. There's got to be another reason.'" Even his local allies had a hard time fathoming what he was up to. "It was way beyond my comprehension," said Rod Noriega, a Chilean bush pilot who flew Tompkins around the continent for decades. "It took me awhile to figure it out, especially when he said he wanted to donate it all. We couldn't understand it."

One purchase at a time, however, the Tompkinses expanded their holdings, amassing more than 1 million acres of temperate rainforests, pristine valleys, and green lagoons. Buying up old cattle ranches, they would then rewild the land. Fences were uprooted, buildings torn down, roads left to crumble and fall into the river. In the land that would become Patagonia National Park, they removed 400 miles of fencing and 25,000 sheep. Chouinard loved the idea of rewilding former grazing lands and paid Patagonia employees to leave their day jobs in Ventura and go spend a couple weeks helping scrub Tompkins's properties of human fingerprints; soon fabric designers were sweating in the sun, chopping up old fence posts and bundling barbed wire to be removed for good. It was all part of Tompkinses' spiritual quest to save the planet. "I see God as nature, in the very simplest terms," Tompkins said. "The great manifestation in the world, in all its forms—from the stars, to the vast night sky, to the oceans, to all the elements that we see and perceive—that is an awesome phenomenon that goes beyond description and words. If there's something that we want to call God that's far greater than ourselves, I would say it's nature. If anything could save the world, I put my money on beauty."

With Tompkins scouring the continent for new acquisitions and laying plans for elegant new visitor centers and expansive trail networks, McDivitt Tompkins was effectively reprising her role as CEO. For 20 years, she had channeled Chouinard's ambitions, turning his creative spirit into the practical work of making Patagonia a profitable, functional company. Now in Chile, she was playing the same role for Chouinard's best friend, who also happened to be the love of her life. Tompkins, like Chouinard, possessed a relentless drive and an unwavering confidence in his own judgment. McDivitt Tompkins was on board and went to work executing their shared vision, managing the finances, coordinating a sprawling legal and operations team, and keeping tabs on projects large and small.

Over the years, the Tompkinses spent nearly $400 million buying land. Some additional funds came from Patagonia; in 2003, the company established the Patagonia Land Trust, which began putting profits from the corporation to work buying up large swaths of South America. And the Chouinards began devoting an ever larger chunk of their own net worth to the grand project of conserving the Patagonian landscape. (Unlike Tompkins, however, Chouinard never advertised his holdings, preferring to keep a low profile and stay out of the headlines.)

Tompkins never stopped harassing Chouinard to make an even bolder move, telling him to sell Patagonia and invest all his winnings into conservation efforts. "He was on my ass to do the same thing," Chouinard said. "Sell the company, come on down here." But Chouinard's reasoning remained consistent. "I thought I could do more good by trying to live up to our mission statement at the time, which was to make the best product and cause no unnecessary harm, and then use the business to influence other companies."

Spending his fortune on conservation efforts in South America was part of Chouinard's ongoing reckoning with what he had built. He was richer than ever, and Patagonia was bigger than ever. Yet already, he was clear he wasn't going to sell the company and cash out or leave the company to his children. Fletcher and Claire were adults, but neither of them harbored ambitions to become CEO of Patagonia. The family had plenty of money, had homes in Ventura and Wyoming, what good would it do for the kids to inherit a corporation?

Discussions about whether to sell the company or take it public still flared up from time to time. At one point, the investment bank Robertson Stephens dangled a $100 million payday in front of the Chouinards. Another time, Chouinard said, he got a call from Warren Buffett, who offered to buy Patagonia. Of all the possible buyers, Buffett might have been a good fit. Known as the Oracle of Omaha, Buffett became one of the richest men in the world by ac- quiring companies and running them with an orientation toward long-term success. Still, Chouinard demurred. He simply could never bring himself to part with Patagonia. He was, however, look- ing for ways to put even more of the company's financial resources toward causes he cared about.

On one of his fishing trips in West Yellowstone, Chouinard got to know Craig Mathews, the founder of Blue Ribbon Flies, a tackle shop on the edge of the park. Mathews was no celebrity and no empire builder, but he ran his business with a sense of purpose. For as long as he could remember, he'd been giving away 2 percent of Blue Ribbon's annual sales to environmental causes he cared about. When Chouinard found out about this, he recognized a kindred spirit and told Mathews that Patagonia gave away 10 per- cent of its profits. From there, the two idealistic anglers started brainstorming: What if they could convince other companies to start giving away a slice of their profits? How big could this get?

A first step toward answering that question was reforming Patagonia's own philanthropic model. Instead of giving away 10 percent of annual profits, Chouinard decided that the company would start giving away 1 percent of sales. In practice, the change wouldn't be all that significant. Patagonia's margins tended to hover around 10 percent, so the dollar figure would be roughly the same in any given year. But the change committed Patagonia to making the contributions in good times and bad. Margins could be futzed with. In the event that profits were down in a bad year, environmental donations could dry up, even if the company had a billion dollars in sales. By committing to giving away 1 percent of revenues, no matter what, Chouinard made meaningful charitable giving a nonnegotiable part of the company's identity.

The money would continue going to the same sort of organizations that Chouinard had been funding since he began bankrolling Mark Capelli's efforts to rehabilitate the Ventura River—grassroots activists working on the front lines of conservation efforts. Chouinard still believed that social change happened not as the result of grandiose actions by great men but through gritty acts of defiance from everyday people. The Vietnam War, he mused, was ended by the hippies in the street. Civil rights were won not by President Johnson but by Rosa Parks. Ditto women's suffrage, gay rights, and any number of other revolutions. It's an oversimplified account of world events to be sure, one that places emphasis on the agitators, not the authorities. Yet it was in keeping with Chouinard's renegade worldview, his lack of faith in the government to solve any of the world's problems, and his hope that even misfits, outsiders, and activists could bend the arc of history.

Wanting to build a movement that would inspire other companies to follow their lead, Chouinard and Mathews founded a new nonprofit organization, 1% for the Planet, in 2002. It was small potatoes at first, just a few of Chouinard's friends agreeing to make some donations. But in time, more and more companies joined on, including big brands like OXO, Flickr, and Tazo. Two decades later, some 6,000 companies are members of 1% for the Planet. Together, the member companies have donated more than $655 million to environmental organizations. "For many of them, Yvon is an inspiration," said Kate Williams, the chief executive of the organization. "Yvon gave them the courage and lit the path, as it were, for them to think about doing business differently." Without Patagonia, a whole generation of socially responsible companies would not have gotten going, Williams said: "A lot of the companies in our network, directly or indirectly, exist because of Patagonia's example."

## "Stretch the Rubber Band of Reason"

Jib Ellison figured he had one last shot. Ellison was one of the Do Boys, and had accompanied Chouinard and Tompkins on countless adventures. For most of his career, if you could call it that, he had been a river rafting guide. His previous job, as a more traditional management consultant, was simple enough: help unorganized companies clean up their operations, hone their market appeal, and make a buck. But assisting pharmaceutical distributors left him dissatisfied. Now he was trying to make a go of it as a sustainability consultant in San Francisco and had set up his own shop, Blu Skye. All he needed was a client.

Ellison went to Peter Seligmann, the head of Conservation International, whom he had met through Tompkins, and requested a meeting with some of the nonprofit's board members. If they were wealthy enough to sit on the board of a big charity, they probably had the cash to hire an upstart consultant. Seligmann obliged, and Ellison met with Rob Walton, the chairman of Walmart, in 2003. Walton, the oldest son of the company's founder, Sam Walton, was the tenth richest person in the world at the time and had a budding interest in the environment. He had begun taking his sons on trips to Madagascar, the Galapagos Islands, and Brazil, seeking to expose them to wild places. And he had begun donating hefty sums of money to conservation efforts, including $21 million to Conservation International. If Ellison could land Walmart as a client, he figured he'd have it made.

When the two men finally connected, Ellison made a simple pitch: let him work with Walmart for a few months and see if he could help executives inside the company identify some changes that might reduce the company's environmental footprint and save some money. Walton was on board and introduced Ellison to the company's CEO, Lee Scott.

Walmart was an unlikely client for a scrappy sustainability consultancy. In the mid-2000s, there was no greater corporate villain than Walmart. Over the previous couple decades, the company had spread across the country, opening thousands of stores, decimating local businesses, and creating a consumerist monoculture. All the while, it was bribing local officials in foreign markets to get permits, stifling employees who tried to raise ethics concerns, and going to war with organized labor.

Yet there were signs that Walmart was open to change. In addition to Walton's personal interest in conservation, all that bad press was finally catching up to the company. Consumers were souring on the brand, regulators were circling, and the company's executives were looking for a way to change the narrative. "We had some real reputational issues, and we had a series of strategies to try and sort of change the perception of Walmart," said

John Fleming, Walmart's chief merchandising officer at the time. "One of them was this initiative around sustainability."

Still, when Ellison finally made his pitch to Scott, it was clear that concern for the environment did not rank high on Walmart's list of priorities. Indeed, when Ellison first described "sustainability" to Scott, the CEO replied: "Do you mean sustaining profits?"

"Yes," Ellison replied, wincing at the misunderstanding and trying to work with Scott. "It is about sustaining profits, but in an entirely different way."

Ellison went on to explain that if Walmart used its enormous influence to help the environment, it could have profound effects in the world. "What if big could be good?" he said. "What if you could actually reach through your supply system and actually make things better? You could make a really big difference here, and only you can do it." Scott was persuaded and soon gave Ellison a mandate to do his thing.

Among Ellison's first tasks was mapping out the myriad ways that a company like Walmart was impacting the planet. The list was endless—from the gas in the delivery trucks to the lights in the stores to the packaging of the goods to the factories where everything was made. As a starting point, however, Ellison simply helped Walmart identify some quick wins that could save money. Here, too, the opportunities were virtually infinite. Just by refining how laundry detergent was packaged, Ellison got Walmart to use 125 million fewer pounds of cardboard for shipping. That reduction in bulk led to savings of a half million gallons of diesel fuel from trucks that didn't need to transport the extra load. Walmart then asked the suppliers of its frozen chickens to send the poultry in unwaxed cardboard boxes that could be recycled instead of unrecyclable waxed boxes, reducing by 2.5 million the number of boxes it was sending into landfills each year. As Walmart expanded its ambitions on the sustainability front, it realized the financial gains could be substantial. Simply improving the fuel efficiency of its massive trucking fleet could save up to $300 million a year. "As we started studying it, we saw that there's a lot of low-hanging fruit," Fleming said. "You can take cost out of your business if you actually focus on efficiency and reducing waste."

Walmart was making initial gains on this front in August of 2005, when Hurricane Katrina slammed into New Orleans. Stormwater breached the levees, flooding the city and leading to an urban catastrophe. State and local officials were unequipped to deal with the magnitude of the destruction, and the federal government was caught flat-footed. But Walmart was ready. Well before the Federal Emergency Management Agency had gotten its act together, Walmart trucks were flowing into New Orleans, delivering food, water, medical supplies, and temporary shelters. It was a watershed moment, demonstrating both the incompetence of the federal government and the surprising power of a well-prepared corporation.

In the wake of the storm, Scott delivered a speech titled "Twenty-First Century Leadership" in which he reflected on the purpose of a company like Walmart. "I saw a company utilize its people resources and scale to make a big and positive difference in people's lives," he said. "Katrina asked this critical question, and I want to ask it of you: What would it take for Walmart to be that company, at our best, all the time? What if we used our size and resources to make this country and this Earth an even better place for all of us: customers, associates, our children, and generations unborn? What would that mean? Could we do it? Is this consistent with our business model?"

After posing that existential challenge, Scott spent the bulk of the speech dwelling on Walmart's responsibility to take care of the environment. "As one of the largest companies in the world, with an expanding global presence, environmental problems are *our* problems," he said. "The supply of natural products—fish, food, water—can only be sustained if the ecosystems that provide them are sustained and protected." Scott went on to articulate a series of lofty goals for the company: to be powered by 100 percent renewable energy, to create zero waste, and to make everything it sold sustainable. It was a radical agenda for 2005, and it stoked the appetite for change inside the world's biggest retailer.

Following Katrina, Ellison's work with Walmart deepened, and he brought in Rick Ridgeway, Chouinard's longtime pal and climbing partner. Ridgeway by this point was working for Patagonia full-time and was responsible for trying to educate the rest of the world about the company's unique culture. Before long, he and Ellison homed in on a wild idea: they needed to get Chouinard to come speak at Walmart headquarters in Bentonville, Arkansas.

It took some cajoling, but eventually the plan was set into motion. One of Walmart's corporate jets arrived at the Jackson Hole, Wyoming, airport, just south of Moose, and ferried Chouinard and Malinda to Arkansas for the day. Malinda was assured that she would be home by dinner. Ridgeway joined, too, but had to be extracted from the wilderness, as he was in the middle of tracking a herd of pronghorn sheep on a 100-mile migration for *National Geographic* magazine. Along with Ellison and a couple Walmart escorts, the Patagonia team made the flight and touched down in Bentonville in time for a tour of the company's headquarters. What they saw appalled them. The architecture was dismal. The color palette was soulless. Most offices had no windows. "It was so claustrophobic and abysmal, and we're just shaking our heads in disbelief," Ridgeway said.

When it came time for Chouinard to speak, the team made

their way to a large auditorium. There, some 1,200 Walmart executives had gathered to hear the septuagenarian dirtbag unspool some mountain wisdom. Introducing Chouinard was Rob Walton, who appeared on a large video monitor above the stage as he beamed in from his beach house in Costa Rica. In the background, the crowd in Bentonville could see waves breaking and a golden beach.

"Yvon, welcome to Walmart," Walton said, waving through the video feed in a dystopian scene, the billionaire looking down on his employees like some sort of deity.

Chouinard didn't miss a beat. "Rob, that's a pretty good-looking cubicle you've got," he said.

The crowd released a spasm of nervous laughter, unaccustomed to the insubordination. Then Chouinard, wearing the one wool blazer he owned—a ratty jacket with leather elbow patches—launched into his stump speech: how he grew up thinking businessmen were greaseballs; how he couldn't believe he was now a businessman himself; how he had redesigned pitons in the name of functionality and discovered along the way the paramount importance of quality; how today Patagonia was trying to minimize the harm it caused the planet by redesigning one product, one supply chain at a time.

Chouinard told the executives that for companies in the business of making stuff, there was no way to get around doing some damage. That was true for Patagonia, and it was certainly true for a behemoth like Walmart. The question was what they wanted to do about it. They could look the other way and ignore the consequences of their actions, deluding themselves that all that cheap merchandise didn't extract a steep tax on the planet. Or they could face up to the toll Walmart was taking on the natural world and try to make it better, bit by bit.

After recounting some of the company's backstory, Chouinard tore into Walmart, accusing his host of being amoral and indifferent to the myriad ways it was making a mess of things. "You're the biggest company in the world," he said. "You're not using your influence." He then took on the country's biggest soda maker, and Walmart's own role in poisoning the American public. "Look at Coca-Cola," he said. "That's what's causing the diabetes epidemic in the United States. Everybody drinking these sugar-sweetened soft drinks." Chouinard turned to Scott, the CEO, and said, "Go to Coke and cut them off," he said. "Just tell them you're not selling this shit anymore." Scott and other Walmart execs squirmed, knowing well that no such thing would happen anytime soon.

As a final bit, Chouinard pulled out a prop: a pair of enormous jeans he had bought at a Walmart. It was denim designed for a morbidly obese person, with billows of fabric and legs wide enough to accommodate the torso of a grown man. Holding the jeans up, he said, "I have to hand it to you. How do you sell something like this for $8.99? The fabric alone must cost that much!" The bean counters in the audience erupted in laughter.

It was an unconventional speech for Walmart, but it broke through the corporate fog of Bentonville. "People could finally connect the dots to 'What does that mean for me and my role at Walmart, and how can I make a difference?'" Fleming said. "It seemed like that was a tipping point. Way more people in line management jobs that could have an impact started to lead after that."

As Chouinard gave his talk, Malinda was getting a closer look at Walmart HQ. She toured Walmart's emergency response center, a compound where the company coordinated disaster relief and managed crises. She marveled at how proficiently the company staged water, food, and supplies, allowing it to respond when a disaster like Katrina hit; how it prepared to clean and repair stores damaged by extreme weather; how it managed fights and shootings on its properties; and how it got employees ("the ones they underpay," she noted) extra hours at other locations in the event that their store was temporarily closed. "There was no emergency they weren't prepared for," she said. "It made FEMA look so weak."

As the Patagonia team departed Bentonville, Mary Fox, Walmart's senior vice president for apparel sourcing, chased down Ridgeway. "We wanted to become more sustainable, but we really didn't know how," she told him. "Please teach us everything you know." Ridgeway said he would try to oblige, and Walmart executives were soon passing through Ventura on a regular basis. Delegations would fly out, spend a few days on campus eating tacos and watching employees come and go with their surfboards, and try to wrap their heads around what Patagonia was up to. Those that arrived for the first time typically came wearing suits, prompting Ridgeway to quip, "Hey dudes, you don't need your jackets."

Some Patagonia employees questioned the merits of the collaboration. Just as many had scoffed at the ethics of making gear for the military, a similar contingent—including Malinda—believed there was no upside to working with Walmart given its abysmal record on the environment, human rights, and more. "Malinda got increasingly uncomfortable with being a bedfellow with a giant multinational like that," Ridgeway said. "They were still doing more harm than good." But Ridgeway—and, critically, Chouinard—believed that the risk was worth the potential reward. If Patagonia could help make Walmart a little greener, wouldn't that be a good thing at the end of the day? "If you changed the trajectory of a giant ship just one degree, it makes a big ripple," Ridgeway said.

The opportunity to make good on that promise came about soon enough. Even before it connected with Patagonia, Walmart had experimented with organic cotton. The results had been middling and nothing came of the effort, but now Ellison wanted them to try again. Taking a page from the Patagonia playbook, he brought Walmart's executive vice president of apparel merchandising to visit cotton farmers in Turkey. First, they visited a conventional cotton farm. It was devoid of insect life, foul smelling, and scarred by herbicides and pesticides. Crop dusters buzzed the fields. Then, Ellison took them to an organic cotton farm, which was brimming with life and smelled like the earth. As it had for the Patagonia executives more than a decade earlier, seeing the contrast firsthand had a profound effect on the Walmart team. The company agreed to ramp up its use of organic cotton and made a large co-purchase agreement with Patagonia. Here they were, the biggest retailer in the world and the little surf company from the coast, locking arms and reshaping the supply chain for one of the nastiest crops on Earth.

Dissenters inside Patagonia continued to fret about the partnership. Patagonia's embrace of organic cotton was one of the things that differentiated it from the competition. If Walmart was going to start selling organic cotton T-shirts for a fraction of the cost, who was going to keep buying Patagonia gear? Still, Ellison and Ridgeway counted the partnership as a win, and the companies kept talking. Walmart began buying organic cotton on its own, and within a year was the single largest customer in the world, instantly eclipsing Patagonia's demand.

The next step in the relationship came when Patagonia helped Walmart develop a scorecard it could use to measure its environmental impact. Walmart had been trying to create such a system, but the early attempts were superficial and didn't drill down into the supply chain. At the same time, Patagonia had been working with the Outdoor Industry Association to develop a scorecard with much more robust standards that was known as the Eco-index. Ridgeway pushed Walmart to toughen its own self-assessment but soon realized it didn't make much sense for each company to be using its own system. Instead, the apparel industry should have a shared set of standards that all companies used.

Ridgeway suggested working together to create a common scorecard that might push the whole industry in the right direction. The proposed code name for the project: David and Goliath. Walmart agreed to fund the endeavor, and in 2009, an invitation went out to 16 other apparel company CEOs that featured both Walmart's logo and Patagonia's logo in the letterhead. Signed by Chouinard and Fleming, the letter included an invitation to gather in the next few months with the intent of creating a new coalition that would promote sustainability. It was an unusual and persuasive combination—the biggest retailer in the world, with all the market power that conferred, in partnership with Patagonia, with its unimpeachable environmental bona fides. Other executives couldn't say no.

The next year, 15 of the 16 companies gathered. Along with Patagonia and Walmart, representatives from Target, Gap, Kohl's, Levi's, Nike, JCPenney, H&M, Hanes, and Marks & Spencer showed up. They quickly agreed that a common set of standards was needed, if only to make things easier for suppliers. When each apparel company had its own code of conduct, reporting system, and inspectors, a supplier could find itself being audited, inspected, and monitored multiple times in a single month. That was a pain for suppliers and meant that apparel companies were performing lots of redundant work. Eventually, the companies agreed to create a new organization called the Sustainable Apparel Coalition that would develop a common set of standards. It took two years, but with the inclusion of a couple hundred data points and a fair bit of arguing about what really mattered, the coalition finally had a system its members could agree on. In need of a name, they seized upon the popularity of the Higgs boson particle, which was in the news after scientists at CERN finally observed the so-called god particle. Their system, introduced in 2012, was called the Higg Index, reflecting, one participant said, "our search for the particles of sustainability." More than three hundred consumer goods companies are now a part of the group that started as the Sustainable Apparel Coalition, which is now known as Cascale.

The collaboration between Walmart and Patagonia didn't go much further than that. After the Higg Index was launched, Walmart withdrew from its engagement with other apparel makers and began focusing on its direct relationship with suppliers. Mike Duke, who succeeded Scott as CEO of Walmart, backed away from the sustainability efforts, and the company never came close to realizing the lofty vision of corporate responsibility Scott outlined in his speech. Chouinard was disappointed by the development, though not surprised. "Walmart did a little bit, and they picked all the low-hanging fruit, and then they realized to go any further is too much work," he said. "To go further, you've got to involve all your suppliers. You've got to clean up your whole supply chain. Well, good luck with that."

## "Turning Over Stones"

Once Patagonia committed to paying close attention to the negative consequences of its work, each bit of growth turned into a mixed blessing. On the one hand, more sales meant more success, more good jobs up and down the supply chain, and ultimately more money for the Chouinards to spend on their growing charitable efforts. On the other hand, it also meant Patagonia was becoming that much more of a drain on the planet's resources, was working in that many more developing markets with ungovernable labor practices, and was having stuff made in still more factories where quality would be that much harder to control. "There's great inherent danger when you start to grow that fast," said Casey Sheahan, who replaced Crooke as CEO in 2005. "You can lose control of social conditions, environmental conditions. I was very nervous about that."

In the few years before Sheahan took over, Patagonia had expanded the number of factories it used in Southeast Asia. Searching for efficiencies, the company started playing suppliers off one another and trying to drive down costs. That had the intended effect of saving money, but it was soon clear that quality was suffering. The new manufacturers didn't have a history of working with Patagonia and didn't share its exacting standards, leading to size irregularities, loose buttons, broken zippers, and other defects. In an ominous sign, return rates were ticking up once again. Worse, when Patagonia sent its employees to inspect the factories, it was clear that some of the new suppliers had substandard labor and human rights practices.

In response to the creeping realization that standards were slipping, Patagonia sharply curtailed the number of factories it worked with. Hoping to avoid more such problems going forward, the company instituted a new policy: before it began working with any new supplier, it would send a team of executives to check out the quality of the products and the factory's social and environmental standards. The inspectors had veto power. If they found anything to be subpar, the factory wouldn't get the contract. Crucially, there were no incentives for the inspectors to offer their stamp of approval; they had the autonomy to blacklist a supplier even if doing so would lead to costly delays. "Nobody ever got fired for it," said Vincent Stanley. "People got praised for doing the right thing."

The next step in Patagonia's journey to become a more transparent company was the launch of a website called the Footprint Chronicles, which debuted in 2007. An unusual bit of corporate storytelling, the site represented Patagonia's initial attempt to come clean about some of the problems it was finding in its sprawling network of suppliers. "The goal is to use transparency about our supply chain to help us reduce our adverse social and environmental impacts—and on an industrial scale," the website read. "We've been in business long enough to know that when we can reduce or eliminate a harm, other businesses will be eager to follow suit."

With one story after another, the Footprint Chronicles detailed Patagonia's attempts to root out hazardous materials and unsavory labor practices. The site recounted how Patagonia figured out how to source chlorine-free wool; how it started using Tencel, a fabric similar to rayon that is made from the pulp of fast-growing eucalyptus trees grown on farms certified by the Forest Stewardship Council; and how it expanded its use of recycled nylon rather than using virgin nylon made with crude oil.

But the closer Patagonia looked, the more problems it found. Examining one factory with an eye toward the working conditions of employees, it discovered that the dyeing process was putting effluent into a river. Some natural materials looked promising at first, until Patagonia realized that treating the fabrics required the use of toxic softeners. As Patagonia learned more about its supply chain, it whittled down the number of its primary suppliers—

those actually making finished Patagonia goods—from 109 to about 75. That made the job of auditing its most important factories easier but also raised new questions about what was happening further down the supply chain.

Self-accountability was a primary motivation behind the Footprint Chronicles. By publishing its trials and errors online, Patagonia was pushing itself to be more transparent and in turn, more responsible. There was also an educational component. Most people don't think twice about where their clothes come from, and Patagonia wanted its customers to know what it took to produce their Baggies, fleeces, and long underwear. "The customer has a right to know what is going on at every level of product creation at a business," Sheahan said. "We were completely transparent around our supply chain by taking video cameras and tape recorders into our factories, publicizing pictures of them, showing the workers that were on the assembly line, in their dorm rooms, in the cafeterias, and just trying to show the world that, 'Hey, we don't actually make clothing downstairs in the basement in Ventura. We make them in China, we make them in Thailand, we make them in Vietnam. And it's a very complex, complicated, connected, global group of people that are contracted to work for us. And we try to keep the standards high everywhere.'"

Patagonia didn't always succeed. A few years after starting the Footprint Chronicles, inspectors auditing one of the second-tier suppliers in Taiwan discovered evidence of human trafficking and indentured servitude. This wasn't a factory making Patagonia clothes; rather it was a mill making the fabrics that were used to create Patagonia's jackets, pants, and more. And it turned out that this second-tier supplier in Taipei was using labor brokers to source workers from other, poorer, Southeast Asian countries.

The brokers would charge migrants as much as $7,000 in exchange for the promise of a job. When the workers finally showed up at a factory, the managers would then deposit their paychecks into company-controlled bank accounts, then automatically deduct fees for living expenses. Workers had their passports confiscated, were told they had to pay off massive debts to their employers before they could leave, and were even made to pay for the privilege of keeping their jobs. "That's not freedom," Sheahan said. "And we started to see evidence of this as we started turning over stones."

Patagonia moved production away from the offending factory. But the deeper it looked, the more it became clear the practice of so-called debt bondage was rampant at its suppliers in Taiwan. The company went public with the revelations on its blog, describing "a form of indentured servitude that could also qualify, less politely, as modern-day slavery." In response to the findings, Patagonia launched an effort to overhaul worker relations at its second-tier suppliers. It hired Verité, a firm that monitors labor conditions, to conduct additional audits. It developed a new set of employment standards for workers in its supply chain with the aim of combating human trafficking. And it started making suppliers reimburse workers for any fees they had paid in order to secure their jobs.

The unsavory revelations didn't stop there. A few years after the Taiwan labor mess, People for the Ethical Treatment of Animals released a video showing inhumane treatment of sheep on a farm in Argentina that supplied wool to Patagonia. The graphic footage from PETA depicted rams getting castrated, tied up, cut, stepped on, and even killed at farms run by Ovis 21, which was considered to be a highly ethical supplier and had been selling wool to Patagonia for years. It was a grotesque violation of Patagonia's professed animal welfare standards, and it led to a wave of negative publicity. "It was such a heavy moment," said Matt Dwyer, the company's vice president of product impact and innovation. "We really thought that we had something in a very, very good place. Then this came up."

As a first step, Patagonia came clean when it learned of the video. "It is as disturbing as anything PETA puts out," the company said in a blog post. And in a matter of days, Patagonia announced it would no longer work with Ovis 21. From there, the company began working with an industry group called the Textile Exchange and helped develop a new set of best-in-class practices, known as the Responsible Wool Standard. It was one more problem with the supply chain, one more complicated mess for Patagonia to clean up. Yet this time, the revelations were laced with an irony Chouinard himself had to appreciate.

For years, Patagonia had been funding environmental activists, including some that used direct action and shock tactics to confront wrongdoers, cause a stir, and make a point. Now, Patagonia itself was on the receiving end of the same tactics. Management bristled at the onslaught, unaccustomed to being portrayed in such a negative light on the public stage. "We weren't used to this kind of attack," Dwyer said. "We don't agree with all the tactics they used. They could have just had a conversation with us that might have worked way better."

Of course, that's not how Patagonia went about trying to make change in the world nor how it expected the activists it funded to operate. Chouinard believed that in order to make change, it was necessary to ruffle a few feathers, and he sympathized with the rabble-rousers who were willing to cause a stir and make a point. That applied to the activists who got arrested while protesting the Maxxam clear-cutting operations, and at the end of the day, it applied to the animal rights activists going after Patagonia, too.

# "Don't Buy This Jacket"

The financial crisis of 2008 rattled the global economy. Shady lenders pushed subprime mortgages on overzealous American borrowers who couldn't afford the loans. Wall Street firms bundled risky debts into instruments that destabilized otherwise sound financial institutions. As banks failed and the stock market crashed, just about every company in the world felt the effects of the downturn. Consumers stopped spending, big brands tottered, and no one was spared from the carnage.

In the first chaotic days of the crisis, Sheahan was tempted to institute a round of layoffs at Patagonia. Preemptively cutting costs and shoring up the company's cash reserves seemed like the prudent thing to do. A company like Patagonia, he figured, was especially vulnerable, given the high price point of most of its items. But the prospect of firing employees was nauseating. The specter of the Black Wednesday layoffs in 1991 still haunted the company, and Sheahan didn't want to let people go unless he absolutely had to. In conversations with his wife, Tara, he unloaded his anxieties and asked for her advice.

"What would you do differently if you were operating the company out of love as opposed to fear?" she said. "Because fear is the opposite of creativity."

"I wouldn't lay off anybody," Sheahan replied. "These people have mortgages, they've got the kids in school, and we've got to keep them going. We've got to find alternative ways to get through this without gutting the company."

So that's what he did. Patagonia would abstain from layoffs, at least for the time being. Instead, it would cut costs wherever it could without sacrificing the quality of the product. International travel, including the paid trips to volunteer with Tompkins, was severely curtailed. A subsidy of $5,000 that was being offered to employees who wanted to buy a hybrid car was taken away. A program to buy carbon offsets was scrapped. There were no bonuses and no annual raises that year. The cost cutting allowed Patagonia to weather the storm. Sales did fall, but not so much that the company was ever in jeopardy, and not even so much that staff cuts were ever seriously considered.

Then something remarkable happened: a few months into the crisis, sales started booming. To be sure, consumers were buying fewer things. But when they did buy stuff, they were buying high-quality items that they expected would last a long time, and they were willing to spend extra. It was yet more validation of one of Chouinard's earliest tenets: making the best products possible always paid off. Even if it was more expensive, customers would pay a premium if they believed they were getting the best.

As Rick Ridgeway and Vincent Stanley got to thinking about it, however, they realized it wasn't enough to just make great stuff; a company also had to convince customers that it had their back if something went wrong. Patagonia needed to assure its community that it would repair damaged items, replace them when needed, and create a system to recycle worn-out apparel.

Some of this work was already underway. After Walmart began using organic cotton, Chouinard had pressed his team to up its ambition and figure out new ways to distinguish Patagonia. That led to a program called Common Threads, later rebranded as Worn Wear, which saw the company buy back used items that were still in good shape and resell them. It also announced that it would accept all worn-out Patagonia gear, even if it couldn't be resold. The company promised that donations wouldn't go into a landfill—the goods would either be recycled or repurposed.

From there, discussions turned to an even more extreme idea: what if Patagonia could encourage customers to buy less stuff, period? It was one thing to promise to repair and recycle; it was way more radical to challenge shoppers to consider whether they needed a new jacket at all. Chouinard liked the idea in principle, but it wasn't clear how to get the message across. Ridgeway floated closing all the stores on Black Friday, the biggest shopping day of the year, and putting up crime scene tape. That didn't fly. But as he kept thinking, Ridgeway eventually returned to "A Plea for Responsible Consumption," the ad that Doug Tompkins had placed in *Utne Reader* back in 1990. Tompkins was way ahead of his time when he prodded consumers to question whether they really needed to buy more clothes. What if now, more than two decades later and with the world reeling from the financial crisis, Patagonia did something similar?

Ridgeway came up with a tagline: "Don't Buy This Jacket," imagining the slogan plastered above an image of a new Patagonia fleece. He made a mock-up of a full-page newspaper ad and presented it to the Patagonia board. Chouinard was open to it, but McDivitt Tompkins, who was still on the board, was skeptical. The message was hypocritical, she worried, and smacked of inauthentic marketing gimmickry. Patagonia was all about selling stuff; how could it tell consumers to buy less with a straight face? There was also the risk of losing sales at the most critical time of the year. Did they really want to do that?

She had a point, of course. McDivitt Tompkins was putting her finger on the paradox that had animated Patagonia for so long, the creative tension she had identified when she was CEO. Ridgeway went back to the drawing board and refined the messaging. He incorporated Common Threads, which promoted Patagonia's efforts to reduce waste and recycle products, and he drew inspiration from *The Limits to Growth,* a 1972 book published by the Club of Rome, which warned that annual, compound economic growth was "the elephant in the room" and would inevitably lead to the collapse of natural ecosystems. When he went back to the board and pitched it again, he got the green light.

On November 25, 2011, Patagonia took out a full-page ad in *The New York Times.* The day was symbolic. It was Black Friday, the day after Thanksgiving and an orgy of consumerism that kicked off the holiday shopping season. The ad was simple, and just as Ridgeway had imagined it: Above a picture of a gray zip-up R2 fleece was the phrase "Don't Buy This Jacket." Below that, the company explained its thinking. "It's Black Friday, the day in the year retail turns from red to black and starts to make real money," the copy read. "But Black Friday, and the culture of consumption it reflects, puts the economy of natural systems that supports all life firmly in the red. We're now using the resources of one-and-a-half planets on our one and only planet. Because Patagonia wants to be in business for a good long time—and leave a world inhabitable for our kids—we want to do the opposite of every other business today. We ask you to buy less and to reflect before you spend a dime on this jacket or anything else." The ad went on to explain that it required 135 liters of water to produce the R2 jacket pictured, even though it was made with 60 percent recycled materials. "Don't buy what you don't need," it concluded. "Think twice before you buy anything."

The response was instantaneous. Trade publications lauded the ad as a brilliantly subversive bit of marketing, using the allure of the taboo to encourage people to buy yet more of Patagonia's gear. Mainstream media outlets wrote news stories about the ad. "For that $57,000 ad in *The New York Times,* we got $40 million to $50 million of free publicity," Sheahan said. As McDivitt Tompkins expected, there was some blowback. Critics accused Patagonia of being hypocritical and using reverse psychology to gin up still more sales. Even some inside the company questioned the motivations. "What was the real intention?" said Grose, the Patagonia consultant. "Was it just really clever marketing?" Either way, the ad worked. In the months following its publication, sales at Patagonia reached new heights.

Chouinard was rattled by the success. He worried that the spike in sales might put the company in the same position it had found itself two decades earlier, when rapid expansion, followed by a downturn, led to the Black Wednesday layoffs. Yet this was no flash in the pan. The "Don't Buy This Jacket" ad was perhaps the purest expression of Patagonia's unconventional philosophy to date, and sales kept on growing. "It was really a culmination of all these internal discussions we were having about what kind of company we wanted to be," said Sheahan. "And it was all driven by the mission statement, which was to make the best product, cause no unnecessary harm, and inspire and implement solutions to the environmental crisis."

Advertising itself as a different sort of company was one thing. But the year after the "Don't Buy This Jacket" ad, Patagonia took steps to codify its status as a corporate outlier. For several years, the so-called B Corp movement had been gaining steam. Benefit corporations, or B Corps, are companies that uphold exemplary social and environmental standards. To become a B Corp, a corporation has to complete a rigorous self-audit, then receive a certification from a nonprofit organization called B Lab. Big companies like Ben & Jerry's and Natura, the largest cosmetics maker in Brazil, were among those that earned the seal of approval. But a half decade after the movement began, Patagonia wasn't part of it.

The B Lab founders had asked Patagonia to become the first company to earn the certification when they started the organization, but Chouinard declined. He and the company's board didn't want to create the impression that Patagonia was inventing a certification to congratulate itself and didn't want to burden themselves with still more auditing when they were already doing plenty on their own, and submitting to a host of other independent audits from organizations like Verité and bluesign. But that changed in 2012, when California began allowing companies to register as so-called benefit corporations. This new legal designation would allow a company to write into their corporate charter a commitment to do more than just make money, but instead also seek to serve the public good. This was something Chouinard could get behind. In becoming a benefit corporation, he saw the chance to do more than advertise Patagonia's social and environmental bona fides. He could legally formalize its commitment to the planet.

As the California state offices came to life on the morning of January 3, 2012, Chouinard, Malinda, and Ridgeway were in Sacramento, waiting to file some paperwork. It was the first day that companies in the state could register as benefit corporations, and Chouinard wanted to make the change in person. Becoming a benefit corporation was a bureaucratic formality, one that would remain invisible to its customers and have no effect on the company's operations. But the move was significant in symbolic terms. For one thing, it paved the way for Patagonia to finally become a B Corp. (B Lab tethered its certification to the benefit corporation designation, and once Patagonia made the legal switch, it was willing to tack on the B Corp designation, too). But for Chouinard, Patagonia becoming a benefit corporation held a deeper significance. For decades, he had been looking for ways to prove to the world that Patagonia was a different sort of company, one that cared about something more than money. With the new designation, that claim was now unimpeachable.

CHAPTER 9

# Fights

## "A Perfect Trap"

Doug and Kris Tompkins had assembled an empire. After two decades of audacious land purchases, shrewd legal battles, and bruising public relations spats, their landholdings stretched from the icy southern tip of Chile to the lush tropical forests of Argentina. Beyond simply acquiring acreage, they had built infrastructure worthy of national parks. Ever the aesthete, Tompkins had insisted that the trails, bridges, and buildings on his properties were of unparalleled beauty and craftsmanship. He hired local artisans to carve intricate woodwork, clad buildings in shingles made from ancient Alerce trees, and insisted that even the trash cans be exquisitely designed. At times, the ornate workmanship struck even his close friends as superfluous. Once, as Tompkins showed off some of the new buildings in what would become Patagonia National Park, Chouinard trailed behind, mumbling his complaints. "This is shit," Chouinard groused. It was too costly, a waste of money, too inaccessible for the locals, and it would be too expensive to maintain.

But while the old Fun Hogs didn't always agree on how to spend their respective fortunes, they remained close confidants.

Not long after touring Chacabuco, they sat together in Pumalín, Chile, and engaged in the same sort of meandering, philosophical conversations they had begun in the California hills when Chouinard was playing hooky from the army. Sipping yerba maté, Tompkins was his strident self, castigating the masses for their casual disregard of the natural world.

"Most people see nature as nothing more than a basket of resources," he said. "A cornucopia to benefit the human economy."

On this day, Chouinard shared his friend's pessimism. "They think we can live without nature," he replied. "Or they think they're better than nature because they can manipulate nature. They don't think we need free-flowing rivers because if the salmon are blocked, no problem, they can just farm the salmon."

Chouinard had wound his buddy up, and Tompkins took it further. "They delude themselves into thinking they can live in a glass box above nature," Tompkins said, gleefully upping the rhetorical ante. "They don't see that civilizations are as fragile as life itself. Bang, one day you're dead. The Ottomans, the Romans, the Greeks, the Mayans. None of the globalists want to look at that possibility."

Chouinard picked up the thread. "Accepting that you're going to die, that we're all going to die—that all societies have a beginning and an end—doesn't mean you have to give up on living, or that you have to become part of accelerating the end," he said. "Doug and I agree on that, but in other ways we're opposites. He is more bothered about the end of society and mankind because he wants to do something about it. I'm just kind of a laid-back Zen Buddhist and just say, 'I'll do what I can and so be it.'"

Tompkins smiled and offered a metaphysical retort: "Well, my buddy Yvon forgets that all good Buddhists have to take their bodhisattva vows and forgo enlightenment until all the world is enlightened."

More than 40 years after they first began prodding each other to climb higher, go further, dream bigger, Chouinard and Tompkins were still egging each other on. And while they were now in their 70s, they were also still testing the limits of their physical endurance.

In December of 2015, Chouinard and Tompkins set out for yet another Do Boys adventure, this one a kayak trip on the north shore of Lago General Carrera, a vast lake on the border of Chile and Argentina. Rick Ridgeway and Jib Ellison were in the area already. Continuing the work that began with Walmart, the pair had brought together 50 chief sustainability officers from companies like Tiffany, Boeing, Disney, and Apple for a retreat designed to get them to actually care about saving the planet. Tompkins dropped in and lectured them on his views that capitalism itself was unsustainable, ruffling some feathers as he effectively accused his guests of greenwashing. Also on the kayaking expedition were Lorenzo Alvarez-Roos, who knew Ellison from whitewater rafting, and Weston Boyles, the son of Edgar Boyles, who had been with Chouinard and Ridgeway during the Minya Konka avalanche in 1981 that killed Jonathan Wright. Ellison and Boyles, who both owned property along the lake, organized the trip, and the plan was to explore the remote north shore, then hike up a valley flanked by a series of stunning peaks.

The night before the trip, they gathered for a meal with Malinda, McDivitt Tompkins, and other friends who were in the area. Over dinner, they joked about their age. No longer were they the Do Boys. They were now the "Done Boys." It wasn't all in jest; Chouinard could see the years wearing on Tompkins. "I was a little shocked to see how frail the old fig looked," Chouinard remembered, employing his longtime nickname for Tompkins. "But then, he probably thought the same of me."

The next morning, as Malinda and McDivitt Tompkins saw the team off, they insisted the men take a satellite phone. Chouinard and Tompkins protested, not wanting to bring any superfluous technology into the remote wilderness. But in the end, they relented, and Ellison stuffed the phone in his pack.

The six men had four boats. Chouinard and Boyles were in single kayaks, Ellison and Alvarez-Roos shared a double, and Ridgeway and Tompkins shared another double with a wonky rudder. For three days, the team enjoyed unusually pristine weather brought on by a high-pressure system. Clear blue skies, a light wind, and not a storm in sight. At night, the men camped on the shoreline, surrounded only by the rocks, water, dirt, and trees. One evening, they dove into the lake, whooping with joy as the bracing glacial runoff stung their aging skin. Chouinard cooked pasta, and they huddled around a campfire, trading stories. Above them, the Milky Way unfurled across the Andes.

On their third night in the wild, the weather began to change. When they woke on the fourth day, December 8, 2015, angry gusts were whipping across the lake. After packing up, they set out paddling, the wind initially at their backs. Tompkins and Ridgeway's boat was slowed by its malfunctioning rudder, and before long the kayaks were getting farther apart, buffeted by the waves, which had rapidly turned into 4-foot swells. With each passing minute, the weather grew more severe. As crosswinds entered the mix, sharp gusts came down the valleys and rocked the boats. "We ran into a perfect trap: a forty-knot wind at our back and an equally strong wind from the side, making for large and confused waves," Chouinard recalled. "We could not even miss one paddle stroke for fear of going over."

Tompkins warned Ridgeway that things were getting serious. "We need to be careful," he said. Ridgeway could barely respond, he was so focused on paddling. The three other boats had made it around a rocky outcropping and were out of sight. Tompkins and Ridgeway were about 200 yards behind, struggling to stay straight as waves rose up beneath them and sent them hurtling down ever steeper faces. The lake was pulsating, and eventually one swell lifted their double kayak up so high that, as they began to descend its face, the boat turned sideways, and a wave swamped them.

Ridgeway was underwater, looking up. In a matter of seconds, he had freed himself and was buoyed to the surface by his life jacket. He was still holding his paddle and had a hand on the kayak, and he was relieved to see Tompkins surface, still wearing his white cap. They made eye contact and shared a knowing glance: they were now fighting for their lives.

"Let's turn the boat over," Tompkins howled through the wind.

They worked together to flip the kayak upright and managed to heave themselves atop it, straddling it like a seesaw. A moment later, another wave crashed, knocking them back into the water. Again, they hoisted themselves onto the boat, and again they were knocked into the lake.

"The wind is taking us away from the point!" Ridgeway screamed.

Tompkins just stared back, the gravity of the situation setting in.

The storm was pushing them deeper into the center of the lake, and Tompkins and Ridgeway decided to swim for shore, which was a few hundred yards away. Ridgeway tried the backstroke, then the breaststroke, fighting against the waves, taking in mouthfuls of water, and coughing them out. Tompkins tried to use his paddle, as if his body were a boat.

Swells, currents, and wind were pushing the men apart. At one point, Ridgeway saw the other men on the shore. But when he waved, they didn't wave back, and between the wind and the distance, it was pointless to yell. Ridgeway kept trying to swim but was barely moving. He began to accept that he was going to die. He looked up at the sky, marveled at the world, and stopped struggling, allowing himself to be subsumed by Patagonia.

Then he snapped out of it. He coughed out water, began yelling again, and soon saw the other men in their kayaks, heading straight for his position. Ellison and Alvarez-Roos arrived in the other double and told him to hold on to the rope loop at the back of the boat. It was too dangerous to try to bring him on top. As Ridgeway held on and they paddled for shore, he asked about Tompkins.

"Weston has him."

Yet Boyles was barely hanging on himself. In his single kayak, he had caught up with Tompkins, who tried to hold on as Boyles paddled for shore. But Boyles could barely move the boat with Tompkins as an anchor, and Tompkins was having a hard time holding on as his body froze. Boyles tried to haul Tompkins atop his kayak, but the boat began taking on water. Boyles avoided capsizing, but by the time Tompkins was out of the water, he was unconscious.

Back on shore, Ellison and the others had called for help using the satellite phone, and a rescue helicopter eventually arrived. Tompkins was flown to Coyhaique Regional Hospital. When the doctors got to him, his internal temperature was 66 degrees Fahrenheit.

The other men, having remained on shore, tried to collect themselves. Ridgeway awoke inside a sleeping bag, his body convulsing as hypothermia set in. Ellison was inside it as well, working to warm Ridgeway with his body heat. Disoriented, Ridgeway asked what was happening, and Ellison explained that Tompkins had been airlifted out. Chouinard was nearby. After a while, voices crackled through Ridgeway's splintered awareness.

"We have Weston, back with Yvon," someone said.

"What about Doug?" Ellison asked.

"Doug is dead."

## "Room for Disaster"

Tompkins's death created a series of unfillable voids. Kris McDivitt Tompkins, now a widow, was bereft. A half century after her father had died in Venezuela, her husband was dead in Argentina. The love of her life, her everyday companion, and her partner in one of the most audacious conservation efforts in the world, was gone, and she slipped into depression. Inside their sprawling nonprofit operation, Tompkins's sudden disappearance upended years of meticulous planning. Efforts to acquire additional properties and transfer huge swaths of land to the governments of Chile and Argentina were destabilized. The fate of some of South America's most exquisite natural landscapes hung in the balance. And within the tight-knit Patagonia community, the loss was a shocking blow. After so many years living such charmed lives and cheating death, the Do Boys had acquired the mystique of something close to invincibility. Now their good luck had run out.

Chouinard had already been present at the death of one of his friends, during the avalanche that killed Jonathan Wright in 1981. A quarter century on, he was there to witness the death of his closest compatriot. It was gutting, yet also somehow fitting. "We were always looking for an adventure, but there is no possibility of adventure without risk," Chouinard said. "We loved life and were not afraid of death—but did not wish to die."

Chouinard acknowledged that the men were cavalier and had

left themselves exposed on the lake. "We just weren't prepared," Chouinard said. "I mean, he was dressed in pressed chinos, a Brooks Brothers shirt, a light sweater, and a rain jacket. Like that Zen painter who always leaves part of his painting unfinished, we always left room for disaster."

Tompkins's death had another tragic consequence: his family descended into bitter wrangling over the fate of his estate. Unlike the Chouinards, who remained a tightly knit unit even as Patagonia prospered and their own net worth soared, the Tompkins family was torn apart by wealth.

Before he died, Tompkins made it clear that in the event of his death, he wished for his remaining fortune to be spent on additional conservation efforts in South America. Nothing was more important to him than protecting as much wilderness as possible. Under no circumstances, he said, should his daughters, Summer and Quincey, inherit his money. "I don't think that inheritances are good for the upbringing of children," he said. "That stunts people's development, it does not motivate them to grow, to develop themselves."

In death, however, Tompkins had no say in the matter. Shortly after he died, Summer sued in a bid to gain access to his fortune and prevent McDivitt Tompkins from using the funds for conservation. Summer, who lived in San Francisco, didn't hesitate to disparage her late father in the press. "We are all very hardworking, productive people not looking for a handout, and he clearly had no trust of us and no respect," she said. "It's definitely an insult. But he is dead, rotting in the ground as we speak." For the previous 20 years, Summer said, the only time she heard from her father was when he passed through town and asked for a place to stay, dirtbagging it until the end. "He was a completely self-absorbed human being," she said. "A narcissist."

Summer's argument in court was simple. Tompkins had organized his estate in California and written a will that included his wishes for how to distribute his assets when he died. According to those instructions, his children were not in line for any inheritance. But because Tompkins lived in Chile, which forbids parents from disinheriting their children, Summer asserted that his estate should have been governed by Chilean law.

McDivitt Tompkins fought the claims. In a legal filing, her lawyer said that Tompkins had disdained his daughter's materialistic lifestyle and values, which were "the very antithesis of everything Doug believed in and stood for during his life." Summer already had plenty of money from her mother, Susie Tompkins Buell, who had made her own fortune from Esprit. Giving her a cut of her father's estate "would only serve to enrich the already rich," while at the same time making it harder for Tompkins to realize his dream of creating national parks in Chile and Argentina. "Doug could never have imagined the cruel irony that Summer would seek to exploit his death and the laws of countries in which Doug had devoted his charity," the lawyer wrote.

After a Los Angeles judge threw out Summer's initial suit, her lawyers sued the Tompkins estate in Chile, arguing that she was entitled to $50 million. McDivitt Tompkins again fought the claims, and again prevailed in court. It was an ugly coda to Tompkins's life and served as a powerful contrast to the Chouinards and their children, who remained suspicious of material wealth and would soon work together to rid themselves of their fortune.

As McDivitt Tompkins moved through her grief and past the lawsuits, she refocused. There was still work to be done creating the parks, and she would now have to finish the job alone. At least the road map was clear. Just months before Tompkins died, his organization had made an offer to the Chilean government: Tompkins Conservation would donate more than 1 million acres to the state if Chile agreed to protect huge swaths of adjacent land and create a new network of national parks.

With that deal on the table, the president of Chile, Michelle Bachelet, went all in. Bachelet was an environmentalist herself, and she agreed to contribute 9 million acres, more than twice what Tompkins had originally proposed. Together, the newly protected areas would form the basis of five new national parks and expand another three. In total, the new Patagonia National Park system would increase the protected land of Chile by more than 40 percent, creating a sanctuary more than triple the size of Yellowstone and Yosemite combined.

On a crisp day in February of 2018, McDivitt Tompkins joined Bachelet in Cochrane, a remote locale in the heart of Patagonia where Tompkins was buried. Chouinard and Ridgeway were there, as were others from the inner circle, all gathered to formally inaugurate Pumalín Douglas Tompkins National Park, the crown jewel of the new parks system. The deal was "good not only for Chile, but for the planet," Bachelet said. "It shows that you don't have to be a rich country to make these kinds of decisions. It only requires will and courage."

McDivitt Tompkins, mournful, pensive, and beaming with pride all at once, her golden-white hair tousled in the wind, reveled in the moment, reflecting on Tompkins and their work, a project that had given her so much but also taken so much. "There is something about the expanse of Patagonia, a kind of haunting soulfulness to it that affects you physically," she said. "Few places like this one grab you and hold on to you like it happened to Doug and I."

## "100 Percent for the Planet"

When Donald J. Trump was first elected president of the United States in November of 2016, Patagonia employees, like so many on the left, were stunned. To the idealistic merchants of surf in Ventura, it seemed inconceivable that after eight years of Barack Obama in the White House, the nation was now going to be run by a philandering reality television star who won the electoral college—but not the popular vote—by demonizing immigrants and spouting lies. And while it was too early to know the details of what a Trump presidency would entail, there was no question that his administration would prove disastrous for the environment. With a pro-business posture, an aversion to regulation of all sorts, and a history of disputing climate science, Trump was poised to roll back many of the pro-environment policies enacted by President Obama. In the days after the election, it was as if a pall had been cast over the Patagonia campus. Employees loitered in the cafeteria in a stupor, as if someone had died.

Eventually work resumed, and a few days after the election the marketing team met to consider how, if at all, the company should respond to the ascendance of Trump. Someone suggested simply shutting down the stores. Another idea was to put up black curtains in all the store windows. Then someone pointed out that Black Friday was coming up. Patagonia had used that day to powerful effect five years ago with the "Don't Buy This Jacket" ad. What if it did something similar this year? Someone suggested they give not 1 percent of Black Friday sales to the planet, but 5 percent. Then a junior marketing employee chimed in: What if Patagonia gave 100 percent of its sales to the planet on that day?

The marketing team loved it and called Rose Marcario, who

had succeeded Sheahan as CEO in 2013. A Tibetan Buddhist who had been arrested during pro-LGBTQ protests when she was younger, Marcario shared Chouinard's antiauthoritarian spirit. She was into it and ran the idea by the Chouinards. They were in, too. Within minutes the decision had been made, and a few days before Black Friday, the company announced that it would donate all of its revenues on America's biggest shopping day to grassroots environmental activists.

Company executives figured they might do about $2 million in sales—a bit more than an average day's revenues, and in line with previous Black Fridays. But after Patagonia publicized the plan and the media picked up the story, the stores and website faced an unprecedented surge of demand. Sales topped $10 million in one day, a record-shattering 24 hours, all of which Patagonia gave away. More than 25,000 people shopped with Patagonia for the first time that day. Customers were scooping up their favorite rain shells and bags, sure. But more than grabbing the newest gear, they were shopping with purpose. The 100 Percent for the Planet gambit was a way for customers to signal their support for Patagonia, and the Patagoniacs didn't disappoint. "You can't buy advertising like that," Chouinard said. "I didn't realize how much power we have. And to not use it would be irresponsible."

Sales kept climbing in the years that followed, buoyed by a wave of goodwill from the environmental community. It helped that the Black Friday sales thinned out much of the excess inventory that had been sitting around in warehouses. With sales booming and a belief that they could sway the debate on national issues, Patagonia executives leaned into politics.

Key to this effort was a new hire who knew how to throw elbows in Washington and beyond. Corley Kenna, a well-connected public relations operative from Georgia with a Beltway insider's understanding of realpolitik, was not a prototypical Patagonia employee. Having previously served in the Obama State Department and worked for Hillary Clinton's 2008 presidential campaign, she was a savvy politico with deep ties in the Democratic establishment. After a few years in the administration, Kenna went to work in the corporate world, ultimately landing at Ralph Lauren. A couple months before Trump was elected, the Chouinards hired her. And once in Ventura, Kenna immediately homed in on an issue where Patagonia could get in the fight.

Not long after Trump took office, he ordered a review of the country's national monuments, areas of pristine wilderness that enjoyed federal protection. Trump argued that the national monuments were too large and that the land should be opened for commercial development, promising to "end another egregious use of government power." That rhetoric obscured a more nefarious agenda: reducing protection for the monuments would mean making areas of untouched wilderness available for oil and gas exploration and mining.

One site threatened by Trump was the Bears Ears National Monument, 1.4 million acres of stunning desert considered sacred by Indigenous tribes. This was land that Patagonia knew well. Since 2012, the company had been funding a small nonprofit working to protect the area, the Friends of Cedar Mesa, through its 1% for the Planet grants. Bears Ears also featured a series of walls that were popular with climbers, further endearing the cause to Chouinard and his team. But now the land was in jeopardy. It was on Trump's list of targets, and Utah's all-Republican congressional delegation supported stripping Bears Ears of its protection.

After Trump announced the review, the Department of the Interior solicited comments from the public. Patagonia organized a letter-writing campaign, and its customers sent in more than

150,000 remarks. The vast majority, along with the more than two million pieces of feedback received by Interior, supported sustained conservation efforts. Marcario, the new CEO, tried to arrange a meeting with Interior Secretary Ryan Zinke but was rebuffed by his office. At the same time Patagonia was putting pressure on the White House, it looked for leverage with the Utah Republicans.

It found what it was looking for in a trade show. Every two years, Patagonia and the country's other major sports apparel brands participated in Outdoor Retailer, an industry conference that took place in Salt Lake City and contributed some $45 million to the local economy. Peter Metcalf, who was still involved with Black Diamond, had the idea to boycott the show if the Utah Republicans didn't come around. Looking to flex their collective power to help save Bears Ears, a group of executives from the outdoor industry held a conference call in February of 2017. Marcario was on the line, as were leaders from The North Face, REI, and other big brands. Also on the call was Gary Herbert, the governor of Utah. The CEOs delivered an ultimatum: if Herbert wouldn't publicly oppose his congressional delegation's efforts to meddle with public lands, they would boycott Outdoor Retailer.

Herbert was unmoved, and after the call, the companies made it clear that they would be looking for a new home for their trade show. Herbert called the move "offensive" and cast the outdoor companies as misinformed corporate citizens playing petty politics. But other governors quickly began courting the companies, hoping to lure Outdoor Retailer to their states, and the trade show found a new home in Denver, where Colorado Governor John Hickenlooper pledged to support the sustained protection of public lands.

Yet even in victory, Chouinard was dissatisfied. Most of the other companies that flexed their muscle to move Outdoor Retailer out of Utah were jumping on the bandwagon when it was politically convenient, he said; none of the others gave much money away to environmental causes. "The whole outdoor industry is just run by a bunch of weenies," Chouinard said. "They're not stepping up. They just suck the life out of outdoor resources and give nothing away." And while other outdoor industry CEOs worried about being too confrontational and fretted about alienating conservative customers, Chouinard fumed that the group hadn't gone further. "Why should we kowtow to these redneck voters and Republican politicians?" he said. "The most you can achieve is a compromise, and that never solves a problem."

Chouinard would soon show how far he was willing to go. In December of 2017, Trump officially announced his plans to sharply reduce the size of several national monuments, including Bears Ears. If Trump's plan went through, Bears Ears would be slashed in size by 85 percent, more than 1 million acres. Another Utah monument, Grand Staircase-Escalante, would be cut in half. Trump framed the decision as an opportunity to reduce federal overreach. "Some people think that the natural resources of Utah should be controlled by a small handful of very distant bureaucrats located in Washington," he said. "And guess what? They're wrong." But there was no disguising who would benefit from the plan; waiting in the wings were fossil fuel and mining interests, primed to exploit the land for oil and gas drilling and mineral extraction.

Sensing what was coming, Patagonia put in motion a scheme it had been quietly working on behind the scenes: it prepared to sue the president. Working with the law firm Hogan Lovells, it dusted off draft complaints, finalized its arguments, and set a drastic plan in motion. Court filings were prepared. The company's legal team

FIGHTS

jumped on an emergency conference call with lawyers in Washington. Kenna prepared to launch a media onslaught. And the graphic design team prepared to do their part in what would be Patagonia's most high-stakes bit of activism to date.

As a first step, the company's website and social media feeds got a stark overhaul. Pictures of athletes and gear were replaced by a grim message against a black background: "The President Stole Your Land."

Next, Patagonia filed its lawsuit. Working with a handful of local environmental groups, the company sued Trump, Interior Secretary Ryan Zinke, the secretary of agriculture, the director of the Bureau of Land Management, and the chief of the Forest Service in US District Court in Washington. The complaint laid out a simple premise: The Antiquities Act of 1906 gave presidents the power to create national monuments. It did not grant the power to reduce them.

Suing the president would have been eventful enough. But within hours of Trump making his announcement, smoke filled the air around Ventura. A brush fire had flared up in nearby Santa Paula, and hot, dry Santa Ana winds rapidly turned it into an inferno. Patagonia's campus emptied out, the city was evacuated, and employees fled, some rushing to salvage whatever they could from their homes as flames raced toward densely populated areas. Among those threatened by the firestorm was Marcario herself. As she drove along Highway 101, she watched the fire encircle Ventura and realized that in addition to a legal battle, she would be facing a simultaneous human resources crisis.

Patagonia had a plan for this, inspired in part by Malinda's trip to Walmart's headquarters in Bentonville. While there, she had seen what a company could do for its people when disaster struck, and she had insisted that Patagonia be prepared. Overnight, employees were told to stay home. The company would pick up the tab for hotels for anyone who needed to evacuate. A skeleton crew stayed on campus, putting out spot fires that flared up as embers landed near the office buildings. "There was ash falling like rain," Marcario said. "It was something I have never seen before."

As the fire spread north, Chouinard and Trump's team sparred in public. Chouinard made a rare media appearance to castigate Trump. "This government is evil, and I'm not going to sit back and let evil win," he said on CNN.

Zinke fired back and told Patagonia to stay in its lane. "They should focus on how to bring manufacturing back to this country, rather than lying to the public about losing federal land," he said on Fox Business Network. The House Committee on Natural Resources joined the fray. "Patagonia is lying to you," the committee wrote on Twitter. "A corporate giant hijacking our public lands debate to sell more products to wealthy elitist urban dwellers from New York to San Francisco." Before long, the hashtag #BoycottPatagonia was circulating on social media.

With Patagonia and Trump supporters trading barbs, the Thomas Fire became the largest wildfire in modern California history, burning for more than a month, destroying more than one thousand structures, and leading to the evacuation of some hundred thousand people. Downtown Ventura and the Patagonia campus were spared, but five employees lost their homes. To Marcario, there was no escaping the connection between the fires, the broader threats to the planet, and Trump. "These are climate disasters, and they're going to get worse," she said. "We have an administration that isn't paying any attention to that."

Bears Ears was a clarifying episode for Patagonia. The company was there to make quality gear. But at the end of the day, Patagonia was an activist company. With that truth clearer than it had been in years, Chouinard decided it was time to revisit Patagonia's mission statement. For years, it had remained unchanged: "Build the best product, cause no unnecessary harm, and use business to inspire and implement solutions to the environmental crisis." Now something simpler, more direct, and more ambitious seemed appropriate. In 2018, he landed on it: "We're in business to save our home planet."

It was the clearest articulation to date of the company's raison d'être. It wasn't enough to try to minimize the deleterious effects of running a business. Instead, counterintuitive as it might be, at Patagonia, the purpose of making stuff was to protect planet Earth.

Stanley was among those who initially had reservations. "I was skeptical at first," he said. "I thought, this is highly aspirational language. Yes, that's a value of the company, but how central is that to us?" More to the point, it was a statement fraught with obvious contradictions. Sure, Patagonia was fighting to protect the environment. But with every fleece, T-shirt, and backpack it made, it was taking a toll on the planet it was trying to save. It still used virgin plastic made from the fossil fuels heating up the globe. Some products still included PFAS, the forever chemicals poisoning the groundwater, people, and animals. Its supply chain was riddled with questionable labor practices.

Chouinard, however, never second-guessed himself. The updated motto became a rallying cry for the company, a reference point it could use to inform decisions large and small. "People say, 'Oh, that's a corny thing. You're not serious about it. It's just a marketing deal,'" Chouinard said of the new mission statement. "Well, it's not. It changed the whole way the company operates. We make all decisions based on: is this the right thing for the home planet?"

# "We Had a Hard Time"

On March 13, 2020, Patagonia became one of the first retailers to shut down in response to the swelling COVID-19 pandemic. All the retail stores closed immediately, the office cleared out, and the e-commerce operations and distribution center in Reno ground to a halt. In a matter of days, sales dried up in North America. The company took measures to preserve cash, including slashing executive pay and furloughing 80 percent of retail staff.

Other retailers were relatively quick to reopen, implementing social distancing policies, encouraging masking, and offering curbside pickup. Not Patagonia. Malinda, ever preoccupied with her employees' well-being, wanted to do nothing that might jeopardize their health. And given the company's prudent financial management (namely, a perennially large cash cushion inspired by the layoffs of 1991), it had the means to ride out the storm. "We were one of the first to shut down, we might be closer to the last to reopen fully—I don't really care," Marcario said. "We are doing everything we can to ensure that our employees are taken care of in the best way possible."

Beyond the safety concerns, there was another reason to potentially delay opening the stores again. As the global economy sputtered, Chouinard saw a silver lining of sorts. Air travel slowed to a trickle, cars vanished from the roads, supply chains ground to a halt. All around the world, people were buying less stuff, using fewer products, burning fewer fossil fuels. The slowdown of human activity became known as the "anthropause." Without smog belching from Indian cities, the skies in Northern India cleared and the Himalayas emerged from their usual haze. Native habitats began to recover. Noise pollution in the oceans decreased. Water and air quality improved. "Nature is healing," a popular meme declared. This was all music to Chouinard's ears. For decades, he had been lamenting the increasingly severe toll humans were taking on the planet. Now, with Patagonia stores closed and the offices empty, Chouinard saw a welcome opportunity for a natural slowdown of the growth the company had been enjoying.

When Patagonia finally did come rumbling back to life, months after most of its competitors, new safety measures were put in place. About half the usual workers manned the distribution center in Reno, those there wore gloves and face coverings, and the facility was routinely sprayed down with disinfectant. The company mandated its employees get vaccinated against COVID. But before any semblance of normalcy could return to the office, Patagonia—along with much of the rest of corporate America—was thrown into further tumult following the murder of George Floyd.

Floyd, an unarmed Black man, was killed by a police officer in Minneapolis, Minnesota, in broad daylight. After the video of the incident went viral, protesters around the country took to the streets. As demonstrations grew and the Black Lives Matter movement took off, many big brands rushed to express their support for the Black community. Patagonia was no exception. "We join with those who call out the name of George Floyd in sorrow and anger against the systemic racism that pervades our land," the company said in a statement shortly after the killing. "We stand in solidarity with African Americans and people of color, including those among our colleagues and their families. And we call on business to work with government and civil society to address racism."

It was a milquetoast statement, the kind of forgettable corporate platitude that so many brands were offering up at the time. But to the few Black employees at the company, and their allies, the statement didn't go nearly far enough. With its gener-alized expressions of sympathy and an absence of specifics, they felt the statement perfectly encapsulated the company's fraught relationship with people of color. Leah Thomas, a Black Patago-nia employee who worked in the marketing department and was furloughed during the pandemic, said the response was too little, too late. Even before Floyd was murdered, she said she had been pressing Patagonia to take a stand on racial justice, to no avail. "I didn't hear much from people that I had gone to marches with to advocate for salmon and other endangered species," she said. "There just didn't seem to be a connection when it came to endan-gered Black and brown lives."

That was hard to argue with. For starters, there were hardly any Black employees at Patagonia. Climbing, surfing, and skiing aren't sports known to attract, let alone embrace, a diverse crowd, and the company reflected this homogeneity. Most employees at headquarters fit the same profile: young to middle-aged, white, outdoorsy, liberal, with a laid-back vibe that seemed chill enough if you were in the know but could seem intimidating and off-putting to outsiders. Dean Carter, the former human resources head, remembered that on his first day of orientation, Chipper Bro Bell took him and a group of new employees surfing on the beach down in Ventura. Carter loved it; he was living an idealized version of the corporate life, making good on Chouinard's prom-ise to let his people go surfing. Then, as Carter caught a wave, he noticed another new hire—a young Black woman—sitting alone on the beach. He paddled in and asked her why she wasn't out in the waves and received a sobering reply: "I don't swim," she said.

It wasn't just the everyday employee base that lacked diver-sity. Senior Black executives were conspicuously absent from the company. In Patagonia catalogs over the years, people of color are hard to find. The lack of diversity was also a problem when it came to convincing Black employees to make a life in a sleepy surf town. "We had a hard time keeping our Black employees in Ventura because there are no Black people in Ventura," Carter said. "They would come, and they would leave."

All of this came to the surface in the months after Floyd's murder. The company was reckoning with generations of privilege and facing tough truths about its own blind spots. "We had a hard time after George Floyd," Carter said. "We really had a hard time admitting that the sports we supported had some level of privilege to them; that surfing, even though it was started in South America, in the US was to some extent an elite sport where you had to have a surfboard and access to a beach, and you had to be able to swim."

The company tried to own up to its failings as agita swelled among employees, issuing a new self-flagellating statement. "The few words we have conveyed fell short and failed to comprehend the pain of our colleagues of color and partners in the outdoor community," the company said. "The Black Lives Matter movement has forced a reckoning of the deep racial injustice around us and laid bare our complicity. We are a white-led outdoor company reliant on recreation on stolen Native lands that are not yet safe for all. Recent months have revealed how much more we need to do to live up to our values as an activist company."

The turmoil didn't end with the Black Lives Matter reckoning. In the midst of the pandemic, Marcario abruptly quit. There was no succession plan in place, and no one had been identified as the next CEO. Marcario and the Chouinards tried to spin the narrative to suggest that her sudden resignation was all part of the plan. "That was a mutual decision," Marcario said. "At some point, the student has to leave the master."

Behind the scenes, the story was more complicated. Insiders

said Marcario ultimately left because she was overwhelmed by pressures from the pandemic, challenges in her personal life, and an increasingly testy relationship with the family. The Chouinards were miffed by Marcario's decision to quit and didn't handle it as strategically as they could have. When she went to Malinda and said she wanted to talk about the timing of her exit, Malinda said: "How about Friday?"

An interim leader was appointed, and the family went looking for a new CEO. But for all practical purposes, the company was leaderless for months as it tried to emerge from the pandemic. At a public company, this kind of chaos would never be tolerated. But at Patagonia, this was just the way it was, the future hanging in limbo as the Chouinards tried to improvise a way forward. Morale suffered, innovation stagnated, and a wave of longtime employees left the company. Chouinard got his wish as sales dipped, yet lasting damage was being done to the company, and it would take years for Patagonia to recover.

Months after Marcario left, the board eventually settled on a permanent replacement: Ryan Gellert, an outdoor industry veteran and expert snowboarder and climber who was running the company's European operations and was serious about environmental activism, too. In Europe, he had helped lead an effort to protect the Vjosa River in Albania, blocking a series of planned hydroelectric dams and preserving it as the last free-flowing river in Europe. Gellert's ascendance provided at least some measure of stability to the company, but more changes were on the horizon.

## "Pay Their Fair Share"

With a new mission statement in place and the company eager to play its part in the resistance to Trump, Patagonia unleashed a flurry of increasingly partisan political activism. In 2020, a post on Twitter went viral showing the inside of a new pair of Stand Up Shorts. Stitched into the backside of the tag was a simple four-word message: "Vote The Assholes Out."

The subversive bit of tailoring was initially done without the knowledge or approval of company higher-ups. A band of rebels in the design team simply added the text to the labels, and the modification made its way through the supply chain unnoticed. Indeed, top executives found out about it only when a reporter called to request a comment after seeing the viral tweet. At other companies, someone would have lost their job. But given that everyone from the CEO to the seamstress was more or less on the same page, Patagonia embraced it. The assholes, in case it wasn't obvious, were the politicians denying the science of climate change and blocking efforts to improve the environment. The voting was coming up on Election Day. When Chouinard learned about the rogue messaging, he said: "These are great. I need them in a size 32."

Then, as Patagonia emerged from the pandemic, it found itself railing against Republican politicians trying to cut taxes. When the Trump administration pushed through a massive corporate tax overhaul, Patagonia, like most companies, enjoyed a windfall. Overnight, its tax bill fell by an estimated $10 million. For most companies, that would have been a cause for celebration. But Gellert, the new CEO, was fuming. In a series of social media posts, he called for the federal government to increase the corporate tax rate. "Companies need to pay their fair share," he said, claiming that Patagonia was "willing to pay a higher corporate tax rate" in order to fund "climate investments."

Gellert didn't stop there. He also called out his fellow business leaders for being hypocritical. In a November 2021 post titled

"Corporate America: Stop Hiding Behind the Chamber of Commerce and Business Roundtable," Gellert lacerated big companies that publicly supported lofty social initiatives, especially the fight against climate change, while privately supporting trade groups that helped maintain the status quo. "Far too many business leaders are saying all the right things on climate while hiding behind business groups that are sabotaging meaningful climate legislation," he said.

At the time, the Biden administration was working to pass the Build Back Better framework, which would have raised corporate taxes and invested the new revenues in efforts to curb dangerous planet-warming emissions. But while many CEOs publicly supported these efforts, some of their trade groups, including the Chamber of Commerce and the Business Roundtable, were working to oppose the law because of the tax hike. The Chamber and the BRT, Gellert said, "have been working to stall and weaken this historic legislation and have spent millions to pressure moderate lawmakers to vote against the planet."

Gellert reserved particular disdain for double-talking chief executives. "These CEOs are happy to tell the public about their ambitions to become 'carbon neutral,' their goal to be a 'regenerative' company and that they are focused on 'equitable climate action,'" he said. "But behind closed doors these companies are sharing a very different story. They are using the power of their brand and their company resources to advocate for their bottom line. This hypocrisy is bad for business. It's bad for everyone."

As Gellert went on the offensive, Patagonia also pared back its business with some of its ideological adversaries. The company had long been referred to as "Patagucci," a smear that took aim at its high prices and popularity with stylish urbanites. And for years, it had done brisk business shipping branded gear to Wall

Street firms. Hedge funds, private equity firms, and banks would pay a premium for bulk orders of Synchilla jackets and Nano Puff vests with their logos embroidered alongside Patagonia's iconic label. The vests were so ubiquitous in Manhattan that the finance bro's signature look—slacks, a blue button-up shirt, and a Patagonia vest—became known as the "Midtown Uniform," with examples documented on an Instagram account that gained 114,000 followers. Many of those vests had relatively short shelf lives. Associates who got them on orientation day would ditch them when they moved on to a new job, and that irked Patagonia execs. They were trying to build products to last, not ones to be handed out during a summer internship and then cast aside. How could the company behind the "Don't Buy This Jacket" ad also be making disposable vests for Wall Street's interns? It couldn't, so the company stopped its co-logo program, and pared back its sales to financial and tech companies.

Not long after that, Patagonia executives cut off another major customer. In 2021, the family that owned the Jackson Hole Mountain Resort, a popular ski area in Wyoming not far from Chouinard's home, hosted a fundraiser featuring Representative Marjorie Taylor Greene and Representative Jim Jordan, among the most virulently right-wing members of the Republican party. Upon learning about the fundraiser, Patagonia decided to pull its offerings from the resort, its largest retailer in the area. It didn't matter that the company would lose a meaningful chunk of sales in one of the country's most iconic resort towns. It wasn't interested in doing business with a family that was raising money for the far right.

All this sharp-elbowed political activity didn't seem to affect Patagonia's reputation. Even as it took aim at Republicans, the company maintained its broad bipartisan support. In 2021 and again in 2023, it was named the most-loved brand in the United States, trusted by Democrats and Republicans alike, according to an annual survey by Axios and Harris Poll, besting popular behemoths like Apple, Amazon, and Costco.

Patagonia's partisan turn was a response to a particular moment in politics. Yet as Kenna explained, its activism wasn't necessarily about backing Republicans or Democrats. Instead, she said, it was about supporting positions that were good for the environment. "We will continue to use our business to advocate for policies to protect our planet, support thriving communities and a strong democracy," she said.

Nearly 50 years after its founding, Patagonia was more political than ever. That was a testament to Chouinard's enduring commitment to his values and his belief that activism could make a difference. Yet even as the spats with the Trump administration were heating up, it was becoming clear that even bigger fights lay ahead. With the planet imperiled and consumer culture running rampant, Chouinard wanted to make sure that Patagonia would be ready for the next 50 years. The founder was entering another one of his periods of creative destruction. Patagonia was going to transform itself again, even if the employees—and the dirtbag billionaire himself—didn't know exactly how. It was time to shake things up, if only for the sake of shaking things up. And this time, it would lead to the biggest changes in the company's history.

# CHAPTER 10

# Giving It All Away

## "The Stars Aligned"

As Tompkins's family fought over his estate and Patagonia grappled with the pandemic, Chouinard, now in his 80s, confronted the complicated reality of his own growing fortune. In 2017, for the first time, *Forbes* magazine placed him on its annual list of billionaires. For most businessmen, inclusion in the prestigious ranking of the world's wealthiest people would have been a badge of honor. For Chouinard, it was a nightmare come true. The dirtbag who grew up loathing greaseball businessmen was now enshrined as one of the biggest moguls of them all. "It really, really pissed me off," he said upon learning of the ranking. "I don't have $1 billion in the bank. You know, I don't drive Lexuses." All day, Chouinard tromped around the office, demanding something be done to rectify the situation. "Get me off that list!" he told anyone who would listen. "I hate that list!"

In the weeks after the *Forbes* rankings were revealed, Chouinard kept stewing about it. Profits were fine when they were keeping the company going and funding activism. But the suggestion that he was hoarding wealth made him nauseous. He resolved to get himself off that list, one way or another. He had never set out to be a billionaire, and he didn't want to die as one. If that meant doing something drastic with the company, so be it.

The pandemic only added more urgency to Chouinard's mission. As the years ticked by, he continued appearing on the *Forbes* list, and as Patagonia grew more successful, his net worth—much to his annoyance—continued ticking up. Finally in 2020, he turned to his inner circle and put forward an ultimatum: either they figured out how to get him off the list, or he would do it himself.

One day in February 2021, Chouinard summoned Gellert to his home in Ventura and threatened to sell the company. "I swear to God, if you guys don't start moving on this, I'm going to go get the *Forbes* magazine list of billionaires and start cold calling people," he said. Gellert was still new to the job, but he quickly understood his boss was serious.

As Chouinard pondered possible options that would relieve him of the burden of owning a multibillion-dollar company, he turned to Charles Conn, a successful entrepreneur and executive who served on Patagonia's board. Conn and Chouinard had met 20 years earlier on a fishing trip. When they arrived at their campsite, it was pouring rain, and Chouinard was preparing to curl up and sleep under a truck. Conn invited him to share his tent, and they had been friends ever since. A few years after that, while standing hip-deep in an Argentinian river, casting flies, Conn asked Chouinard what would happen to Patagonia when he died. "Well," Chouinard said, "we're going to have to shut the company down, because I don't trust anyone else to run the company." In search of more palatable alternatives, Gellert and Conn brought in Patagonia's general counsel, Hilary Dessouky, and her deputy, Greg Curtis. Together, it would be up to this group to help Chouinard figure out what to do with his company.

From the start, it became clear that there were no obvious solutions to a problem like this. Conn told Chouinard as much in a memo synthesizing his thinking on the situation. "Here are your options," he wrote. "None of them are good." As Conn, Gellert, Dessouky, and Curtis began testing different options, they conducted a series of conversations with the family and in time, a handful of overarching priorities emerged.

- Patagonia had to survive, despite Chouinard's earlier threat to shut it down. The company, with all its quirks and curiosities and flaws, needed to emerge from whatever happened as more or less the same independent company it had always been. It wouldn't do for some other conglomerate to swallow it whole and start stripping it for parts. Patagonia had survived for 50 years. It deserved the chance to make it for another 50 years.

- A larger share of the profits being generated by the company—which by this point were more than $100 million a year—had to go to environmental causes. Giving away 1 percent of sales was fine. And the Chouinards had funneled much of their personal earnings into land preservation efforts in South America and beyond. But one of the main outcomes Chouinard wanted to accomplish with whatever transaction took place was turbocharging the philanthropic efforts, giving as much money as possible to activists and conservationists around the world.

- Whatever solution the team came up with needed to be done in a way that downplayed the family's public profile going forward and protected the privacy of Fletcher and Claire Chouinard, as well as their children. The Chouinards weren't interested in burnishing their reputation by starting a foundation in their name or endowing some university. And their

239

children didn't want to inherit the company, didn't want a ton of money, and didn't want to be famous.

Beyond those three priorities, several other requirements came into focus, as well. Simultaneously preserving Patagonia's independence and ridding the Chouinards of their wealth would necessitate a creative approach to the handling of the company's equity. While the family owned all the shares in the company—worth some $3 billion—it didn't want to keep that stock and didn't want anyone else to have it, either. This made a conventional sale of the company all but impossible. There had to be an alternative. This was an essential piece of the puzzle, and one with no obvious solution. "What motivates everyone else in the world does not motivate them," Curtis said. "They just don't give a fuck."

At the same time, the Chouinards wanted to stay involved with Patagonia. They had no desire to own the stock that made them billionaires. But they did expect to have an ongoing relationship with the company. Fletcher and Claire still worked there full-time. Chouinard and Malinda still rattled around the office. All four of them were on the board. Patagonia was all the family had ever known. Leaving abruptly would have been disorienting for them and the company.

Finally, whatever would happen needed to happen soon. Chouinard was as vigorous as an octogenarian could be, but he didn't want to die with the situation unresolved. Doing so would leave too many loose ends and, more importantly, he believed, would jeopardize the company's integrity.

With these criteria in mind, the team got to work. Starting in early 2021, Conn, Gellert, Dessouky, and Curtis began meeting every two weeks to consider different options and map out possible scenarios. They would trade ideas, sometimes sharing hand-drawn sketches with proposed plans. As is often the case with sensitive corporate missions, the endeavor got its own code name: Project Chacabuco, a reference to the pristine valley in Chile that the Chouinards and the Tompkinses partnered to preserve decades earlier. Deliberations were confidential, and even longtime insiders like Ridgeway and Stanley didn't know what was in the works.

The Chouinard children were in the fold, however, and their input would be key. Over the years, Chouinard had distributed Patagonia's voting and nonvoting shares between himself, Malinda, Fletcher, and Claire. Both children now worked at the company—Fletcher running the surfboard business, FCD, and Claire working in the design department. Both were in their 40s and had their own families. It would be reasonable for them to expect some financial benefit from their long association with the company or even to inherit Patagonia someday. Yet neither of them had any such ambitions. The Chouinard children didn't just understand their parents' vision, they shared it. "My kids didn't want to own it," Chouinard said. "Both are ambivalent about becoming public figures, and both believe that billionaires represent a policy failure. They were brought up right."

With the family's priorities in focus, the Project Chacabuco team went looking for a solution that would honor all Chouinard's wishes. One relatively straightforward option would be selling the company to the employees. For decades, Patagonia workers had groused about not participating in the upside of all the value they were creating. Turning the company into an employee-owned cooperative would be a grand gesture and a way of rectifying that situation. Yet there were obvious problems with going that route. With a collective of employees in charge, there was no guarantee that profits would be distributed to environmental causes and no assurance that over time, Patagonia's willingness to forego short-term gains for the sake of its values would endure.

The team considered relocating the company to another country, maybe Switzerland or Denmark, where different legal models permitted the operation of charitable corporations. Another scenario had the Chouinards selling the company, ideally to a like-minded billionaire or a benevolent private corporation. But all the same concerns applied in this situation. Even if they sold Patagonia to an idealistic owner who was a good steward of the company for the next decade, what was to stop that person from selling it to someone else? And then what happened? This was hardly idle speculation. At one point, Malinda said they had an offer on the table to acquire the company for $6 billion. But she had no faith that the buyer would keep Patagonia intact. "We took a $6 billion bet that we could use the business to save the planet," Malinda said. "If we had left with $6 billion for the environment, there would have been 3,000 people out of a job in a year."

And of course, Chouinard had totally given up on the idea of taking Patagonia public. An initial public offering—which lets institutional investors and individuals acquire shares in a company—would have created a series of entanglements that permanently handicapped Patagonia's ability to live up to its values. Investors would have been expecting endless growth, executives would have been thinking about quarterly profits, and activist hedge funds would have surely pounced. "I don't respect the stock market at all," Chouinard said. "Once you're public, you've lost control over the company, and you have to maximize profits for the shareholder. You lose all control, and then you become one of these irresponsible companies." The Chouinards wouldn't hand Patagonia over to the employees, wouldn't sell, wouldn't take it public, and absolutely did not want to own the thing. Just as Conn had predicted, there were no good options.

After months of research, the Project Chacabuco team arrived at the same unsatisfying conclusion: there was no obvious solution to this multibillion-dollar problem. Even at other companies founded by executives with a strong sense of purpose—think Ben & Jerry's or Newman's Own—the ownership transitions have rarely led to happy endings. Ben & Jerry's was acquired by Unilever, the big consumer goods conglomerate. The ice cream maker maintained many of the original quirks that made it a pioneer in the realm of socially responsible business, but it has made compromises along the way, and is hardly the beacon of social responsibility it was while under the control of its founders. Newman's Own, meanwhile, remained an independent private company that donated its profits to charity, per the wishes of its founder, the actor Paul Newman. But because of the way the company and its related philanthropies were structured, the Newman family was forced to step away. And in recent years, Newman's daughters had sued the company, arguing its leadership was not donating as much money to charity as it was supposed to. Patagonia would need a bespoke solution, something that had never been done before. But what?

In search of answers, the biweekly meetings veered into the philosophical as the team debated existential questions:

"How and when do we know if the Patagonia experiment has succeeded or failed?" read the minutes of one meeting.

"If the company can't succeed without the Chouinards, isn't that a failure?"

"How do we stop or reverse the negative effects of business and even affect change in capitalism in order to save our whole planet?"

Conn said it was like being in therapy. "It sounds ridiculous," he said. "But it was like Gestalt sessions every week or every other week for more than two years."

## "Let's Do It"

Fittingly, it was one of Chouinard's expeditions that forced the issue. The family had a trip planned for August of 2021. Worried they all might die together in an accident and leave the company directionless, they asked Gellert, Conn, Dessouky, and Curtis to come up with some kind of plan before they left.

The Project Chacabuco team put together their best solution and presented it to the family. The rough outline called for the Chouinards to donate all their shares in Patagonia to a private foundation, which would then sell the stock over time, at a rate of perhaps 5 percent a year. Proceeds from the sale of those shares would then be given away to environmental groups, providing a steady stream of charitable giving for decades. In a best-case scenario, it would be one buyer—a benevolent billionaire, perhaps—who would acquire all the shares, and who would agree to certain terms that would preserve the features of the company that Chouinard and Malinda cared about most. It left unanswered the question of what would happen when this new owner had full control of Patagonia, but at least it was something. The team got a rough term sheet together and had the family sign it before they went on their trip, but everyone involved knew it was an imperfect solution.

The Project Chacabuco team's work wasn't done. The proposed plan simply kicked the can down the road. "We weren't happy with that choice," Curtis said. "We thought of it as defective because it sort of led to some consequences that if we had had more time, we would want to structure around." Crucially and unacceptably, the current plan would have compromised the integrity of the company by gradually handing control to someone else. "It became clear that the biggest thing that Patagonia had done wasn't the money that the family had been giving away, which was a big, big, big thing," Conn said. "It was simply running Patagonia as something different from any other business. Patagonia's biggest contribution was being an iconoclast." At this point, Conn thought to bring in a new set of eyes.

Dan Mosley has spent his career as a kind of fixer for the very rich. Early in his career, as a partner at Cravath, Swaine & Moore, one of the most prestigious corporate law firms in New York, he fixed problems for multinational corporations: litigation, mergers and acquisitions, patent disputes. There wasn't much he couldn't sort out on behalf of his clients. After 30 years at Cravath, Mosley moved to BDT, a financial advisory firm founded by Byron Trott, who is best known as Warren Buffett's banker, and was now focused on helping wealthy people manage their estates.

Once Conn brought Mosley into the fold and got him up to speed, the Wall Street veteran was astonished by the Chouinards' sincere desire to part with their fortune. "It's hard to find a family that owned and controlled a phenomenal company like this that are willing just to give it away entirely during their lifetime," he said. He quickly homed in on an option that the Patagonia team had not considered.

Mosley suggested investigating the use of a purpose trust, a noncharitable entity that is established and operates for the benefit of a special purpose, rather than a specific individual. Purpose trusts have been around for decades as part of the arcane laws governing how estates are managed. But for the most part, they had been used for relatively small tasks—caring for a pet after its owner died, or funding the management of a piece of property, or a cemetery plot. Mosley encouraged the Project Chacabuco team to think bigger. What if they used a purpose trust to enshrine the values of Patagonia itself? What if that was the linchpin that made possible an entirely new form of corporate succession planning? If done right, using a purpose trust might allow the Chouinards to accomplish all their goals without forcing a sale of the company.

Within a couple months, the contours of a final arrangement came into focus. The Chouinards would irrevocably transfer all the company's voting stock, equivalent to 2 percent of the company's overall shares, into a newly established entity known as the Patagonia Purpose Trust. The trust would be overseen by family members and their closest advisors, and it would ensure that Patagonia the company made good on its commitment to be socially responsible and give away all its profits.

The Chouinards would then irrevocably donate the other 98 percent of Patagonia's stock, the nonvoting shares, to a group of newly established 501(c)(4) nonprofit organizations called the Holdfast Collective. The Holdfast Collective would serve a number of purposes. Crucially, it would be the permanent custodian of the vast majority of Patagonia's stock. But while it would take possession of those shares, which could have been worth billions, it would not sell them. Instead, it would be the recipient of all of Patagonia's earnings that weren't reinvested in the company and then give those funds away on an ongoing basis to groups working to fight the climate crisis. A board, composed of the family and some of its closest advisors, would approve the broad strokes of the philanthropic strategy. And because it was structured as a 501(c)(4) and not a more traditional 501(c)(3) nonprofit, Holdfast would be able to make donations to political groups. "Patagonia has every incentive to continue operating profitably so it can maximize benefit for all of its stakeholders and push out more dividends to the Holdfast Collective to use to save the planet," Dessouky said.

With the voting shares locked up in the purpose trust, there was no chance that some spineless billionaire or amoral corporation would be taking over. Patagonia's independence would be preserved. "From the family's perspective, and Yvon's perspective in particular, it's not all about profits," Mosley said. "He wants this company to run pursuant to the principles that he has established, even if it makes less money. His goal was to ensure that it operated the way it operated, and then it will make whatever profit it makes."

Crucially, the children approved. Fletcher, who is even more press shy than his father, issued a rare statement: "Generational succession is a risky continuity plan for any business, and it does little to assure that a company's values will remain intact into the far future," he said. "This is the first truly durable option. It brings a sense of relief for Patagonia, my family, and I'm also just happy to stop talking about death and get back to work!"

Claire, who is similarly private, was also at peace with the solution. "The climate and biodiversity crises are the existential threats to life on our planet and must be the focus of our work to protect them," she said. "But in going after root causes, we realized that these are symptoms. They are the direct result of an extractive model of capitalism. We need to change the entire system and make it regenerative. All of us, and generations to come, depend on our swift action now."

With the planning mostly complete, it was time to get buy-in from the whole team. On a brilliant December morning in 2021, McDivitt Tompkins welcomed Patagonia's inner circle to her home in the golden hills of Santa Paula, just outside Ventura. Chouinard and Malinda were there, along with Fletcher and Claire. Gellert, Conn, Dessouky, and Curtis—the Project Chacabuco team—were there, along with Mosley. Byron Trott, the legendary banker who founded BDT, had flown in for the meeting, sensing the momentousness of the occasion. Also in attendance was Dan Emmett, a close family friend and Patagonia board member. McDivitt Tompkins served homemade quiche, and the team sat in Adirondack chairs under an oak tree in the backyard, next to an avocado orchard. Two Labrador retrievers bounded around the yard. It was the first time in years that Patagonia's inner circle had gathered in person, the pandemic having forced even the closest of friends to go remote. Now, they had reunited in order to give the company away. Mosley and the Project Chacabuco team described the plan in detail, then described it again. Questions were fielded, concerns aired, and one by one, the reservations fell away. When it came time to secure the final blessing from everyone in attendance, the consent was unanimous.

"Yeah, this feels good. This feels right."

"I like everything that you said."

"This is exactly what we were looking for."

"Let's do it."

A question more than 50 years in the making finally had its answer. "That was a day where it actually seemed like the stars aligned and you could see the solution starting to line up," Gellert said. "We still had a million and one things to figure out, but it started to feel like, 'Holy shit, this might actually work.' And I think you really felt everybody involved go 'Wow, I get this. I trust this. I actually think I'm seeing how this solves the things that are most important to me.'"

A few months of back-office paperwork followed, all in preparation for one last meeting to make the transaction official. In August of 2022, Curtis traveled to the Chouinards' home in Moose, Wyoming, to finalize the deal. With a few strokes of the pen, the family authorized the transfer of all their shares to the Holdfast Collective and the Patagonia Purpose Trust. One moment they were the sole owners of a private corporation that could have sold for $6 billion, the next moment they were not.

After Chouinard and Malinda signed the documents, they made the short drive to Dornans, a restaurant and general store at the gateway to Grand Teton National Park. Chouinard sat at a picnic table in the fading sunlight, eating a hamburger and drinking a Guinness. He raised a toast to the Project Chacabuco team. Then, with dusk gathering, Chouinard and Malinda slipped away and headed for home, arms around each other in their matching Patagonia jackets.

## "Billionaire No More"

A month later, it was time to reveal the news to the rest of the company, and the world. The secret had been remarkably well kept. Outside of those few who had planned the ownership change and those who had to sign off on it, no one else knew. When the moment finally came to inform the staff, Patagonia threw itself a party. On the evening of September 13, employees had an all-day hold put on their calendars. When those in Ventura showed up at the office the next morning, they were greeted by food trucks in the parking lot, an interactive exhibit charting the company's half century of milestones, and a stage set up with cameras broadcasting the event to the rest of the company's offices around the world. Former employees had been invited, too. Rumors swirled. Some staffers said that Beyoncé was coming to give a speech.

As the morning's proceedings began, Chouinard sat in the front row of the audience alongside Malinda, the children, McDivitt Tompkins, Gellert, and Ridgeway. Then the comedian Trevor

Noah appeared on a large screen, riffing on what a unique company Patagonia was and teeing up the big reveal. A montage of the company's history played, followed by footage of Chouinard, who looked into the camera and explained what he and the family were doing. With his brief remarks, he tried to make a complex series of trusts, nonprofit organizations, and advisory boards comprehensible to a few thousand surfers and climbers. It wasn't altogether successful. After the film ran, many employees were still confused. Had the company been sold? Did they still have a job? Were they getting any of the money? The executive team fielded questions from the audience and tried to simplify it all, and bit by bit, the contours of the transaction became clear to most of those inside the company.

Then Chouinard himself took the stage. Wearing jeans and a Hawaiian shirt, he reflected on his career, and the significance of the moment. "By turning over the ownership of the corporation to our home planet, we are now reinventing capitalism," he said. "I believe we will not only survive but thrive because of this new structure. It does two of the most important things. It locks in our values, and it gives away more money to the environmental crisis." As he concluded his remarks, Chouinard teared up. "I never cry at funerals," he said. "I only cry at rodeos and days like this."

As the event was unfolding in Ventura, my story in *The New York Times* published online under the headline: "Billionaire No More: Patagonia Founder Gives Away the Company." The article went viral, garnering millions of views online. Other news outlets picked up the news, celebrities shared the story on social media, and a wave of Patagonia fans flooded the internet with tributes to the company, which started pushing out a new marketing tagline: "Earth is now our only shareholder."

It was a triumphal moment for the Chouinards and their allies, and within Patagonia's inner circle, it was also an occasion to reflect on the legacy of Doug Tompkins. For years, Tompkins had pushed Chouinard to sell the company and devote his winnings to conservation efforts, just as he had done with Esprit. But now Chouinard had found an entirely new solution that created not just a onetime payout but a durable stream of earnings that would fund environmental causes for decades to come. McDivitt Tompkins said her late husband would have approved. "What Doug did was perfect. He wanted out of business. But I was glad that Yvon didn't follow Doug," she said. "Doug would be really so proud of Yvon, just like Yvon was so proud of us every time we created a new national park."

With the donation, Chouinard joined a short list of billionaires who have donated substantially all their money to charity. Warren Buffett, the legendary investor, has donated billions to charitable organizations through the Giving Pledge, a movement he founded with Microsoft cofounder Bill Gates that gets billionaires to pledge to give away most of their money. Gates himself has donated over $50 billion through the Bill & Melinda Gates Foundation, focusing on global health, education, and poverty reduction. George Soros, the billionaire investor, donated over $32 billion to the Open Society Foundations, a network of charities supporting democracy, human rights, and social justice causes. Chuck Feeney, the cofounder of Duty Free Shoppers Group, gave away his entire $8 billion fortune through the Atlantic Philanthropies, completely divesting himself of his wealth to support education, health care, and human rights. MacKenzie Scott, the former wife of Jeff Bezos, has rapidly donated billions to various charitable causes, focusing on historically underfunded organizations and addressing inequity. And now, alongside these titans was Yvon Chouinard.

Outside the company, some commentators perceived a dark motivation to the corporate restructuring: tax avoidance. "Patagonia's $3 billion corporate gift is also a convenient way to avoid taxes," wrote Quartz. "Patagonia's founder rejects his billionaire status, but he's still saving $700 million in taxes with a legal loophole," wrote *Fortune*. "It's a massive tax avoidance scheme," tweeted Jesse Eisinger, an editor at ProPublica who covers taxes.

There was no question that the Chouinards would be paying a relatively modest sum to the Internal Revenue Service given the size of Patagonia. When business owners sell their companies, state and federal taxes can add up to more than 33 percent of the sale price. Had the Chouinards sold the company, that could have amounted to $1 billion or more. But capital gains taxes are, by definition, owed only when there are profits. With the family's transfer of their shares to the Patagonia Purpose Trust and the Holdfast Collective, they had no capital gains. They were not selling the company, and they were not making a profit.

Instead, by donating the vast majority of their shares to the Holdfast Collective, they were able to relinquish their ownership of the company without accruing a tax bill. That was a definite perk. Yet the family also sacrificed what could have been an enormous tax advantage. Had they structured the Holdfast Collective as a 501(c)(3), they could have claimed a massive tax deduction by donating their shares to the nonprofit. But because they made Holdfast a 501(c)(4), which enabled it to engage in political activity, they couldn't claim a deduction.

Instead, the Chouinards were taxed only on their donation of the voting shares to the Patagonia Purpose Trust, a bill that amounted to just $17.5 million. "There was a meaningful cost to them doing it, but it was a cost they were willing to bear to ensure that this company stays true to their principles," Mosley said. "And they didn't get a charitable deduction for it. There is no tax benefit here whatsoever." At the end of the day, it was practically a wash. The Chouinards realized no great profit, generated no great tax break, and paid no huge tax bill.

Although it was a unique structure without any real precedent, critics continued to say it all looked like a savvy tax dodge. The Chouinards were effectively keeping control of Patagonia while paying a pittance in taxes. If that wasn't gaming the system, what was? Just weeks earlier, Barre Seid, a Republican donor, made headlines when he pulled off a somewhat similar move. Seid, who was the sole owner of a computer hardware company called Tripp Lite, donated his firm to a conservative 501(c)(3) called the Marble Freedom Trust, earning himself an enormous tax deduction. Once Marble Freedom Trust had control of Tripp Lite, it immediately sold the company to an Irish conglomerate for $1.65 billion, retaining all the proceeds from the sale, while Seid paid no taxes.

At first glance, it looked as if the Chouinards had done virtually the same thing. In Patagonia's case, however, there was a crucial difference. Whereas Seid donated his shares in Tripp Lite to a nonprofit, which then sold them to another company, the value of Patagonia's equity was never monetized. The stock—worth billions of dollars—was effectively frozen forever. And whereas in Seid's case, the proceeds from the sale of Tripp Lite would be funding a wave of conservative activism through the Marble Freedom Trust, in the Chouinards' case, the funds for their environmental work would come from the ongoing profits made by Patagonia, not the sale of its equity.

There's no question that the Chouinards could have structured the deal in a way that would have caused them to pay more in taxes. For example, if they had donated all their stock to the Patagonia Purpose Trust—instead of just the 2 percent of voting shares—they would have faced a tax bill in the range of $850 million. But there was no obvious way to come up with that much cash. With no proceeds from a sale of the company, where would the funds for that kind of tax bill come from? Finding that kind of cash would have meant selling shares to an outside investor, which is precisely what they were trying to avoid.

Critics of the transaction remain flummoxed by the whole thing, insisting that it was an elaborate scheme that revealed Chouinard to be a rapacious capitalist after all. Yet that critique lacks any substantive evidence. Chouinard and his family never monetized the value of the company. They could have pocketed billions of dollars in profits, but they didn't. They didn't go off to buy new houses and yachts. Instead, they gave it all away, unburdening themselves of a fortune they had built from scratch. "Now we can die in peace," Malinda said.

## "An Existential Exit Strategy"

Rarely in the history of capitalism has a company restructured itself in a way that would ensure all its profits go toward charitable causes. There is Newman's Own, which has distributed the earnings from Paul Newman's salad dressings and cookies since the early 1980s. Some European companies, including IKEA and Lego, donate most of their profits to foundations. And there is surprisingly, Rolex, the Swiss watchmaker that funnels its proceeds to the Hans Wilsdorf Foundation, which supports environmental and educational causes. But with Patagonia now sending its proceeds to the Holdfast Collective, and with the Chouinards expecting immediate results, the pressure was on to make an impact.

Money began moving even before news of the ownership change was public. Soon after the ink was dry on the contracts, Patagonia wired $50 million in cash to the Holdfast Collective, seeding the organization with an initial dividend that instantly made it one of the most formidable environmental philanthropies in the country. Now Holdfast had to figure out how to give it away. Typically for the Chouinards, there was no real plan. After spending so much time figuring out how to get rid of their wealth, they had given only fleeting thought to the complex work of figuring out where the money would actually go.

In the end, it came down to one man to start writing the checks: Greg Curtis, Patagonia's former deputy general counsel, who was tasked with running Holdfast. Curtis left Patagonia and became the sole full-time employee of Holdfast. He was given no staff, just some part-time legal and finance help. But starting in late 2022, working from office space leased from Patagonia on its Ventura campus, he started writing checks.

The Holdfast Collective had no website and no way for non-profits to apply for grants. It had no media presence, and Holdfast, Patagonia, and the Chouinards made no efforts to publicize Curtis and the pot of money he was now controlling. There was also no public indication of how Holdfast would approach its giving. Chouinard himself had only the roughest idea of what he did and didn't want Curtis to do with the money. "I don't think we're going to invest in any kind of technology that captures carbon," he said, dismissing a process favored by techno-optimists who believe it will be possible to cool the planet by sucking $CO_2$ out of the atmosphere. "I think we understand nature more than we understand technology, so these carbon capture things that are going to cost millions and millions of dollars, I don't believe in them." Instead, Chouinard said he wanted to support natural processes. "You can capture a lot of carbon through changing the way we do agriculture, so that'll be one focus," he said. "We're helping to buy up large areas of the planet that are carbon sinks and keep them from being developed."

With little more than that to go on, Curtis got to work. Just as Paul Tebbel had done when he began giving away Patagonia's profits decades before, Curtis brought Chouinard recommendations for donations and got him to sign off on the giving strategy's general direction. Using this model, Holdfast made 690 grants and commitments totaling more than $61 million in its first year of operation. There were big donations for conservation efforts, including grants to help protect the Vjosa River in Albania. The Nature Conservancy got $5.2 million to buy 8,000 acres in the Mobile-Tensaw Delta to protect a fragile waterway.

And not long after setting up shop, Curtis heard about a campaign to impede the construction of Pebble Mine, a proposed gold and copper mine in Alaska, by buying up some critical parcels of land. Within days, Curtis had committed to providing the final $3.1 million needed for the plan, finalizing the purchase and scuttling the mining project.

In total, the funds helped protect 162,710 acres of wilderness around the world. There were sizable grants to environmental organizations such as Earthjustice, the nonprofit legal group that works to curb pollution and address climate change. And there was a flurry of handouts to eclectic groups such as Hot Pink Dolphins, a band of activists working to protect the Indo-Pacific bottlenose dolphins near Jeju Island, South Korea. For the most part, it came down to making relatively small donations to grassroots groups, perpetuating, with an almost manic level of consistency, the approach Chouinard first took when he gave his initial grants to Capelli and the Friends of the Ventura River some 50 years earlier.

Holdfast also waded into politics. There were major contributions to Senate Majority PAC and House Majority PAC, both of which work to elect Democrats to Congress, as well as smaller gifts to grassroots groups such as the Black Voters Matter Fund, the Center for American Progress Action Fund, and the Georgia Investor Action Fund, all of which support Democrats. In all, about $1 million went to help elect Democrats around the country during the group's first year in operation. Curtis said there was no intention to be partisan. "We are not aiming to be an extension of the Democratic Party," he said. "The sole purpose in engaging in politics and policy is to advance stronger environmental policy. We would be really interested in supporting any climate leader— Republican, Democrat, or independent. It just so happens that a lot of those folks are Democrats."

The professions of nonpartisanship fell flat, however, and Republicans pounced, claiming the donations to Democratic causes were evidence of clear partisan bias. A conservative activist group filed a complaint with the Federal Elections Commission alleging that the Holdfast Collective misidentified some of the donations it made to Democratic groups in 2022.

Caitlin Sutherland, the executive director of Americans for Public Trust, a conservative group, tried to cast Chouinard as the left's next George Soros, framing him as a political mastermind bent on shaping public opinion. "It is unacceptable that a for-profit company posed as a donor to mask a network of nonprofit organizations working to quietly influence our political system," she said. "By misreporting the source of the donations, Holdfast is trying to hide its true organizational structure that operates as a $1.7 billion ATM for liberal groups." Sutherland's critique smacked of hypocrisy. Americans for Public Trust was itself a dark money group seeking to shape the political debate. The problem, in her eyes, was that Holdfast was using its resources to support Democrats.

Inside Patagonia, the initial confusion over the ownership

change cleared up relatively quickly, the minor furor over employees not getting a piece of the pie subsided, and the work of Holdfast soon became a point of pride. "It's a motivator, and it's something that gives Patagonia's employees a real sense of purpose every day," said John Sterling, who worked on the environmental grants team. "They're not just going in to make the best fleece jacket. They're going in to save the planet."

As other moguls assessed what Chouinard had pulled off, some came looking for advice. Dozens of rich people approached the company seeking guidance on how they might accomplish something like that, too. Beyond the Ventura campus, similar conversations were taking place. 1% for the Planet, the nonprofit organization Chouinard founded with his fishing buddy Craig Mathews, said it was starting to advise other companies on how they might restructure themselves in a way to maximize charitable giving.

And at least a few other magnates said they were going to follow Chouinard's lead, although the details were fuzzy. Michael Bloomberg, the founder of Bloomberg L.P. and the former mayor of New York City, put to rest years of speculation and confirmed that he would give the vast majority of his $22.5 billion company to his Bloomberg Philanthropies, which he already used as a tool to give away huge sums of money.

And then David Green, the founder and CEO of Hobby Lobby, said he was going to give away the $4.6 billion company to the Lord Almighty. Green had already used Hobby Lobby as a vehicle for his conservative Christian activism. Years earlier, Hobby Lobby won a case before the Supreme Court after the company refused to provide its employees with health insurance that covered birth control. Now, Green said, "I chose God," he wrote in a guest essay on the Fox News website, drawing a direct parallel to

Patagonia. "Like Chouinard said, 'Instead of "going public," you could say we're "going purpose."'"

Details were scarce, but Green said he had transferred all of Hobby Lobby's voting stock to a trust and that he would be using the proceeds from the company to "fund Christianity." Green wasn't as transparent as Chouinard about the specifics of his plan, and the two men were supporting very different causes with their funds. But Green was nevertheless professing the same sort of selflessness and disdain for materialism that had animated Chouinard for so long. "We really wanted to do something that mattered a hundred years from now," Green said. "Instead of just absorbing things ourselves, we wanted to do things in various ministries."

For company insiders, the moves by Green, Bloomberg, and others proved that Chouinard had once again opened a new route. "We all knew this wasn't just about the company," Ridgeway said. "It was about how the company could show the entire world that there's other ways to do this. That's what it was about. This was a potentially historic moment in the evolution of business. I can easily imagine that 50 years hence, people will recognize this is as an inflection point around how we all thought about capitalism in the past."

Or as Malinda Chouinard put it: "Imagine if all the rich people did this. But they keep buying boats instead."

Even Jim Collins, the celebrated management guru and author of business bibles like *Good to Great*, gave Patagonia's ownership overhaul his tentative seal of approval. "Let's call it a big and wonderful experiment," he said. "Even more profound than product innovation is organizational innovation. If the Chouinard family's restructuring works, if it's successful, it could be a new evolution for some companies and how they evolve over time . . . When people ask: What's your exit strategy? Boy, Chouinard just rede-fined that. This is like an existential exit strategy. He's saying: This is what my life is about."

More than an exit strategy, however, the ownership change was Chouinard's way of finishing the job on his own terms. For decades, the question of what would happen to this most unusual company had hung in the air. Until it was resolved, there could be no final accounting of Patagonia's legacy, no real way to measure the impact of Chouinard's lifetime of work. But by giving it all away, Chouinard made an emphatic statement. There was indeed another way to do business. He had created lasting value, not for himself, but for the planet. He had resisted the allure of mate-rial wealth until the end and plowed his fortune into protecting something truly priceless: the natural world. And by devising a structure that insulated the company from outside meddling, he had codified this arrangement in perpetuity, forging an ironclad guarantee that Patagonia would endure, its profits going to pro-tect the planet, even after he was gone.

CHAPTER 11

# The Next 50 Years

## "Doing the Right Thing"

As the sun disappeared behind the Andes, I watched Chouinard emerge from a river in Argentina, sopping wet after spending the day wading through frigid waters. We had spent the past week at Las Pampas Lodge, a remote hotel that caters to wealthy fly-fishing enthusiasts and also serves as the unofficial testing ground for Patagonia's fishing team. Chouinard had recently celebrated his 85th birthday but was undiminished. Each day, he would set out early, eating a hearty breakfast before piling into a pickup truck and enduring a bumpy hourlong ride on rutted-out roads. Then he would fish for at least eight hours straight, breaking only briefly to take lunch in the bushes. Each evening, he would be the last one out of the river. He was the best angler around. One day, he caught 101 fish, a personal record. The next day, he hauled up 25 large brown trout, a feat that stoked the envy of his companions, some of whom were lucky to get one brownie in the course of a week.

This trip was about more than just catching trout, however. Chouinard was also trying to perfect Patagonia's fishing offerings. Just as he had used his own first ascents to tweak the specifications of pitons and carabiners when he was a climber in his 20s, he was still at it now, using his time on the river to improve his products. Having emerged from the water, Chouinard made his way over to Eric Noll, one of Patagonia's designers. Before the trip, Noll had made Chouinard a handful of prototype jackets, each one featuring slightly different materials and designs. Chouinard tried out a new one each day, then offered Noll feedback as the sun set.

On this day, Chouinard was mostly pleased. His body and base layers were dry. The waders hadn't absorbed any water. Even better, a new gutter system on the jacket's hood that Noll designed was working well, carrying water away from the brim without letting it drip onto Chouinard's face. But there was one problem, Chouinard told Noll: a strip of Velcro that cinched the cuffs tight was too close to the end of the sleeve, and it was scratching his skin. The designers should add a few millimeters of fabric to fix the problem. It was the same sort of perfectionism Chouinard had brought to his work for a half century, and he was still sweating the small stuff, refining materials and designs in an attempt to create the Platonic ideal of whatever product had his attention.

For now, this attention to detail seems to be working. In the years since the pandemic and the ownership change, Patagonia's revenues have continued ticking up. There have been some fluctuations, as is natural at a company now doing more than $1 billion a year in sales. But if Patagonia is to survive another 50 years, it will require sustaining that sort of commitment to quality even after Chouinard is gone. And it will require much more than simply making a better fishing jacket.

As Patagonia's offerings have improved, so too have its rivals' counterofferings. The market for well-made outdoor gear is more crowded than ever. If you don't fancy Patagonia's winter line, there are plenty of other options from Arc'teryx, Black Diamond,

Bogner, Canada Goose, Columbia, Cotopaxi, Fjällräven, Helly Hansen, Jack Wolfskin, L.L.Bean, Marmot, Norrøna, Osprey, Outdoor Research, The North Face, REI, Salomon, and more. Not to mention cheaper offerings from Amazon, Temu, or any number of other discount retailers. In order to keep standing out, Patagonia will need to stay several steps ahead of its rivals, and that will mean continuing to seek out—and solve—the hard problems.

A few days after my time at Las Pampas with Chouinard, I was straddling a surfboard in Punta de Lobos, Chile, testing a new piece of gear Patagonia had devised in an attempt to address one of its long-running problems. Since 2006, Patagonia has been producing wetsuits for surfers. The first ones were made in Japan and featured a merino wool lining, drawing inspiration from the wool sweaters that Chouinard wore when he was surfing back in the '60s. They also featured a neoprene that was made from limestone, an innovation that Patagonia believed was more environmentally friendly than traditional neoprene, which is made from petrochemicals. The wetsuits were good enough, and they earned Patagonia some street cred with surfers.

But the team in Ventura quickly learned that the wool-lined, limestone-based suits had major shortcomings. The neoprene wasn't as environmentally friendly as the company initially thought, the suits weren't as durable as they should have been, and the wool didn't age well. A few years later, some of the surf team heard about a new material, Yulex, that was made from natural rubber derived from the hevea tree. After a few years of work, Patagonia had developed its first batch of Yulex wetsuits. The supply chain was set up to scale, a media plan was in place, and the surf community was receptive to the promise of the new suits. But when the first units started getting to customers, they all fit wrong. The factory had switched the chest panels during the fabrication process, with small parts going into medium suits, and vice versa. Customers were livid, the launch was a bust, and years of work to arrive at that moment had been squandered by one manufacturing snafu. The next batch fit right, and while it's taken time, Patagonia has since found a growing market with its Yulex wetsuits.

As the sun set off the coast, rays of light illuminating the two giant rock thumbs that give Punta de Lobos its iconic break, I paddled out with Ramón Navarro, one of the best big wave surfers in the world and a Patagonia ambassador. The Pacific waters were cold, but we were warm in our Yulex suits. The swell was easy on this day, and we mostly bobbed in the froth, admiring the coastline, listening to the gulls. Then, as we were about to call it a day, a small wave came along and I hopped aboard, riding it for a few seconds before getting tossed into the surf.

More than a thousand miles north of Punta de Lobos is the seaside town of Chincha, Peru. Chincha is unremarkable save for its largest employer, a vertically integrated textile factory called Textil del Valle, or TDV. The quality of Patagonia's clothes will only ever be as good as the quality of the factories where they are made, and it is at factories like TDV that Patagonia is pushing the limits, trying to find out just how responsible it can be in an inherently irresponsible industry.

Less than a decade ago, TDV was in bad shape; it was competing with other conventional garment factories on price, paying workers a pittance, and cutting corners in an effort to find profits wherever it could. Quality and profits were suffering, so in 2018, the owners hired Juan José Córdova, a construction executive, to come in and try to revive the operations. Córdova quickly ascertained that the status quo wouldn't let the company succeed.

Instead, he picked up on a growing demand from big brands for eco-friendly clothes and decided to lean in.

TDV, which also had its own fields of cotton, started transitioning its crop to be organic. It began exploring regenerative practices. It improved its wastewater treatment, purchased carbon offsets, and reduced its energy consumption. Critically, TDV also began improving the factory, providing additional services and better pay to its thousands of workers. Córdova's goal, he said, was to create nothing less than "the most sustainable textile plant in the world." At first, this required a fair bit of investment. Its current customers weren't asking for these premium features, and TDV had to spend millions to upgrade its operations. But within a few years, the focus on quality had paid off. With its organic cotton, natural dyes, and a loyal and motivated workforce, TDV won lucrative contracts with Lululemon and Lacoste, leading to a sharp uptick in earnings for the company.

Once it had its own house in order, Córdova's team pitched Patagonia. It was well known among textile manufacturers that Chouinard's company upheld the strictest standards for its suppliers, and TDV believed it could rise to the challenge. No such luck. When Patagonia inspectors visited TDV, they left dissatisfied. There were questions about the traceability of its organic cotton, its water usage, and the working conditions. A year later, TDV came back to Patagonia, claiming it had resolved those concerns. This time, Patagonia agreed, and gave TDV a contract to make some of its T-shirts. Since then, TDV's share of Patagonia's output has grown annually, and the factory is now making rugby shirts and sweatshirts as well. It was further confirmation that not just Patagonia, but its suppliers too, could reap financial rewards when they put the quality of the products and the health of the planet first. "The money was not the point," Córdova said of TDV's transformation. "The profit was a consequence of doing the right thing."

Even as Patagonia makes strides in reforming its waterproof materials, its wetsuits, and its factories, it is still confronted with problems for which there are no easy solutions. In 2019, it learned that some of the organic cotton it was sourcing from the Xinjiang region of China was being produced by the Uyghur people under slave labor conditions. After a public relations flare-up, it stopped using organic cotton from Xinjiang. But the episode was a painful reminder of how challenging it is to protect vulnerable workers. Years after it believed it had rooted out forced labor in its Taiwan factories, it was facing a similar situation in China.

Another enduring sore spot for the company: microplastics. Using so much recycled polyester is a win for the environment in many ways. It avoids the consumption of virgin petroleum products, lessening demand for fossil fuels ever so slightly. But every polyester garment Patagonia makes is also polluting the planet, shedding microscopic particles of plastic that are invisible to the eye but pose a long-term environmental hazard. As awareness about microplastics has grown, Patagonia has tried to redesign its fabrics to shed less particulate matter. It has tried educating consumers about proper care, encouraging them to wash their fleeces less and in cold water, which can reduce shedding. It even collaborated with Samsung, the Korean appliance maker, to design a washing machine that has special filters to remove microplastics. But these efforts have helped only so much; a recent analysis found that Patagonia fleeces shed large quantities of microplastics. Meanwhile, the plastic haze is spreading around the globe, turning up everywhere from snow on the South Pole to the breath of dolphins in the Pacific.

And when it comes to fossil fuels, Patagonia limits the use of single-use plastics when it can, but there is no way to ship its wares around the world without burning huge amounts of jet fuel, shipping fuel, and gasoline. Its factories also continue to wrap many items in individual plastic bags. The company has made great strides since it began its environmental journey so many years ago, and yet with every step it takes forward, it finds new problems it must address. Even after a half century's work, Chouinard understood that the elusive goal of a business that was actually good for the planet remained out of reach. "Patagonia is not a sustainable company," he said. "There's no such thing. I look at our philanthropy as not charity but as the cost of doing business."

The imperative to save the planet has never been more urgent. I traveled to South America with Chouinard and the Patagonia team during what was the hottest year in recorded history. The level of carbon dioxide in the atmosphere had reached an all-time high as planet-warming emissions and fossil fuel production continued unabated. All around the world, storms made worse by climate change were pummeling vulnerable communities. As we traveled, wildfires raged in Chile, and drought ravaged the Amazon rainforest. And a few months after our trip, Donald Trump won his second presidential election. After four years of a Biden administration that had prioritized climate action, Trump was storming back into office, intent on rolling back environmental protections and expanding fossil fuel production.

This time, there was no great panic inside Patagonia. Instead, as was the case across much of the progressive world, there was simply a collective sigh of defeat. And then the Patagonia team got back to work. They would sell their clothes and their gear, take the money they earned, and plow it into efforts to protect the planet. They wouldn't be able to defeat Trump on their own, but if they could make it harder for the president to muck up the natural world, well, that was something.

"Every advancement in this society has been done through activism," Chouinard said just days after the election. "It's grass-roots movements. It's nongovernmental organizations operating where there's no market, no shareholders, no bullshit. It's businesses being courageous and doing their part . . . It's simple: every business should be committed to people and the planet, above all else—for future generations and any future economy."

## "Bigger Than the Apparel Business"

If Chouinard has his way, Patagonia may be best known as a food company 50 years from now. Improbable as that might sound, it's a future the company is actively pursuing with the help of Paul Lightfoot, an entrepreneur who shares Chouinard's disdain for the conventional food system.

I first met Lightfoot at the Rusty Duck, the only bar in Dawson, Minnesota, a one-stoplight town surrounded by megafarms. Lightfoot is the general manager of Patagonia Provisions, the company's nascent food business, and we had come to the epicenter of industrial agriculture to see if we could peer into the future. All around us, stretching for hundreds of miles in every direction, were endless rows of soybeans and field corn—the kind of corn used to make ethanol and high-fructose corn syrup, not eat off the cob. These are the biggest cash crops in the United States, and producing them at this scale requires a host of unsavory practices. The use of chemical pesticides and synthetic fertilizer is rampant. The lack of genetic diversity makes plants more susceptible to diseases and pests. And the soil and groundwater wind up polluted from runoff. But on this summer day, our destination was not one of those problematic megafarms. It was A-Frame Farm, a 1,200-acre oasis in the middle of the heartland.

A-Frame is run by Luke Peterson, a farmer who was working in conventional agriculture before he grew disillusioned and decided to go organic. While his plot of land is just a blip in this expanse of megafarms, it stands out for its diversity. Bees and bugs hummed in the air. Flowers bloomed in the margins between the crops and the grass. There were sunflowers, cattle, and barley. And about 15 percent of the land was dedicated to kernza, a perennial grain that can be used like wheat and is at the center of Patagonia's food strategy.

Unlike traditional wheat—or most crops, for that matter—kernza isn't an annual; it doesn't need to be replanted every year. Instead, one kernza plant can stay in the ground and be productive for several years in a row, delivering a cascading series of benefits to farmers and the planet. For farmers, perennials like kernza mean using less labor, less fuel, less water.

As for the planet, kernza works miracles with the soil. Because it lives for so long, its roots go deep—burrowing down 15 feet, compared to about 5 feet with conventional wheat. That allows kernza to sequester far more carbon dioxide, a promising development that points to the role agriculture can play in the fight against global warming.

Those intertwined benefits—good for farmers, good for the planet—explain why Lightfoot is one of the country's biggest champions of kernza, using it in the beers and pastas sold under the Patagonia Provisions brand. "The mission of Patagonia is to save our home planet, which is a beautifully simple mission," he said as we sipped a kernza lager under the stars. "And if you think about all the different ways that the business can help fulfill that mission, food is the most important lever that Patagonia can pull."

Chouinard started thinking about creating a food company more than 40 years ago. In 1984, he hired Lorenz Schaller, an expert in ancient grains, to lead the project. Schaller was tasked with creating a division that would sell blends of roasted grain such as barley, known in Tibet as tsampa. The idea for the packaging was that it would resemble the Celestial Seasonings tea logo but feature "ethnic folklore and recipes for the mountains and travel." By the next year, the company was working on selling Japanese rice, Chinese Dragon Claw Millet, and South American grains with Aztec and Inca origins. But it quickly became clear that starting a food company from scratch was no easy feat. Sourcing exotic grains in bulk was tough, the market was limited, and distribution was a headache. The effort fizzled.

Decades later, Chouinard tried again. In 2012, he hired Birgit Cameron, a food entrepreneur, to start Patagonia Provisions. His hypothesis was simple: At the end of the day, there was no way to make clothing in a way that was truly good for the planet; even if you use recycled, eco-friendly materials and renewable energy while upholding high labor standards, the best clothes in the world won't heal nature. But food can. The right kind of farming practices can improve soil health. The right kinds of plants can absorb carbon dioxide. The right kind of grazing animals can help restore wild lands. The right kinds of seafood can clean the oceans. "We need a revolution in society, and it's not gonna come from any other way except from agriculture," Chouinard said. "People don't care about how cotton is grown in Turkey, but they really care about their food."

With the lofty mandate to create a profitable business that would promote regenerative agriculture and also deliver meaningful sales at a company the size of Patagonia, Cameron set to work. In a matter of years, Patagonia Provisions introduced dozens of products. In addition to crackers and tinned fish, there were soups, chilis, fruit bars, and grains. Aggressive expansion plans called for the rapid-fire launch of baby food, oils, sauces, and more. In 2021, Patagonia launched its own wine. (The reviews were not kind.) Before long, the company was making more than 70 different items and was racing to introduce more.

It was an audacious expansion strategy, but it spread Provisions thin. After several years, only a few of the offerings—mostly the tinned fish—were selling much. And yet even as most of the items in the portfolio failed to catch on, Patagonia kept producing them. The result was a catalog of zombie offerings with little distribution and minimal brand awareness that were taxing the resources of a small division within a company that still knew almost nothing about food. By 2022, Chouinard had had enough. Cameron was out, and Lightfoot was brought in with the mandate to make Patagonia Provisions profitable.

Lightfoot's first move was rightsizing the portfolio. He and his team went through the product lineup one item at a time and evaluated each offering on four criteria: Was the quality good? Was it nutritious and tasty? Did it have a positive environmental impact? And was it profitable? Some items failed on all fronts. Crackers made from breadfruit, a tropical plant native to Barbados, were out; they weren't selling well, and there were no other breadfruit items in the works. So were all the items with barely any sales. So was the buffalo jerky that was being made in limited quantities. Goodbye to the fruit bars and soups and chilis and grains. Instead, Lightfoot focused on three initial categories: crackers, pasta, and tinned seafood.

Seafood is the biggest part of the business, and in some ways, the easiest. Tinned fish is enjoying a renaissance among consumers, and Patagonia Provisions has a strong brand with a loyal following, plus distribution in big chains like Whole Foods. Having spent more than a decade building out the supply chain, the company also had a reliable stable of fish farmers. And the sardines, anchovies, mackerel, and mussels it sells all have a good environmental story to tell. Mussels actually clean the ocean, filtering out algae and silt. (Provisions now sells more than a million tins of mussels a year.) Sardines, anchovies, and mackerel are small fish that are quick to repopulate and in less danger of overfishing, as is the case with larger species like tuna. And the whole enterprise is simply on brand for Chouinard himself, who loves catching fish, cooking fish, eating fish, and talking about fish.

Then there's kernza. While the grain is not yet well known, its proponents say it has the potential to be something like a miracle worker on American farmland. Once yields improve and costs come down, they believe it could displace wheat in a number of products. But first it needs a market. Current production is minuscule, fewer than 50,000 acres. Compare that to some 37 million acres of conventional wheat that are grown in the US. But Patagonia has faced down such problems before. Just as it did when it wanted to see organic cotton go mainstream, it is paying a premium for kernza in the short term, integrating it into its supply chain, and helping other companies come along for the ride.

As a first step, Patagonia Provisions partnered with a handful of breweries around the country, including Sierra Nevada, Topa Topa, and Aslan. Those brewers made Patagonia-branded beer with kernza, helping create a market for the perennial grain, extending the Patagonia brand, and perhaps making an iota of difference on the climate front, too. It helps that the beer tastes good. One of the varieties, the Non-Alcoholic Kernza Golden

Brew made by Patagonia Provisions and Deschutes Brewery, won a gold medal at the Great American Beer Festival. And Patagonia beer can now be found at Whole Foods. "You can't win just with environmental impact," Lightfoot said, channeling Chouinard. "If you don't get the quality right, you're not going to win."

In food, Chouinard sees a path to an entirely new sort of business model. With the right kind of agriculture, there is the possibility—however hard it might be to realize—to actually do some good for the Earth. At scale, shellfish, kernza, and other regenerative crops can actually sequester carbon dioxide, purify waters, and remove pollutants from the atmosphere. If Chouinard could snap his fingers, he said, he would make the clothing business disappear and just sell fish, crackers, and beer. Fifty years from now, he said, "I could see the food business being bigger than the apparel business."

## "A Spiritual Connection with Nature"

Chouinard and I were up before dawn. We had spent the past several days at Las Pampas, fishing under rainbows, breaking for lunch and wine in the bushes, then enjoying hearty dinners of Argentine steak and potatoes back at the lodge. The power went out for 48 hours, we dined by candlelight, and we had no contact with the outside world. Now it was time to leave. It was still dark, and as we tossed our duffel bags into the bed of a pickup truck, I looked up and saw the Milky Way spilled out across the sky.

We were headed north to Bariloche, the lakeside city where the Fun Hogs had mustered their supplies all those years ago before ascending Fitz Roy. After an hour of navigating backroads, we connected with Route 40, the same highway Chouinard had driven on that trip in 1968. The road was now paved, but little else had changed. Fifty-six years after he had embarked on that pivotal journey, he was still on the move, still seeking out the wild corners of the planet.

Crammed in the backseat of an old Toyota pickup, we passed a cup of yerba maté back and forth, taking sips of the bitter brew through a metal straw, and Chouinard told me what was bugging him these days. He was proud of Patagonia, of course he was. But Chouinard had always been a curmudgeon, harboring a glass-half-empty view of the world even as he lived a charmed life. Now, in his old age, he seemed to have grown even more dour, sometimes unable to appreciate that Patagonia was one of the most popular, influential companies in the world. Sure, the company was more successful than he could have imagined. Yes, the culture remained relentlessly weird, the campus was still full of kids, the cafeteria still served up organic food, and idealistic professionals still clamored to work in Ventura. Yet despite all this, Chouinard couldn't help but feel like the company was losing its way.

Some of the challenges were easy to see. There was the dip in sales growth after COVID, the reckoning over race, the abrupt departure of Marcario. More recently, workers at the retail store in Reno had voted to form a labor union, and a restructuring led to a small round of layoffs. There was also tension among the company's senior ranks. Even after the ownership change, challenges between the board and the management team endured. Gellert and the other executives face what can sometimes feel like irreconcilable objectives. On the one hand, they are told to generate profits to support environmental causes; at the same time, they're told to limit growth.

The company was trying to uphold its high standards when it comes to its employment practices, but doing so can slow down product development and create a culture that lacks a sense of urgency. The board wanted the company to be nimble, yet too often, major decisions still needed to be cleared by the Chouinards. And while Patagonia gear is generally regarded as among the best on the market, Chouinard was still quick to complain about durability and materials and fit. "We've got managers that are just managing," he told me. "They're not taking us to the next place."

At the core of Chouinard's complaints was his sense that today's employees simply didn't understand quality. There were too many different versions of similar items. The clothes didn't always work like they should. The company was making too many things that lasted a season or two, not a lifetime. "The secret of our success has been quality," he said. "We really are trying to make the best quality product, and our definition of quality includes environmental responsibility. And every time we make a decision based on either quality or environmental responsibility, we make more money. It's really that simple."

He still held out some hope for humanity. On the one hand, he worried that young people were spending too much time inside looking at screens. "There's a nature deficit disorder," he said. "Nothing's going to happen until all of us get a spiritual connection with nature." But he thought the general populace must be on the brink of some sort of collective revelation. With the quality of modern life so trashy, how could folks not realize that the system was broken? When would they realize that spending all their time and money chasing material goods was a dead-end proposition? "If a customer buys a cheapo blender made out of plastic and puts an ice cube in and it blows up and shorts out, maybe they'll save up and buy a blender to last the rest of their life," he said. It was a simple analogy, but it spoke to his grander aspiration: that consumers would get as obsessed with quality as he had been his whole life, that they would buy less stuff, but buy things that were built to last.

"What we're trying to do is convince the customer to buy less, buy better," he said. If consumers do that, "that'll force corporations to change. And then if corporations change, then government will change." And if governments change, then maybe the world could change. The details might have been fuzzy, but Chouinard's values remained clear.

More grandly, Chouinard wanted people everywhere to recognize that the world was facing an environmental crisis and do something about it. He'd seen the destruction with his own eyes, the melting glaciers, the polluted rivers, the urban sprawl. He had done his part to try and protect the planet. Why wasn't everyone else doing their part, too? "I think every single person has to make it their number one priority," he said. "During World War II we grew a garden, we rationed sugar, we ate horse meat. It rallied the entire country together. That's what we have to do to save the planet. Each one of us has to dig down deep and say, 'Okay, what can I do?'" He then turned the mirror on himself. "Am I doing enough?" he said. "The answer is no. So how can we do more good with this company?"

As for how to do more good with Patagonia, the playbook hadn't changed. The company remained committed to saving the home planet. That was still his North Star, and with the ownership change and the establishment of the Holdfast Collective, he had institutionalized his priorities, ensuring that Patagonia's profits would be going to conservation efforts as long as the company survived.

And yes, the company needed to be profitable. On this front, Patagonia was set up for success. It had no long-term debt, no antsy investors, no greedy shareholders. Customers were more stoked about the brand than ever, thanks in part to Chouinard's own story and the activism and the conservation. It just had to keep hitting those roughly 10 percent margins and there would be ample resources for Holdfast each year.

Quality was the tough one. Chouinard wanted the company to double down on its craftsmanship. Not just the stitching and the blend of its fabrics, but the sustainability of its materials, the ethics of its suppliers, all of it. Unless Patagonia kept pushing itself to be more responsible, what was the point? "We're not a perfect company," he said. "But at least we're recognizing it, and we're doing something about it."

And it was undeniable that with its focus on sustainable business, the activism, and the coalition building, Patagonia had made an impact well beyond Ventura. The company may not be able to singlehandedly change capitalism, but Chouinard's fingerprints are all over the business world. When companies take better care of their employees, when they provide childcare, when they let employees be themselves in the office, that is the legacy of Patagonia. When corporations push their vendors to treat their workers well, when they try to root out toxic materials in the supply chain, when they do the right thing even when it costs a bit more, there, too, is the legacy of Chouinard. When CEOs take a stand, talk back to the president, and encourage customers to vote, that's in part Patagonia's doing, too. And then there were the national parks in Chile and Argentina, all the sustainability groups Patagonia had cofounded, the 1% for the Planet grants, the ownership change, and now the money flowing from Holdfast.

Was Chouinard satisfied? After so many years, so many close

calls, so much gained and so much lost, so much given away, was he at peace?

"I feel like I could die tomorrow, and the company is going to continue for the next 50 years, and it's going to continue doing the right thing, and I don't have to be around," he said. "I've never been a micromanager. I'm the company philosopher. I'm the entrepreneur that comes up with crazy ideas. Sometimes they worked, sometimes they didn't. But I feel a big relief that I've put my life in order. And now I'm going to work on making everything simpler and simpler for myself."

After a six-hour drive, we arrived in Bariloche, where we were inspecting the newest Patagonia outpost. The company had recently purchased a verdant estate overlooking Nahuel Huapi Lake and was in the process of turning the property into a store, bunkhouse, and all-purpose home base for the Patagonia team in the region. The centerpiece was an exquisite historic home built in 1916 by Emilio Frey, an Argentinian explorer who helped draw the country's border with Chile. Now the house, clad in alerce shingles, was being turned into a Patagonia store. A nearby building would serve as a hostel for employees and athletes passing through town. All around, there were gardens, forests, and hiking trails.

Chouinard spent a half hour poking around the house, marveling at the joinery and the craftsmanship, appreciating the quality of a building that had been constructed before he was born, and that was now finding a new life. He then walked outside and strolled through the orchards. It was early afternoon, and we hadn't eaten much, so Chouinard picked an apple off a tree, took a few bites, then threw it in the dirt. We stood in the garden, staring out at the lake. Then it was time to go. I had a flight to catch, and Chouinard's adventure was just beginning. He was switching out some gear, maybe taking a shower. After that, he was headed off to walk around another mountain, to fish another river, to find himself—somewhere in Patagonia.

# ACKNOWLEDGMENTS

Endless thanks to so many who helped make this book happen. First and foremost to my family, who give me the time and space and love I need to do this work. Ali is my biggest fan, Franny and Clark are my smallest fans, and I love you all so much.

Eamon Dolan is a brilliant editor and author and friend who publishes books that change people's minds, and I'm forever grateful for his support. The entire team at Simon & Schuster, including Jon Karp, Priscilla Painton, Jackie Seow, Tzipora Chein, Ingrid Carabulea, Brianna Scharfenberg, and Patty Romanowski, operate the best publishing house in the world; it's an honor to be part of their roster. I'm fortunate to have the world's greatest agent and agency in my corner; thank you, Binky, Helen Manders, and everyone at CAA. Thanks to my colleagues at *The New York Times*, an essential institution that seeks the truth and helps people understand the world; it's a privilege to work in that newsroom every single day. Hannah Fairfield and Lyndsey Layton understood the importance of the ownership change story when I first pitched it, and Ryan McCarthy contributed invaluable edits on a late draft of this book that helped me find my voice. Friends including Rimjhim Dey and her team at DEY, Alan Fleischmann and Dafna Tapiero, Sam Potolicchio, Erin Allweiss, Jolie Hunt, Margaret Richardson, Daphne Wang, Deb Greenspan, Joe and Christie Marchese, Ash Chang, Anand Giridharardas, Ted Oberwager, Pete Stavros, Adam Met, Adam Grant, Nick Bilton, Charles Duhigg, Conrad Anker, Lynn Forester de Rothschild, Paul Hawken, John Vaillant, Darren Walker, the Lader family, Jay Simpson, Greg Behrman, Susan McPherson, Susan MacTavish Best, Sharon Johnson, Kevin Delaney, Raj Shah, Aron Cramer, and others offered essential support along the way. And I wouldn't be a reader and writer if my parents weren't readers and writers, too; thanks, Mom and Dad.

Books and articles written by Yvon and Malinda Chouinard, Vincent Stanley, Rick Ridgeway, and other longtime Patagonia employees and associates were an essential part of my research. I particularly recommend *Some Stories, Let My People Go Surfing, The Responsible Company, Family Business*, and *Life Lived Wild*. *A Wild Idea* by Jonathan Franklin provides a rich portrait of Doug Tompkins's life and includes a comprehensive description of the Fun Hogs trip.

This book would not have been possible without the cooperation of the Chouinard family and Patagonia. Particular thanks to Yvon and Malinda for welcoming me into their lives, to my fellow travelers Corley Kenna and Alex Perry (*todo sí!*), and to Kris McDivitt Tompkins, Vincent Stanley, Rick Ridgeway, Ryan Gellert, Val Franco, Terri Laine, Corey Simpson, and Alexa Liccardi for invaluable help with research, reporting, and fact-checking. Thanks also to early readers, including Chris Van Leuven, Michael Peppard, Edward Sullivan, Sabrina Shankman, Sali Christeson, Seth Boyd, and Ali, all of whom helped improve this manuscript. Thanks to Rascal, who loves me unconditionally. And most of all, thanks to you, my readers, for entrusting me with your time.

Now please put this book down and go outside.

# NOTES

## CHAPTER 1: A RHYTHM ALL HIS OWN

17 *"I hated head-to-head competition"*: Yvon Chouinard, in discussion with the author, 2024.

19 *"It was lucky"*: Jeremy Bernstein, "Ascending," *The New Yorker*, January 31, 1977.

22 *"I was a dirtbag climber"*: Grayson Haver Currin, "Yvon Chouinard on Why He Gave Away Patagonia to Save the Planet," *National Geographic*, "National Geographic 33 2025," March 18, 2025, https://www.nationalgeographic.com /culture/article/yvon-Chouinard-nat-geo-33-2025.

25 *"Crazy as it was"*: Karen Frishman, in discussion with the author, 2023.

26 *"He taught me"*: Greg Dalton, "Yvon Chouinard: Founding Patagonia & Living Simply," November 27, 2016, in Climate One, https://www.climateone.org /audio/yvon-Chouinard-founding-patagonia-living-simply.

27 *"I thought, 'What kind of a business'"*: Paul Bruun, "Yvon Chouinard Profile," *Fly Rod & Reel*, September 25, 2008.

28 *"Chouinard's equipment was that much better"*: John Steinbreder, "He's in His Element in the Elements," *Sports Illustrated*, February 11, 1991, https://vault.si .com/vault/1991/02/11/hes-in-his-element-in-the-elements-yvon-Chouinard -the-man-behind-patagonia-outfitters-does-his-best-work-in-the-rugged -outdoors.

29 *"A poetic soul"*: Royal Robbins, "The North America Wall," *American Alpine Journal* (1965):331–38, AAC Publications, https://publications.americanalpineclub .org/articles/12196533100/The-North-America-Wall.

33 *"It was almost like not being in the army"*: Bernstein, "Ascending."

35  *"Early on, we recognized"*: Yvon Chouinard, *Some Stories: Lessons from the Edge of Business and Sport* (Patagonia Press, 2019), 335.


## CHAPTER 2: DIRTBAGS

37  *"It is 3,300 feet high"*: John Muir, "The Approach to the Valley," 1912, https://vault
.sierraclub.org/john_muir_exhibit/writings/the_yosemite/chapter_1.aspx.

38  *"Two meals a day"*: Chouinard, *Some Stories*, 101.

38  *"We learned that our minds"*: Chouinard, *Some Stories*, 106.

38  *"The new philosophy"*: Chouinard, *Some Stories*, 105.

39  *"Just why is Yosemite climbing"*: Yvon Chouinard, "Modern Yosemite Climbing,"
*American Alpine Journal* (1963):319–27, AAC Publications, https://publications
.americanalpineclub.org/articles/12196331900/Modern-Yosemite-Climbing.

41  *"What a collection of people"*: David Browne, "The North Face's Epic 1966
Store Opening, Starring the Grateful Dead," *Men's Journal*, December 4, 2017,
https://www.mensjournal.com/gear/north-faces-epic-1966-opening-party
-featuring-the-grateful-dead-w446385.

41  *"I've always considered Doug"*: Dick Dorworth, in discussion with the author, 2023.

43  *"Designing was as much fun"*: Bennett Barthelemy, "Remembering Tom
Frost (1937–2018): The Full Perspective Interview," *Climbing*, April 8, 2009,
https://www.climbing.com/news/tom-frost-the-full-perspective-interview/.

50  *"Doug and I were the only ones"*: Chouinard, interview, 2024.

51  *"Doug convinced him"*: Dorworth, in discussion with the author, 2023.

52  *"Well, now"*: Jonathan Franklin, *A Wild Idea* (New York: HarperOne, 2021).

53  *"I always thought of rock climbing"*: Bernstein, "Ascending."

53  *"I love this planet"*: Chouinard, interview, 2022.

54  *"It was widely felt"*: Tom Frost, "Preserving the Cracks!," *American Alpine Journal* (1972):1–6, AAC Publications, https://publications.americanalpineclub
.org/articles/12197200100/Preserving-the-Cracks.

55  *"A perfection of means"*: Chouinard Equipment Catalog, 1972.

58  *"the effect of a pane of glass"*: Daniel P. Moynihan, "Daniel P. Moynihan to John
Ehrlichman, September 17, 1969," https://www.nixonlibrary.gov/sites/default
/files/virtuallibrary/documents/jul10/56.pdf.


## CHAPTER 3: PUSHING THE LIMITS

60  *"Been away from civilization"*: Chouinard, *Some Stories*, 115.

61  *"Almost everything I have"*: Haver Currin, "Yvon Chouinard on Why He Gave
Away Patagonia to Save the Planet."

# NOTES

62 *"We just invented our own way"*: Chouinard, interview, 2024.

63 *"We were both marching"*: Mark Capelli, in discussion with the author, 2023.

65 *"Every time he went climbing"*: Hall Stratton, in discussion with the author, 2024.

66 *"That epiphany made it"*: Davey Agnew, in discussion with the author, 2024.

69 *"We knew the pile would capture"*: Val Franco, in discussion with the author, 2022.

70 *"Animals have the fur"*: Franco, interview.

72 *"How dare you countermand"*: Vincent Stanley, in discussion with the author, 2023.

74 *"The people working with him"*: Stratton, interview.

75 *"Here's Chouinard Equipment"*: Yvon Chouinard, *Let My People Go Surfing* (New York: Penguin, 2006), 38.

76 *"I've been given this responsibility"*: Kris McDivitt Tompkins, in discussion with the author, 2024.

79 *"Oh man"*: Rick Ridgeway, in discussion with the author, 2024.

80 *"Nobody knew what they were doing"*: Billy Kulczyzki, in discussion with the author, 2022.

## CHAPTER 4: PATAGONIACS

83 *"The photographs really suck"*: Ridgeway, interview.

84 *"But I don't know anything"*: Jennifer Ridgeway, "Capture a Patagoniac," Patagonia Stories, September 9, 2020, https://www.patagonia.com/stories/capture-a-patagoniac/story-91628.html.

87 *"like tiny fireflies"*: Malinda Pennoyer Chouinard and Jennifer Ridgeway, *Family Business: Innovative On-Site Child Care Since 1983* (Patagonia Press, 2016), 22.

90 *"No matter where you were"*: Ridgeway, interview.

90 *"Language changes in the presence of babies"*: Chouinard and Ridgeway, *Family Business*, 32.

91 *"and not one of them has ended up"*: Chouinard, interview, 2024.

92 *"When you value families"*: Dean Carter, in discussion with the author, 2023.

93 *"We would be running around"*: Mary Ellen Smith, in discussion with the author, 2023.

95 *"We knew we were dead"*: Greg Dalton, "Yvon Chouinard; Founding Patagonia and Living Simply," *Climate One* podcast, October 28, 2016, https://www.climateone.org/audio/yvon-Chouinard-founding-patagonia-and-living-simply.

# NOTES

96 *"Fuck these mountains"*: Rick Ridgeway, *Life Lived Wild* (Patagonia Press, 2021), 82.

96 *"I've had a lot of close calls"*: Dalton, "Yvon Chouinard."

97 *"When I came out of it"*: Craig Vetter, "He's Not Worthy," *Outside*, January 1997, https://www.outsideonline.com/outdoor-adventure/hes-not-worthy/.

97 *"There are a million holes"*: Vetter, "He's Not Worthy."

98 *"I don't want to see it"*: Chouinard, interview, 2024.

101 *"If you wear the same underwear"*: Trust for Public Land, "A Conversation with Yvon Chouinard—Land & People," November 1, 2001, https://www.tpl.org /resource/conversation-yvon-Chouinard-landpeople.

101 *"I can't make it through"*: Smith, interview.

103 *"We didn't need to hedge"*: Henry Barber, in discussion with the author, 2023.

103 *"For many, many years"*: Hilary Greenbaum and Dana Rubinstein, "The Evolution of Fleece, from Scratchy to Snuggie," *New York Times*, November 25, 2011, https://www.nytimes.com/2011/11/27/magazine/fleece-scratchy-to-snuggie.html.

## CHAPTER 5: WINNING BACK THE WILD

106 *"It is time to stop waffling"*: Philip Shabecoff, "Global Warming Has Begun, Expert Tells Senate," *New York Times*, June 24, 1988, https://www.nytimes.com /1988/06/24/us/global-warming-has-begun-expert-tells-senate.html.

107 *"People realized that if you"*: Paul Tebbel, in discussion with the author, 2023.

111 *"Our politicians are running"*: Joanna M. Miller, "Campus Faces Opposition Despite CSU's Warning," *Los Angeles Times*, December 28, 1989, https://www .latimes.com/archives/la-xpm-1989-12-28-ve-1342-story.html.

112 *"Everything we make pollutes"*: "Reality Check," Patagonia catalog, Spring 1991.

113 *"We know this is heresy"*: Connie Koenenn, "Esprit Surprises Industry with 'Don't-Buy-It' Ad," *Tampa Bay Times*, October 17, 2005, https://www.tampabay .com/archive/1990/07/02/esprit-surprises-industry-with-don-t-buy-it-ad/.

114 *"What we were doing"*: Kevin Sweeney, in discussion with the author, 2023.

115 *"We are deepening a lifestyle"*: Lost Arrow Corporation, Business Update, November 1990.

116 *"We were setting customers up"*: Stanley, interview.

117 *"No equipment failed"*: Denise Hamilton, "Suits Force Mountain Gear Firm to File for Bankruptcy," *Los Angeles Times*, May 11, 1989, https://www.latimes .com/archives/la-xpm-1989-05-11-we-3605-story.html.

117 *"I've taken a lot of pride"*: Hamilton, "Suits Force Mountain Gear Firm to File for Bankruptcy."

118 *"I sold the climbing company"*: Chouinard, interview, 2023.

# NOTES

118 *"We thought we were doing them"*: Malinda Chouinard, in discussion with the author, 2023.

120 *"It wasn't a great time"*: Email from Malinda Chouinard, 2024.

121 *"By the mid-1980s"*: Franklin, *A Wild Idea*, 103.

121 *"I found myself caught"*: Michael O'Donnell, "Review: 'A Wild Idea' and the Conservationism of Douglas Tompkins," *The Atlantic*, August 5, 2021, https://www.theatlantic.com/magazine/archive/2021/09/douglas-tompkins -wild-idea-patagonia/619495/.

122 *"I left that world of making stuff"*: Jason Mark, "The Fashion Executives Who Saved a Patagonian Paradise," *Sierra*, September 4, 2019, https://www .sierraclub.org/sierra/2019-5-september-october/feature/fashion-executives -who-saved-patagonian-paradise-doug-kris-tompkins.

122 *"What are you going to do"*: Franklin, *A Wild Idea*, 112.

124 *"some sort of demented real estate guy"*: Mark, "The Fashion Executives Who Saved a Patagonian Paradise."

124 *"You never know"*: Chris Malloy, director, *180° South*, 2010.

125 *"Chouinard's not financially driven"*: Craig Vetter, "He's Not Worthy."

125 *"There have been a few times"*: Chouinard, *Some Stories*, 130.

126 *"We really had a bond"*: Barber, interview.

126 *"There was a sense"*: Libby Ellis, in discussion with the author, 2023.

126 *"Things get idealized"*: Lynda Grose, in discussion with the author, 2023.

126 *"Yvon was always very clear"*: Kulczycki, interview.

127 *"Yvon has no respect"*: Vetter, "He's Not Worthy."

127 *"You kept track of how"*: Randy Harward, in discussion with the author, 2023.

128 *"Is that a quality coffee bean?"*: Harward, interview.

130 *"We're sleazeballs"*: Harward, interview.

130 *"I didn't know anything"*: Jason Blevins, "Pat O'Donnell, the 63-year-old CEO of Aspen Skiing Co," *Denver Post*, December 18, 2001.

### CHAPTER 6: A CRITICAL TIME

133 *"Our bottom-line reason"*: Chouinard, *Let My People Go Surfing*.

134 *"If I did sell the company"*: Chouinard, interview, 2024.

134 *"We aren't going to sell"*: Chouinard, interview, 2022.

134 *"I really believe this is a movement"*: Steinbreder, "He's in His Element in the Elements."

137 *"That was rough"*: Vetter, "He's Not Worthy."

137 *"There's one thing I know"*: Alison May, in discussion with the author, 2023.

138 *"Whatever you do"*: McDivitt Tompkins, interview.

139  *"a wake-up call"*: Dalton, "Yvon Chouinard."

140  *"We were just going for growth"*: Guy Raz, "Patagonia: Yvon Chouinard," December 11, 2016, *How I Built This* podcast, https://podcasts.apple.com/us/podcast/patagonia-yvon-Chouinard/id1150510297?i=1000378841890.

141  *"Can a three-star French restaurant"*: Yvon Chouinard, "The Next Hundred Years," 1995, https://thedesignofprosperity.se/2009/press/Chouinard/TheNext100Years-YvonChouinard-Patagonia-Inc.pdf.

141  *"There's two kinds of growth"*: Raz, "Patagonia: Yvon Chouinard."

142  *"I'm building this very successful"*: Christine Lagorio-Chafkin, "He's Spent Over 40 Years at Patagonia. Here Are His Tips for Growing a Company and a Social Mission at the Same Time," *Inc.*, May 23, 2024, https://www.inc.com/christine-lagorio/hes-spent-more-than-40-years-at-patagonia-here-are-his-tips-for-growing-a-company-and-social-mission-at-the-same-time.html.

143  *"Yvon Chouinard touts his company"*: Alex Bhattacharji, "Peak Patagonia: The Story Behind the Mic Drop Heard Round the World," *Inc.*, December 5, 2022, https://www.inc.com/magazine/202212/alex-bhattacharji/patagonia-story-behind-mic-drop-heard-round-world.html.

145  *"People would come back"*: Stanley, interview.

146  *"I'll get out of the sportswear business"*: Stanley, interview.

146  *"When we got Yvon out there"*: Jill Dumain, in discussion with the author, 2023.

148  *"If we continue to make clothes"*: Patagonia Archives, Environmental activism timeline wall, 2023.

148  *"We have realized for years"*: "Patagonia to Switch to Organic Cotton," Patagonia news release, Fall 1995.

149  *"I was prepared to lose"*: Dave Olsen, in discussion with the author, 2022.

150  *"It let a lot of companies"*: Dumain, interview, 2023

150  *"I started going deeper"*: Chouinard, interview, 2022.

150  *"Why would I want to do that?"*: Tebbel, interview.

152  *"We did research to try"*: Olsen, interview.

154  *"We've spent the last ten"*: Sweeney, interview.

### CHAPTER 7: LEAPS OF FAITH

156  *"Absolutely not"*: McDivitt Tompkins, interview.

157  *"It really hurt my feelings"*: May, interview.

158  *"Woman or man wanted"*: "Patagonia Advertises for New Chief Executive," *Los Angeles Times*, January 30, 1996, https://www.latimes.com/archives/la-xpm-1996-01-30-fi-30240-story.html.

# NOTES

159  *"I didn't know how to spell"*: Chipper Bro Bell, in discussion with the author, 2023.

161  *"Wake this company up"*: Olsen, interview.

165  *"I think I have the best workers"*: Bell, interview.

169  *"Those are the people"*: John Sterling, in discussion with the author, 2023.

169  *"You're going to get terrible press"*: Tebbel, interview.

171  *"They more than doubled"*: Dani Burlison, "Headwaters Forest Reserve and the Battle That Saved It," *Earth Island Journal*, February 27, 2019, https://www.earthisland.org/journal/index.php/articles/entry/headwaters-forest-reserve-humboldt-california/.

172  *"As we went deeper"*: Tebbel, interview.

173  *"I'd feel a lot more comfortable"*: Conference on Corporate Citizenship Panel, May 16, 1996, Clinton Archives, https://clinton.presidentiallibraries.us/files/original/5dc57aaba10cbe09f947858584764d33.pdf.

174  *"He had lost the cap"*: Chouinard, *Some Stories*, 265.

175  *"There seems to be a disconnect"*: Chouinard, *Some Stories*, 413.

175  *"I thought, 'Humane letters?'"*: Vetter, "He's Not Worthy."

178  *"Not everyone at the company"*: Carter, interview.

179  *"If you make clothes"*: James Stout, "Outdoor Brands Make Big Bucks Selling Gear for War—But Can't Always Control Who Uses It," *Backpacker*, March 22, 2021, https://www.backpacker.com/stories/issues/outdoor-brands-make-big-bucks-selling-gear-for-war-but-cant-always-control-who-uses-it/.

179  *"Bras don't kill people"*: Chouinard, interview, 2024.

179  *"He always seemed very slick"*: Elissa Foster, in discussion with the author, 2023.

179  *"Michael Crooke was the only one"*: Chouinard, interview, 2024.

180  *"We've rushed through a lot"*: Forest Reinhardt, "Patagonia," Harvard Business School case study, October 19, 2010.

180  *"Once Kris stepped down"*: Kulczycki, interview.

## CHAPTER 8: LEADERSHIP

182  *"I've got to find $2.5 million"*: McDivitt Tompkins, interview.

183  *"In Latin America"*: Jimmy Chin and Elizabeth Chai Vasarhelyi, directors, *Wild Life*, Little Monster Films/National Geographic Documentary Films, 2023.

183  *"It was way beyond"*: Rod Noriega, in discussion with the author, 2024.

183  *"I see God as nature"*: "Doug Tompkins," Fundación Rewilding Chile, Facebook, December 8, 2024, https://www.facebook.com/watch/?v=887416780254945.

184  *"He was on my ass"*: Chouinard, interview, 2022.

# NOTES

187 *"For many of them"*: Kate Williams, in discussion with the author, 2024.

188 *"We had some real reputational"*: John Fleming, in discussion with the author, 2024.

189 *"Do you mean sustaining"*: Jib Ellison, in discussion with the author, 2024.

190 *"I saw a company utilize"*: Lee Scott, "Twenty-First Century Leadership," Walmart, October 23, 2005, https://corporate.walmart.com/news/2005/10/23/twenty-first-century-leadership.

194 *"There was no emergency"*: Malinda Chouinard, interview.

194 *"We wanted to become"*: Marc Gunther, "Behind the Scenes at the Sustainable Apparel Coalition," *Trellis*, July 26, 2012, https://trellis.net/article/behind-scenes-sustainable-apparel-coalition/.

194 *"Hey dudes, you don't"*: Ridgeway, interview.

197 *"Walmart did a little bit"*: Chouinard, interview, 2024.

198 *"There's great inherent danger"*: Casey Sheahan, in discussion with the author, 2024.

199 *"Nobody ever got fired"*: Stanley, interview.

200 *"The customer has a right"*: Sheahan, interview.

201 *"a form of indentured servitude"*: Corey Simpson, "Patagonia and Human Trafficking," Patagoniaworks.com, June 3, 2015, https://www.patagoniaworks.com/press/2015/6/3/patagonia-and-human-trafficking.

202 *"It was such a heavy moment"*: Matt Dwyer, in discussion with the author, 2024.

203 *"What would you do"*: Sheahan, interview.

207 *"What was the real intention?"*: Grose, interview.


## CHAPTER 9: FIGHTS

210 *"This is shit"*: McDivitt Tompkins, interview.

211 *"Most people see nature"*: Ridgeway, *Life Lived Wild*, 373.

212 *"I was a little shocked"*: Chouinard, *Some Stories*, 336.

213 *"We ran into a perfect trap"*: Chouinard, *Some Stories*, 336.

214 *"The wind is taking us"*: Ridgeway, *Life Lived Wild*, 390.

216 *"We have Weston"*: Ridgeway, *Life Lived Wild*, 395.

216 *"We were always looking"*: Chouinard, *Some Stories*, 336.

217 *"We just weren't prepared"*: Daniel Duane, "Rebel with a Cause: Yvon Chouinard on the Passing of His Lifelong Friend, Doug Tompkins," *Men's Journal*, December 4, 2017, https://www.mensjournal.com/adventure/rebel-with-a-cause-yvon-Chouinard-on-the-passing-of-his-lifelong-friend-doug-tompkins-20160106.

217 *"I don't think that inheritances"*: Michael Hiltzik, "A San Francisco Socialite Sues for a Share of the Esprit Fortune Her Conservationist Father Left to Char-

# NOTES

ity," *Los Angeles Times*, October 27, 2017, https://www.latimes.com/business
/hiltzik/la-fi-hiltzik-tompkins-will-20171027-story.html.

217 *"We are all very hardworking"*: Phil Matier and Andy Ross, "Daughter Seeks
Millions from Esprit Co-Founder," *San Francisco Chronicle*, October 30, 2017,
https://www.sfchronicle.com/bayarea/matier-ross/article/Daughter-seeks
-millions-from-Esprit-co-founder-12314126.php#photo-10406686.

219 *"good not only for Chile"*: Pascale Bonnefoy, "With 10 Million Acres in Patagonia, a National Park System Is Born," *New York Times*, February 19, 2018,
https://www.nytimes.com/2018/02/19/world/americas/patagonia-national
-park-chile.html.

219 *"There is something about"*: Bonnefoy, "With 10 Million Acres in Patagonia, a
National Park System Is Born."

221 *"You can't buy advertising"*: Abe Streep, "Patagonia's Big Business of #Re-
sist," *Outside Online*, July 24, 2017, https://www.outsideonline.com/outdoor
-adventure/environment/big-business-resist/.

224 *"The whole outdoor industry"*: Streep, "Patagonia's Big Business of #Resist."

224 *"Some people think"*: Julie Turkewitz, "Trump Slashes Size of Bears Ears and
Grand Staircase Monuments," *New York Times*, December 4, 2017, https://www
.nytimes.com/2017/12/04/us/trump-bears-ears.html.

226 *"There was ash falling"*: David Gelles, "Patagonia v. Trump," *New York Times*,
May 5, 2018, https://www.nytimes.com/2018/05/05/business/patagonia-trump
-bears-ears.html.

227 *"I was skeptical"*: Stanley, interview.

227 *"People say, 'Oh, that's'"*: Chouinard, interview, 2022.

228 *"We were one of the first"*: Sapna Maheshwari, "Patagonia, Quick to Close,
Could Be Last to Reopen," *New York Times*, May 12, 2020, https://www.nytimes
.com/2020/05/12/business/patagonia-reopening-coronavirus.html.

229 *"We join with those"*: "Patagonia Statement on Social Injustice," Patagonia.com,
May 31, 2020, https://www.patagoniaworks.com/press/2020/5/31/patagonia
-statement-on-social-injustice.

230 *"I didn't hear much"*: Maxine Wally, "Green Girl Leah on Why Environmentalists Must Speak Up for Black Lives Matter," *W Magazine*, July 22, 2020,
https://www.wmagazine.com/culture/green-girl-leah-thomas-intersectional
-environmentalism-the-people-interview.

230 *"I don't swim"*: Carter, interview.

231 *"The few words we"*: "Our Acknowledgment," Patagonia.com, September 4, 2020,
https://www.patagonia.com/stories/our-acknowledgment/story-91580.html.

231 *"That was a mutual decision"*: David Gelles, "Rose Marcario, the Former C.E.O.
of Patagonia, Retreats to the Rainforest," *New York Times*, February 18, 2021,

https://www.nytimes.com/2021/02/18/business/rose-marcario-patagonia
-corner-office.html.

233 *"These are great"*: Jonathan Evans, "The Full Story Behind Patagonia's 'Vote the Assholes Out' Tags," *Esquire*, September 19, 2020, https://www.esquire.com /style/mens-fashion/a34078539/patagonia-vote-the-assholes-out-shorts-tag -meaning/.

233 *"Companies need to pay"*: Ryan Gellert, "Corporate America: Stop Hiding Behind the Chamber of Commerce and Business Roundtable," LinkedIn, November 4, 2021, https://www.linkedin.com/pulse/corporate-america-stop-hiding -behind-chamber-commerce-ryan-gellert.

236 *"We will continue to use"*: Andrew Blake, "Patagonia Severs Ties with Wyoming Ski Resort After Its Owner Hosted a Freedom Caucus Fundraiser," *Washington Times*, August 21, 2021, https://www.washingtontimes.com/news/2021/aug /21/patagonia-boycotts-wyoming-ski-resort-after-co-own/.

## CHAPTER 10: GIVING IT ALL AWAY

237 *"It really, really pissed"*: Chouinard, interview, 2022.

237 *"Get me off that list"*: Carter, interview.

238 *"I swear to God"*: Ryan Gellert, in discussion with the author, 2022.

238 *"Well, we're going to have"*: Charles Conn, in discussion with the author, 2022.

241 *"My kids didn't want"*: Bhattacharji, "Peak Patagonia: The Story Behind the Mic Drop Heard Round the World."

242 *"We took a $6 billion"*: Malinda Chouinard, interview.

242 *"I don't respect"*: Chouinard, interview, 2022.

243 *"How and when"*: Hilary Dessouky, in discussion with the author, 2022.

245 *"It's hard to find"*: Dan Mosley, in discussion with the author, 2022.

246 *"Patagonia has every incentive"*: Dessouky, interview.

247 *"Generational succession is a risky"*: Email from Fletcher Chouinard, 2022.

247 *"The climate and biodiversity"*: Email from Claire Chouinard, 2022.

248 *"Yeah, this feels good"*: Bhattacharji, "Peak Patagonia: The Story Behind the Mic Drop Heard Round the World."

248 *"That was a day"*: Gellert, interview.

250 *"By turning over the ownership"*: Video of internal event, Patagonia, 2022.

251 *"What Doug did was perfect"*: McDivitt Tompkins, interview.

251 *"Patagonia's $3 billion corporate"*: Scott Nover, "Patagonia's $3 Billion Corporate Gift Is Also a Convenient Way to Avoid Taxes," Quartz, September 16, 2022, https://qz.com/patagonia-s-3-billion-corporate-gift-is-also-a-conveni -1849543678.

252 *"Patagonia's founder rejects"*: Alicia Adamczyk, "Patagonia's Founder Rejects His Billionaire Status, But He's Still Saving $700 Million in Taxes with a Legal Loophole," *Fortune*, September 16, 2022, https://fortune.com/2022/09/16/patagonia-founder-legal-tax-loophole/.

252 *"It's a massive tax avoidance"*: Jesse Eisinger, Twitter, September 15, 2022, https://x.com/eisingerj/status/1570382234514767872.

252 *"There was a meaningful cost"*: David Gelles, "Patagonia Founder Gives Away the Company to Fight Climate Change," *New York Times*, September 14, 2022, https://www.nytimes.com/2022/09/14/climate/patagonia-climate-philanthropy-Chouinard.html.

254 *"Now we can die"*: Malinda Chouinard, interview.

257 *"It is unacceptable that"*: Thomas Catenacci, "Major Outdoor Clothing Company Quietly Operating Liberal Dark Money Group Hit with FEC Complaint," Fox Business, February 21, 2024, https://www.foxbusiness.com/politics/major-outdoor-clothing-company-quietly-operating-liberal-dark-money-group-hit-fec-complaint.

258 *"It's a motivator"*: John Sterling, in discussion with the author, 2023.

258 *"I chose God"*: David Green, "My Decision to Give Away Ownership of Hobby Lobby: I Chose God," Fox News, October 20, 2022, https://www.foxnews.com/opinion/decision-to-give-away-ownership-hobby-lobby-chose-god.

259 *"fund Christianity"*: Laura Carrione, "Hobby Lobby Founder Explains Decision to 'Give Away Ownership' of Company: 'Joy in Giving What We Have,'" Fox Business, November 14, 2022, https://www.foxbusiness.com/retail/hobby-lobby-founder-explains-decision-give-away-ownership-company-joy-giving.

259 *"We all knew this wasn't"*: Ridgeway, interview.

259 *"Imagine if all the rich people"*: Malinda Chouinard, interview.

259 *"Let's call it a big"*: Stephanie Mehta, "Why Is the Patagonia Sale a Big Deal? Jim Collins, Author of 'Good to Great,' Weighs In," *Fast Company*, October 7, 2022, https://www.fastcompany.com/90793822/why-is-the-patagonia-sale-a-big-deal-jim-collins-author-of-good-to-great-weighs-in.

### CHAPTER 11: THE NEXT 50 YEARS

266 *"The money was not"*: Juan José Córdova, in discussion with the author, 2024.

267 *"Patagonia is not a sustainable company"*: Haver Currin, "Yvon Chouinard on Why He Gave Away Patagonia to Save the Planet."

268 *"Every advancement in this"*: Yvon Chouinard, "A Letter from Our Founder," 1% for the Planet, November 14, 2024, https://www.onepercentfortheplanet.org/stories/a-letter-from-our-founder.

# NOTES

269 *"The mission of Patagonia"*: Paul Lightfoot, in discussion with the author, 2023.

270 *"We need a revolution"*: Chouinard, interview, 2024.

273 *"I could see the food business"*: Chouinard, interview, 2023.

275 *"We've got managers"*: Chouinard, interview, 2024.

278 *"I feel like I could die"*: Chouinard, interview, 2022.

# INDEX

ABC, 95, 108

*ABC's Wide World of Sports*, 95

acrylic fabric, 70, 71

advertising, 205–7. *See also* marketing

Afghanistan, US invasion of, 177

A-Frame Farm, 269

Africa, 96

Agnew, Davey, 66

agriculture, regenerative, 269–70, 273

Alabama, 80

Alaska, 94

Albania, 256

Albuquerque, New Mexico, 31

Alcoa (manufacturer), 27

Alps, 44

Alvarez-Roos, Lorenzo, 212–16

Amazon, 236, 263

*American Alpine Journal*, 39

Americans for Public Trust, 257

Ancient Forest International, 119

Andes, 8–9, 11, 45–46, 49, 138–39, 212–16, 261. *See also specific locations*

Androscoggin River, 13

animal welfare standards, 201–2

Antarctica, 110

"anthropause," 228–29

antigrowth issues, 111

anti-odor technologies, 153

Antiquities Act of 1906, 225

apparel. *See* clothing

Apple, 212, 236

Araucaria (tree), 119

Arc'teryx, 262

Argentina, 7, 8, 45–46, 48–49, 182, 210, 212–16, 218, 261, 277. *See also specific locations*

Patagonia management retreat in, 155–56

Arkansas, 191

Army Rangers, 177

Aslan (brewery), 272

Atlantic Philanthropies, 251

Audubon Society, 107

auto mechanics, 19–20

axes, 92, 118. *See also* ice axes ("piolets")

ice axes ("piolets"), 44–45, 175–76

pickaxes, 92

Axios, 236

Bachelet, Michelle, 219

backpacks, 67

Baez, Joan, 41

Baggies (shorts), 98, 200

Barber, Henry, 80, 103, 125, 126

Bariloche, Argentina, 48–49, 273–74, 277–78

barley, 269, 270

Baumgartner, Jo Ann, 144–45

B Corp movement, 6, 207–9

BDT, 245

Bears Ears National Monument, 222–24, 225–27

# INDEX

Beat generation, 40, 41
the Beatles, 43
Beckey, Fred, 30
beer, 272
Bell, Chipper Bro, 159–60, 230
Ben & Jerry's, 207, 243
benefit corporations, 208–9
Bentonville, Arkansas, 191–93, 225
Berkeley, California, 41
Berry Amendment (Department of Defense
    rule), 178
Bezos, Jeff, 251
Bhutan, 1
Biden administration, 234, 267
Bill & Melinda Gates Foundation, 251
B Lab founders, 208
Black Diamond, 82, 119, 164, 223, 262
Black Friday, 205, 206–7
    2016, 220–22
Black Lives Matter movement, 229–31
Black Saturday, 106
blacksmithing, 25–28, 31, 33, 82
Black Voters Matter Fund, 257
"Black Wednesday" (1991 Patagonia financial
    crisis), 135–38, 139, 203, 207
Bloomberg, Michael, 258, 259
Bloomberg Philanthropies, 258
Bloomingdale's, 68
Blue Ribbon Flies, 185
bluesign (independent supply chain auditor), 208
Blu Skye (sustainability consultancy), 187
Boeing, 4, 212
Bogner, 263
bolts (rock climbing), 54
Bondurant, Rob, 103
Bossier, Tex, 80
Boston, Massachusetts, retail store in, 143–44
boxer briefs, 178
#BoycottPatagonia, 226
Boyles, Edgar, 212
Boyles, Weston, 212–16
Brailsford, John, 54
branding, 98–104
breweries, 272
British free climbing, 54
Buckley, Peter, 124
Buell, Susie Tompkins (née Russell), 41, 42, 46,
    47, 49, 77, 122, 218

Buffett, Warren, 185, 245, 251
Bugaboos, 30
Buhl, Hermann, 22
Build Back Better, 234
bunting (synthetic pile), 98, 102, 103
Burbank, California, 15–16, 25, 36
business, as force for good, 8
business journalism, 4–5, 7–8
Business Roundtable, 234
Bussiere, Bill, 125, 130, 137, 143
buttons, made from tagua nuts, 115–16
buy-back program, 204–6

Cade, Tom, 18, 19
Calamai family, 153
California, 31. See also specific locations
    benefit corporations in, 208–9
    maternity leave and, 87
    overdevelopment in, 97
    Proposition 9: Clean Energy Act, 62
    whitewater kayaking in, 92–93
California State University, plan for new
    campus in Ventura, 110–11
California Supreme Court, 64
Cameron, Birgit, 270–71
Campbell, Joseph, *The Hero with a Thousand
    Faces*, 50
Canada, 30, 175
Canada Goose, 263
Canadian Rockies, 30
Cañi mountains, 119
Cañi Sanctuary, 119–225
Capelli, Mark, 63–64, 186
Capilene (textile), 101, 102, 103, 176, 256
capitalism, 7, 134, 212
carabiners, 27–28, 29, 31, 36, 41, 51, 66, 71, 118
carcinogens, 153
Carson, Rachel, *Silent Spring*, 57
Carter, Dean, 92, 178, 230, 231
Cascale (Sustainable Apparel Coalition), 196–97
Casitas Municipal Water District, 64
Cassady, Neal, 40
catalogs, 82–86, 92, 111, 120
Catholic Church, 182
Center for American Progress Fund, 257
CERN, 197
Cerro Fitz Roy, 45–52, 67, 82, 97–98, 273
Chacabuco Valley, Chile, 181–84, 211, 241

# INDEX

Chamber of Commerce, 234
Chamonix, France, 44
  Patagonia retail store in, 135
charitable giving, 107–11
Chengdu, China, 95–96
Chico Hot Springs resort, 168
childcare, 86–92
childcare center at Patagonia, 87–92, 115, 173, 277
Chile, 1, 7, 46–48, 119, 156, 181–84, 210, 212–16, 218–19, 241, 277. *See also specific locations*
China, 1, 95, 200, 266
Chincha, Peru, 264
Chinese Dragon Claw Millet, 270
chocks, 53–54, 64, 66
Chouinard, Doris, 13
Chouinard, Gerald (Jeff, brother), 13, 14, 24, 27, 43–44, 80
Chouinard, Gerard Lorenzo (father), 12–13, 25
Chouinard, Rachael, 13
Chouinard, Yvonne, 13
Chouinard, Celanire, 12
Chouinard, Claire, 60–61, 174, 185, 239, 240, 241, 247, 249
Chouinard, Fletcher, 60, 87, 185, 239, 240, 241, 247, 249
Chouinard, Jacques, 12–13
Chouinard, Malinda. *See* Pennoyer, Ellen Malinda
Chouinard, Yvonne, 14, 15, 25
Chouinard, Yvon Vincent, 11–35, 36, 83, 179, 202, 237
  adventures of, 1–2, 5, 13, 32, 92, 212–16, 244 (*see also specific locations*)
  announces Patagonia Purpose Trust, 249–54
  article in *American Alpine Journal*, 39
  athleticism of, 17
  auto mechanics and, 19–20
  in avalanche, 95–96
  in Bariloche, Argentina, 277–78
  Bears Ears National Monument and, 222–24, 225–27
  becomes businessman, 28, 40–45
  Bell and, 158–59
  birth of, 11–12, 13
  birth of his children, 60–61
  Black Friday 2016 and, 221
  blacksmithing and, 25–28, 82

"Black Wednesday" and, 136, 137–38
Cañi Sanctuary and, 119–25
celebrates 85th birthday, 261
Cerro Fitz Roy trip and, 45–52
Chacabuco Valley, Chile, and, 181–82, 183, 211, 241
childhood of, 13–16
chooses Patagonia name, 67
clarity about Patagonia's mission, 133–34
climbing and, 13, 37–39, 92, 94–96, 103–4, 161, 174
cofounds 1% for the Planet, 186–87
commitment to his values, 236
considers expanding into apparel, 51
considers selling Patagonia, 185
Corporate Citizen Conference and, 173–75
COVID-19 pandemic and, 228–29
craftsmanship and, 277
creative tension and, 164
creativity of, 29
Crooke and, 177, 180
declines B Lab founders' request, 208
depressed after avalanche in Himalayas, 96
desire to sell less, 112–13
desire to stay involved with Patagonia, 240
dirtbag roots of, 168–69
discharged from the army, 36
disdain for conventional food system, 268
diving, 16, 159–60
divorces Lamb, 36
dreams of becoming a fur trapper, 14
education of, 15, 16, 24, 33
elusive goal of sustainability and, 267
exit strategy and, 254–60
extreme sports and, 92
falconry and, 17–18
first brush with death, 22–23
fishing and, 7–9, 92, 261–62
as founder, 2
gifts and limitations of, 17, 19
growing ambitions of, 27–28
hiking and, 20
holding out hope for humanity, 275–76
ice climbing, 92
injuries of, 50, 92–93, 174
innovative designs by, 28–29
irked by sales reps' commissions, 125–26
irreverence of, 174–75

297

# INDEX

Chouinard, Yvon Vincent (*cont.*)
    kayaking and, 1, 97, 212–16
    at Lago General Carrera retreat, 212–16
    at Las Pampas Lodge, 261–63, 273
    lawsuits against Chouinard Equipment and,
        117–18
    layoffs and, 137, 138–43
    legacy of, 239–40, 243, 260, 277–78
    *Let My People Go Surfing*, 143
    library of, 22
    local politics and, 62–63
    maintains control of Patagonia, 2–3
    makes change to benefit corporation, 208–9
    makes his own gear, 24–29
    management style of, 5, 92–98, 165
    Marcario's exit and, 231–32
    marries Lamb, 32
    marries Pennoyer, 60
    in military, 32–35, 179
    mission to give everything away, 237–60
    "Modern Yosemite Climbing" (essay), 39–40
    money and, 21–22, 164, 165
    as mountaineer aid, 179
    moves company to Ventura, California, 42
    Patagonia National Park and, 181–82, 183, 210
    pessimism of, 5, 141–42, 211, 274
    plans for future of Patagonia, 240–49
    quality standards and, 128, 275–76
    rappelling and, 18–19
    "Reality Check" (essay), 111–13, 114, 115
    receives honorary degree from Yale, 175
    regrets selling Chouinard Equipment, 164
    relinquishes ownership of Patagonia, 3–5
    rock climbing and, 1–2, 18–20, 22–23, 28,
        33, 92
    second home in Moose, Wyoming, 60–61,
        106, 130, 185, 235, 248
    sells Chouinard Equipment to employees,
        118–19
    sense of mortality and, 96–97, 211
    settles on purpose trust, 245–49
    spars with Trump, 226
    speech at Walmart, 191–93
    spontaneity of, 103–4
    surfing and, 1, 27, 83, 263
    taxes and, 251–53
    Tompkins and, 33–35, 123, 124–25, 133,
        157, 184, 210–11, 212–17

Tools conference and, 168–69
    Utah boycott and, 223–24
    vision of corporate responsibility, 111–17
    wealth of, 2–3
    "A word . . ." (essay), 56–57, 111
    working after high school, 23–24
    worldview of, 39, 51–52, 56–57
    Zen Buddhism and, 4
Chouinard Equipment for Alpinists, 42–45, 46,
        47, 65–71, 164. *See also specific products*
    becomes Black Diamond, 119
    catalog of, 55–56, 111
    childcare at, 86–92
    "clean climbing" ethos and, 55–58
    environmental activism and, 62
    establishes permanent home base, 60
    expansion of, 44–45, 58
    files for Chapter 11 bankruptcy protection, 118
    founding of, 2
    "hardware" and "software" categories, 66
    incorporated into new entity, 58
    insurance premiums and, 118
    largest maker of climbing gear in US by
        1970, 52
    lawsuits against, 117–19
    overhauled to avoid harming environment, 54
    Pentagon and, 176
    reputation of, 67
    rethinking the workday, 62
    touchmark for, 82
    workforce of, 43–44
Chouinard family, 244. *See also specific family
        members*
    cohesion of, 217, 218
    family history, 12–13
    moves to California, 15
    taxes and, 251–53
Christensen, Clay, 102
Christian Action Council, 110
City Lights (bookstore), 40
Civilian Conservation Corps, 21
civil rights, 186
clear-cutting, 170
climate change, 11–12, 96–97, 267
climbing, 92, 94–96, 103–4, 161, 174. *See also*
        ice climbing; rock climbing
    "clean climbing" ethos, 55–58
    growing popularity of, 111

# INDEX

climbing equipment, 73, 80. *See also specific products*
Clinton, Bill, 172, 173–75
Clinton, Hillary, 222
Clogwyn du'r Arddu, 53–54
clothing, 51, 65–71, 82–86. *See also specific products*
marketing of, 82–86
Club of Rome, *The Limits to Growth*, 206
CNN, 174, 226
coalition building, 109–10, 111, 277
Coca-Cola, 193
Collins, Jim, 259–60
Colombia, 48
Columbia (brand), 263
Common Threads, 204, 205–6
competitors, 149–50, 161–62, 262–63. *See also specific competitors*
Condor Club, 40
Conn, Charles, 238, 241–49
Conservation Alliance, 6, 109–10
conservation efforts, 30, 34, 57, 61, 107–11, 119–25, 123, 181–84, 187–90, 217, 276. *See also specific projects and locations*
Conservation International, 115, 187–88
consistency, 128
consumerism, 113, 120–21, 142, 205–6
consumers
education of, 266
financial crisis of 2008 and, 203
Córdova, Juan José, 264–66
corduroy pants, 65
Corporate Citizen Conference, 173–75
corporate responsibility, 111–17
corporate tax cuts, 233–34
Costa Rica, 48
Costco, 236
Cotopaxi, 263
cotton, 65, 112, 115
organic, 143–50, 153, 193, 204, 265–66
toxicity of nonorganic, 143–45
treated with formaldehyde, 143–44
COVID-19 pandemic, 228–32, 233, 237, 274
Coyhaique Regional Hospital, 215
craftsmanship, 68, 277
crampons, 92
Cravath, Swaine & Moore, 245
credit, securing, 68–69

Crooke, Michael, 177–78, 179–80, 198
Crooked Thumb, 23
Curtis, Greg, 238, 241–49, 255, 257
customers, 277
contributions to catalog, 85–86
education of, 200
encouraging to buy less, 205–6
customer service, 204

Darien Gap, 48
Darwin, Charles, 46
Dawson, Minnesota, 268–69
Day, Dale, 80
DDT (insecticide), 19, 57
debt bondage, 200–201
deep ecology, 121–22
Delta Force, 177
Democrats, 236, 256–57
Denali, 94
Denver, Colorado, 223
Deschutes Brewery, 273
Dessouky, Hilary, 238, 241–49
Disney, 212
"Do Boys," 92–93, 187, 212–16
"Don't Buy This Jacket" ad, 114, 205, 206–7, 220
Dorworth, Dick, 41, 47, 48, 49, 51
Douro River, 151
drugs, 94
Duke, Mike, 197
Dumain, Jill, 146, 147, 148, 149, 150
Dunbar, Robin, 127, 135
Duty Free Shoppers Group, 251
Dwyer, Matt, 202
Dyersburg Fabrics, 152
dyes, 146–47, 150, 151
dyeing process, 199
recycled plastic and, 153

Earth First! 123, 168, 172
Earthjustice, 256
Eastern Europe, 11
Eastern Mountain Sports, 67
Eco-index, 196
Ecuador, 48
Einstein, Albert, 55
Eisinger, Jesse, 252
El Capitan, 37–39, 111
elevation, 74

# INDEX

Ellis, Libby, 126
Ellison, Jib, 187–90, 195, 212–16
El Paso, Texas, 177–78
Emerson, Ralph Waldo, 22
emissions, 267
employees, 165, 277
employee stock ownership plans (ESOPs),
    158, 166
employment standards, 201, 277
*The Endless Summer* (documentary), 42, 46
environmental activism, 3–4, 34–35, 62,
    105–31, 134, 141–42, 168–69, 222–27,
    236, 246–60, 267–68, 274, 276, 277. *See
    also specific projects and locations*
    environmental grants, 64, 138
    environmental responsibility, 111–17
    Patagonia on receiving end of, 202
Environmental Defense Fund, 107
environmental destruction, 96–97
environmentalism, 22, 51–58. *See also*
    environmental activism
Esprit, 34, 49, 78, 79, 113, 114, 115, 121, 122,
    155, 158, 218
extreme sports, 92

fabrics. *See also specific fabrics and materials*
    development of new, 176
    environmental analysis of, 150–54
    life-cycle assessments of, 115
factories, 198–202, 264–66. *See also*
    manufacturing; supply chains
fair labor standards, 173
falconry, 17–18
Fan Fire, 105
FBI (Federal Bureau of Investigation), 123
Federal Emergency Management Agency
    (FEMA), 190, 193
Feeney, Chuck, 251
Ferlinghetti, Lawrence, 40
fertilizers, 112
Feuerstein, Aaron, 99–100
Feuerstein, Henry, 98–99
financial crisis of 2008, 203–9
fishing, 7, 8–9, 21–22, 92, 261–62
FitzRoy, Robert, 46
Fjällräven, 263
fleece, 99–100, 152, 200, 266
Fleming, John, 189–90, 196

Flickr, 187
Floyd, George, murder of, 229–31
"The Flying Baby" (photograph), 85–86
Foamback jacket, 69
food production, sustainable, 268–73
Footprint Chronicles, 199
*Forbes* magazine, 237
Foreman, Dave, 123, 168–69
Forest Stewardship Council, 199
formaldehyde, 112, 143–44
Fort Ord, California, 32
*Fortune* magazine, 252
fossil fuels, 57–58, 71, 97, 106, 152, 228, 267
Foster, Elissa, 179
Foundation for Deep Ecology, 123, 170, 182
Fox, Mary, 194
Fox News, 226, 258–59
Franco, Val, 67, 69, 70
free diving, 159–60
Free Speech movement, 40
Frey, Emilio, 278
Frey, Glen, 171
Friends of Cedar Mesa, 222
Friends of the Bow, 170
Friends of the Ventura River, 63–64, 256
Frishman, Karen, 25
Frost, Doreen, 46, 73, 87
Frost, Tom, 21, 28, 29, 37, 44, 46, 54, 72, 74, 87
    bought out by Chouinards, 73
    as business partner, 43–44
    Cerro Fitz Roy trip and, 45–52
    tensions with Chouinards, 72–73
    "A word . . ." (essay), 56–57, 111
Fun Hogs, 45–52, 82, 97, 114, 120, 125, 181,
    210–11, 273
fur, fake, 99

Gannett Peak, 20
Gap, 196
Gates, Bill, 251
gear, 41
    fishing, 261–62
    market for, 262–63
    marketing of, 82–86
    quality of, 98
    rappelling, 18–19
    rock climbing, 24–29, 73, 80 (*see also specific
    products*)

tested by US military, 175–76
testing, 93
Gellert, Ryan, 232, 233–34, 238, 239, 241–49, 274
Gelles, David
    in Bariloche, Argentina, 273–79
    "Billionaire No More" story, 250
    covering Patagonia, 4
    at Las Pampas Lodge, 261–63
    *The Man Who Broke Capitalism*, 4
    *Mindful Work*, 4
    research for this book, 7–8, 261–63
General Electric, 4
Georgetown University, 173–75
Georgia Investor Action Fund, 257
Ginsberg, Allen, 40, 41
Giving Pledge, 251
glaciers, 96–97
Glen Canyon Dam, 168
global average temperatures, 11–12, 267
globalization, 36–37, 175. *See also* supply chains
global warming, 57–58, 96–97, 267
gloves, 66
Gore, Al, 110
grains, 269–70, 272
Grand Staircase-Escalante, 224
Grand Teton National Park, 61, 249
Grateful Dead, 41
Great Pacific Child Development Center, 89
Great Pacific Iron Works, 58, 89
Green, David, 258–59
Greene, Marjorie Taylor, 235
greenhouse gases, 58, 106
Greenpeace USA, 107
greenwashing, 212
Grose, Lynda, 126, 207
growing pains, at Patagonia, 79–80
Guatemala, 48

H&M, 196
Habitat for Humanity, 107
Hackett, Peter, 94
Hanes, 196
Hansen, James E., 106
Hans Wilsdorf Foundation, 254
hardware (rock climbing). *See also* gear; *specific products*
    lawsuits and, 117–19
    marketing of, 82–86

Harley-Davidson, 133
harnesses, 117–18
Harrelson, Woody, 171
Harris Poll, 236
Hart, Gary, 108
Harward, Randy, 127–28, 129
hats, 66
Hawaii, 174
Headwaters Forest, 170, 171, 172
Heagle, Ray, 72, 73
Hells Angels, 41, 87
Helly Hansen, 263
Hennek, Dennis, 155
Herbert, Gary, 223
Herbert, TM, 21, 30
hexes (rock climbing), 71
Hickenlooper, John, 223
Higg Index, 196–97
Higgs boson particle, 197
hiking, quest of, 56
Himalayas, 94, 95–96, 155
HMS *Beagle*, 46
Hobby Lobby, 258–59
Hogan Lovells, 224–25
Holdfast Collective, 246–60, 276, 277
Hollister Ranch, 159–60
Hong Kong, 68, 151
Hot Pink Dolphins (activist group), 256
HSBC, 136–37, 138
Hughes, Howard, 24, 43
human rights practices, 94, 198–202, 251
human trafficking, 200–201
Humboldt County, California, 170
hunting, 21, 50
Huntsville, Alabama, 32
Hurricane Katrina, 190–91, 193
Hurwitz, Charles, 170–71, 172
hybrid fabrics, 153

ice axes ("piolets"), 44–45,
    175–76
ice climbing, 44–45, 92
IKEA, 254
imports, 65–66
*Inc.* magazine, 143
indentured servitude, 200–201
Industrial Revolution, 11
"innovator's dilemma," 102

insulation, 100–101
investors, potential, 51–52

jackets, 66, 69, 70, 100, 116, 235, 262
Jackson Hole, Wyoming, 191
Jackson Hole Mountain Resort, 235
Jack Wolfskin, 263
Japan, 116
JCPenney, 196
Jenny Lake, 21
Johnson, Lyndon, 57, 186
Jones, Chris, 48, 49
Jones, Ron, 136
Joplin, Janis, 41
Jordan, Jim, 235
J. P. Stevens & Co., Inc., 36–37
Jumbo Pique (sweater), 146–47
Jursch, Eve, 180

K2, 94
Kami, Michael, 133–34
Kamps, Bob, 23
Kat Pinnacle, 28
kayaking, 92–93, 97, 212–16
Kelty, 110
Kenna, Corley, 221–22, 225, 236
Kennedy, John F., 57
kernza, 269, 272–73
Kerouac, Jack, *The Dharma Bums*, 40
Kettenhofen, Bob, 100
Klein, Rick, 119, 120
knee pads, 176
Kohl's, 196
Korea, 33
Korean War, 33, 179
Kulczycki, Billy, 80, 125–27, 180

Lacoste, 265
Lago General Carrera, retreat in, 212–16
La Jolla, California, 16
Lamb, Carol "Peanut," 32, 36
Las Pampas Lodge, 261, 263, 273
layering, 71
layoffs, 135–38, 139, 203, 207
leadership, 160, 181–209
leaps of faith, 155–80
Level 9 Combat Pants, 178
Level 9 Combat Shirt, 178

Levi's, 196
Lewiston, Maine, 11–12, 13
Lightfoot, Paul, 268–69, 271
Lily's Cafe, 108
limits, pushing, 59–81
Lisbon, Maine, 12, 13, 36–37
L.L.Bean, 76, 81, 153, 263
logging, 170
London, England, 136
long underwear, 98, 200
Los Angeles, California, 15–16
Lost Arrow line, 178
Lost Arrow Project, 178
Lululemon, 265

Madoff, Bernie, 4
Maine, 36–37, 76, 81
Malden, Massachusetts, 98
Malden Mills, 98–99, 103
Mallory, George, 46–47
management, by absence, 92–98
Mander, Jerry, 139–40, 142
Manufacturers Bank, Los Angeles, 76
manufacturing, 68, 151. *See also* factories;
    supply chains
  in Asia, 127–28, 129, 151, 198–202
  globalization and, 36–37
Marble Freedom Trust, 253
Marcario, Rose, 220–21, 223, 225–26, 231–32,
    274
Marin Headlands, 143
marketing, 55–56, 82–86. *See also* catalogs
  Black Friday 2016 and, 220–22
  of clothing, 82–86
  "Don't Buy This Jacket" ad, 114, 205–7, 220
  eco-friendly, 113–14, 115, 149, 153
  of gear, 82–86
  of hardware for rock climbing, 82–86
Marks & Spencer, 196
Marmot, 263
Marsh, Paul, 80
maternity leave, 87–88, 91
Mathews, Craig, 185–87, 258
Maxxam, 170–72, 202
May, Alison, 137–38, 157–58, 166,
    179
Mays, Denny, 80
Mazatlán, Mexico, 48

# INDEX

McDivitt, Kris, 44, 73, 74, 75–77, 80, 81, 83, 87, 138, 205, 207
  "Black Wednesday" and, 136, 137, 155
  burnout and, 130, 155
  catalog and, 84–85
  as CEO for Tompkins' holdings, 184
  Chacabuco Valley purchase and, 181–82
  childcare center and, 88–89, 90
  creative tension and, 164
  "creative tension" caused by Patagonia footprint, 108
  at Lago General Carrera, 212–13
  leaves operational role at Patagonia, 157, 180
  marriage to Tompkins, 157, 210
  Patagonia Purpose Trust and, 247–48
  plans to retire, 130
  ready for reset, 155
  reclaims control of Patagonia, 136–37
  recruitment of new executives and, 130–31
  Reef Walkers and, 116
  on self-auditing, 115
  Tompkins Conservation and, 219
  Tompkins's death and, 216–19
  Tompkins's legacy and, 219, 249–51
McDivitt, Roger, 44, 73, 74, 75, 79
*Men Against the Clouds*, 95
Metcalf, Peter, 85, 118, 164, 223
Mexico, 22, 48, 175
Mexico City, 48
microplastics, 266
"Midtown Uniform," 235
millet, 270
Milliken, 101
Minnesota, Patagonia's food team in, 7
Minya Konka, 94
  avalanche at, 95–96, 212, 216, 217
mittens, 66
Mobile-Tensaw Delta, 256
Mojave Desert, 20
Moloka'i, Hawaii, 174
Montana, 7
Mont Blanc, 156
Montessori, Maria, 89
Moose, Wyoming, 60–61, 106, 130, 185, 191, 248
Morey, Tom, 42
Mosley, Dan, 245, 248, 252
Mount Edith Cavell, 30
Mount Everest, 47

Mount Fitz Roy, 7
Mount Sir Donald, 30
Moynihan, Daniel Patrick, 57
Muir, John, 22, 37
Munich, Germany, 136

Næss, Arne, 121, 124
Nahuel Huapi Lake, 278
Nano-Air hoody, 178
Nano Puff vests, 235
*National Geographic* magazine, 191
National Labor Relations Board, 78
Natura, 207
nature, reverence for, 56–57
Nature Conservancy, 256
Nautica, 165
Navarro, Ramón, 264
Navy SEALs, 177
neoprene, 263
New Deal, 21
Newman, Paul, 243, 254
Newman's Own, 243, 254
New Mexico, 31–32
New Orleans, Louisiana, 190–91, 193
*The New York Times*, 4, 106, 206–7, 250
*Nightline*, 108
Nike, 196
Nixon, Richard, 57
Noah, Trevor, 249–50
Noll, Eric, 262
nontoxic dyes, 146–47
nontoxic fabrics, 145–53
Norrøna, 263
North America, 11. *See also specific locations*
North American Free Trade Agreement, 174–75
North American Wall, El Capitan, 37–39
North Beach, 40
The North Face, 40–42, 45, 77, 110, 223, 263
nylon, 71, 99, 115, 151, 199

Obama, Barack, 220
Obama administration, 222
O'Donnell, Pat, 130, 135, 143, 157, 179
offshoring, 78
Old Faithful, 105
Olsen, Dave, 149, 152, 160–67, 177, 179
1% for the Planet, 6, 186–87, 222, 258, 277
Open Society Foundations, 251

# INDEX

organic cotton, 143–50, 153, 193, 204, 265–66
Osprey, 263
Outdoor Industry Association, 196
Outdoor Research, 263
Outdoor Retailer (conference), 223
overdevelopment, 35, 97–98
overseas manufacturing, 36
Ovis 21, 201–2
OXO, 187

Pacific Lumber, 170, 171
Palo Alto, California, 41
pants, 65, 178
Parks, Rosa, 186
Patagonia (company), 34, 49–52, 96, 176, 184,
    220, 274
  applies stricter standards with suppliers,
      198–202
  bailed out by Tompkins, 34
  B Corp movement and, 207–9
  Bears Ears National Monument and,
      222–24, 225–27
  becomes benefit corporation, 208–9
  Black employees at, 229–31
  Black Lives Matter movement and, 229–31
  "Black Wednesday" financial crisis at,
      135–38, 139–40, 207
  boycotts of, 170, 226
  on brink of failure, 136
  as burden, 2
  buy-back program and, 204–6
  catalog of, 36, 82–86, 92, 111, 120
  childcare at, 86–92, 115, 173, 277
  Chouinard chooses name, 67
  Chouinard's desire to transition into
      environmental foundation, 134
  Chouinard weighs selling, 124–25, 133, 184,
      185
  cleaning up supply chains, 150–54
  coalition building, 6–7, 134, 149–50,
      185–86, 277
  cofounds Conservation Alliance, 109–10
  companies interested in acquiring, 164–65
  competitors of, 161–62, 262–63 (see also
      specific competitors)
  confusion over ownership change, 258
  contradiction of, 167, 172–73
  corporate taxes and, 233–34

COVID-19 pandemic and, 228–32, 233,
    237, 274
craftsmanship and, 277
credit issues, 136–38, 140–41
critical time for, 132–54
culture of, 164, 177, 179–80
customer service, 36
debt crisis in, 136
distribution center in Reno, 163
diversifying product line, 98
"Don't Buy This Jacket" ad, 114
employee diversity at, 230–31
employee retreats at, 142–43, 155–56
employees and, 4, 142–43, 155–56, 170–71,
    230–31, 274–75
employees arrested, 170–71
employment standards at, 274–75
ends co-logo program, 235
environmental activism and, 3–4, 110, 138,
    222–27, 232–36, 246–60, 267–68, 274, 277
    (see also specific projects and locations)
environmental footprint of, 107–8, 111–17,
    130, 199–200
environmental review process, 115
equestrian line, 135
exceptionality of, 7
expands offerings, 68
expansion plans, 135
financial crisis of 2008 and, 203–9
first board of directors, 139–40
as food company, 268–73
forced to close offices and showrooms, 136
fossil fuels and, 267
founding of, 2
future of, 141–42, 238–49, 261–79
future profits directed to protecting the
    planet, 3–4
governance structure, 3–4
grant making by, 109, 138, 222, 258, 277
growing pains and, 79–80
growth of, 82–83, 127, 129–30, 140–41,
    163–64, 207, 262, 274
headquarters in Ventura, California, 3
holds suppliers conference, 153–54
hypocrisy of, 5–6, 172–73, 207
identity of, 86
insulated from lawsuits against Chouinard
    Equipment, 117

# INDEX

IPO possibility and, 242–43
as its own harshest critic, 111–17
launches Footprint Chronicles, 199–200
launches online store, 163
layoffs and, 137–40, 207
legacy of, 260
legal incorporation of, 80
letter-writing campaign for Bears Ears, 222–23
limits to growth of, 141–42, 274
local politics and, 110–11
manufacturing moves to Asia, 127–28, 129
market share of, 102
May as general manager of, 157–58
microplastics and, 266
mission statement of, 133–34, 207, 227, 232
as model for other companies, 6–7, 134, 149–50, 185–86
as more than a corporation, 6
named most-loved brand in US in 2023, 236
nonviolent civil disobedience training for employees, 172
Olsen as CEO of, 161–67
1% for the Planet grants, 222, 258, 277
pares back business with ideological adversaries, 234–35
partnership with Walmart, 187–97
as part of environmental problems, 172–73
"Patagucci" smear and, 234
philanthropy and, 107–11, 185–86, 237–60
planning for continued growth, 135
plans to sue Trump, 224–25
political activities of, 7
profitability of, 276–77
quality standards and, 98, 128–29, 277
on receiving end of environmental activism, 202
reputation of, 79–80, 235–36
retail stores, 135, 143 (see also specific locations)
sailing line, 135
scaling of boutique operation, 36–37
second Trump term and, 267–68
self-accountability and, 6, 111–17, 200
self-auditing by, 111–17, 150, 207–9
sewing shop at, 67
stock donated to Holdfast Collective, 246–49
stock equity of, 240
succession planning for, 3, 130–31, 132–34, 238–60

success of, 127, 129–30, 143, 166, 197–98, 207, 262, 276–77
supply chains and, 68, 114, 127–28, 135, 143–54, 264–66, 277
sustainability efforts and, 6, 111–17, 127–28, 135, 143–50, 150–54, 200, 207–9, 264–66, 277
switch to organic cotton, 143–50
Textil del Valle and, 264–66
Thomas Fire and, 225–26
time card machines incident, 76–77
"tithing" program, 107–11
Tompkins's death and, 216
as tool for social and environmental change, 130
at Tools conference, 168–75
touchmark for, 82, 98
transparency and, 199–202
Trump administration and, 220–25, 232–36
US military and, 175–79
Utah boycott and, 222–24
values of, 138–43, 154
worker pay and, 107
Patagonia (region), 46, 124, 156–57, 181–84, 219, 277–78. See also specific locations
Patagoniacs, 85–86, 221, 277. See also customers
Patagonia Land Trust, 184
Patagonia National Park, 181–84, 210, 219, 277
Patagonia Provisions, 268–73
Patagonia Purpose Trust, 246–60, 276
Peak District, England, 65
Pebble Mine, 256
Peckham Vocational Industries, 178
Peet's Coffee, 128
Pennoyer, Ellen Malinda, 59–60, 69, 84, 93, 99, 108, 125, 130, 145–46, 168, 208
Chacabuco Valley purchase and, 181–82
childcare and, 87–92
COVID-19 pandemic and, 228
desire to stay involved with Patagonia, 240
disapproves of McDivitt-Tompkins relationship, 157
empathy for the working class, 88
employees and, 165
environmental activism, 246–60
exit strategy and, 254–60
and formation of purpose trust, 247–49

Pennoyer, Ellen Malinda (*cont.*)
  Frost and, 72
  at Lago General Carrera, 212–13
  legacy of, 239–40, 243, 260
  local politics and, 62
  Marcario's exit and, 231–32
  Patagonia's environmental footprint and, 108
  philanthropy and, 246–60
  Planned Parenthood and, 109
  plans for future of Patagonia, 240–49
  on sale of Chouinard Equipment, 118–19
  succession planning and, 132–34
  Walmart and, 191, 193–94, 225
People for the Ethical Treatment of Animals, 201–2
peregrine falcons, 19, 37, 57
Peru, Patagonia's factories in, 7
pesticides, 112, 147
Peterson, Luke, 269
Peterson, Steve, 127
petrochemicals, 152, 263
petroleum, 152
philanthropy, 107–11, 123, 186, 198, 246–60.
  *See also specific projects and locations*
  giving it all away, 237–60
  groundbreaking, 3–4, 7
pickaxes, 92
Pickett, Karen, 171
pile jackets, 70
pile sweaters, 69
pitons, 24, 25–29, 31, 36, 39, 41, 51, 52, 53, 54,
    64, 80, 128
  phasing out of, 53, 54, 102
Plain Jane, 42, 46, 49, 51, 68, 77–78
Planned Parenthood, 109, 110, 142, 170
plastic haze, 266
plastics recycling, 152–53
"A Plea for Responsible Consumption" ad, 205
politics, 7, 62–63, 110–11, 222, 222–25, 223,
    232–36, 233–34, 235–36, 257, 267
polyester, 71, 99–100, 101–2, 115, 152
  recycled, 266
polypropylene fiber, 71, 98, 101, 102, 103
Pope, Karl, 42
Portugal, 151
post-consumer recycled plastics, 152–53
Prato, Italy, 153
Pratt, Chuck, 32, 37

Pray, Montana, 168
Prentice, Don, 18
Presidio, San Francisco, 33, 35
product design, 44–45, 54, 66–67, 69–70 *See
    also specific products*
product durability, 117
product quality, 117. *See also specific products*
professionalism, 87
professionalization, 77
Project Chacabuco, 241–49
pro-life activists, 110
Proposition 9: Clean Environment Act, 62
ProPublica, 252
public relations, 110
Pumalín Douglas Tompkins National Park, 219
Punta de Lobos, Chile, 263–64
purpose trust, definition of, 245–46. *See also
    Patagonia Purpose Trust*

quality control, 128–29, 277
Quartz, 252

rain shells, 116
rain slickers, 66
Raitt, Bonnie, 171, 172
Ralph Lauren, 165
rappelling gear, 18–19
rayon, 199
Read, Al, 94–95
Reagan, Ronald, 106
Real Cheap Sports, 80
Realized Ultimate Reality Piton (RURP), 29
Rébuffat, Gaston, 22
recessions, 142
recycled polyester, 266
Reef Walkers, 116
REI, 67, 110, 223, 263
Reñihué farm, 124
Reno, Nevada
  Patagonia distribution center in, 163
  Patagonia retail store in, 274
reproductive rights, 110
Republicans, 233–34, 235–36, 257
Responsible Wool Standard, 202
retail stores, 107, 135, 274. *See also specific
    locations*
Retro Pile fleece jackets, 100
rice, 270

# INDEX

Ridgeway, Carissa, 86–92
Ridgeway, Jennifer, 87–88, 90
Ridgeway, Rick, 83–84, 86–88, 94–96, 191, 193, 195, 204–8, 212–16, 219, 241, 249, 259
Robbins, Royal, 21, 28, 37–38, 66
Robert, Yvon, 13
rock climbing, 1–2, 18–20, 22–23, 28, 33, 37–39, 65, 92, 94–96, 103–4, 161, 174. *See also* climbing; ice climbing
   "clean climbing" ethos, 55–58
   costs of, 56–57
   effect on the environment, 51–58
   growing popularity of, 111
   as identity, 23
   new approach to, 38–39
   in the nude, 34
   rock climbing gear, 24–29, 73, 80 (*see also specific products*)
   rock climbing subculture, 29–30
   style of, 56–57
Rockefeller, John D. Jr., 61
The Rolling Stones, 55
Route 66, 15
"rucksack revolution," 40
Ruckus Society, 172
rugby shirts, 65–66, 68, 69, 80
Russell, Susie, 41, 42, 46, 49, 77, 122, 218. *See also* Buell, Susie Tompkins
Russia, 97
Rusty Duck, 268–69

Saint-Exupéry, Antoine de, 55
Saks Fifth Avenue, 68
Salathé, John, 25–26, 37
sales reps, commissions and, 125–26
Salk, Jonas, 74
Salomon, 263
Salt Lake City, Utah, 223
Salvation Army, 107
Salzer, Jim, 111
Samsung, 266
San Francisco, California, 33, 40, 46, 49
San Francisco, California, Police Department, 78
*San Francisco Chronicle*, 49
*San Francisco Examiner*, 41
Santa Barbara, California, 159–60
Savings and Loan crisis, 135–36
Schaller, Lorenz, 270

Schmitz, Kim, 95, 96
Schultz, Howard, 173
Scott, Lee, 188, 190–91, 193, 197
Scott, MacKenzie, 251
seafood, 271–72, 273
seamstresses, 67
Security Pacific National Bank, 136
Seid, Barre, 253
Seligmann, Peter, 187–88
Selkirks, 30
Sentinel Rock, 30
Sespe Wilderness, 161
sewing machine, 129
Shawangunks, 31, 34
Sheahan, Casey, 198, 201, 203, 207
Sheahan, Tara, 203
sheep, 201–2
shirts
   Level 9 Combat Shirt, 178
   rugby shirts, 65–66, 68, 69, 80
   T-shirts, 178
shoes, 66
shorts, 66–67, 76, 98
Shoshone Fire, 105
Sierra Club Legal Defense Fund, 107
Sierra Nevada (brewery), 272
Sierras, 175–76
Sievert, Jane, 85
Silicon Valley, 4
Simon and Garfunkel, 43
simplification, 74
Slack, Jocelyn, 82
slavery, 200–201
Sloan, Howard, 80
small game, 21
Smith, Mary Ellen, 93
Smith & Hawken, 115
Snake River, 61
Snowdon Railway, 54
software (rock climbing), 65–71. *See also* clothing; *specific products*
Soros, George, 251, 257
sourcing, 68
South America, 8, 34, 45–52, 181–84. *See also specific locations*
   conservation efforts in, 217–19
   land use in, 120
   surfing's origins in, 231

Southeast Asia, 198, 200
Southern California Falconry Club, 17, 19
South Howser Tower, 30
Soviet Union, 97
spandex, 99
Spence, Gerry, 123
sports bras, 176
Stand Up Shorts, 67, 80, 233
Stanley, Vincent, 43, 72–73, 116, 145, 199, 204, 227, 241
Starbucks, 173
Steiner, Rudolf, 89
Sterling, John, 169, 171–72, 258
Stoney Point, 21
stoppers (rock climbing), 71
Storm Creek Fire, 105
Stratton, Hall, 65, 74
success, defining, 143
suppliers, 68, 277. See also supply chains
    in Asia, 198–202
    conference for, 153–54
    standards for, 198–202
supply chains, 36, 68, 114–15, 127–28, 135, 143–50, 199–200, 264–66, 277
    cleaning up, 145–54, 201–2
    interrogating, 134, 143–53, 198–202
    remaking, 153–54
surfboards, 27
surfing, 27, 48, 83, 92, 231, 263
sustainability efforts, 187–97, 212–13, 223–24, 267, 277. See also conservation efforts
sustainability groups, 277. See also specific groups
Sustainable Apparel Coalition (Cascale), 6, 196–97
Sustainable Cotton Project, 144–45
sustainable materials, 115–16
Sutherland, Caitlin, 257
sweaters, 69, 146–47
Sweeney, Kevin, 108–9, 110, 114, 150, 154, 169
Synchilla, 100, 101, 102, 103, 176
    Synchilla jackets, 235
    Synchilla Snap-T, 100–101
synthetic materials, 70–71, 98, 99, 102, 112, 150. See also specific materials

tagua nuts, 115–16
Tahquitz Rocks, 21
tailoring, subversive, 233

Taiwan, 200–201
Target, 196
tax cuts, 233–34
Tazo, 187
Tebbel, Paul, 107, 150, 151, 173, 256
Tejada-Flores, Lito, 47, 48, 49, 78
Temu, 263
Tencel, 199
Terray, Lionel, 46
terrorist attacks of September 11, 2001, 177
Tetons, 21, 22, 31, 43, 52, 61, 106, 130
Textil del Valle (TDV), 264–66
Textile Exchange, 6, 202
textile industry, 98–99
textiles, 98–102. See also specific fabrics and materials
Tehachapi Mountains, 19
Thailand, 147–48, 200
Thomas, Leah, 230
Thomas Fire, 225–26
Thoreau, Henry David, 22, 74
Tiffany, 212
Tijuana, Mexico, 43
Time to Vote, 6
Tingwick, Quebec, 12
Tise, Jane, 49
Tokyo, Japan, retail store in, 135
Tompkins, Doug, 33–35, 40–42, 45–46, 49, 51, 68, 77–79, 89, 113, 168, 179, 187, 204, 212–16
    bails out Patagonia, 34
    burial of, 219
    Cañi Sanctuary and, 120
    Cerro Fitz Roy trip and, 45–52
    Chacabuco Valley, Chile, and, 181–82, 211, 241
    conservation efforts and, 124, 181–84, 210, 211, 217–19, 241 (see also Pumalín Douglas Tompkins National Park; Tompkins Conservation)
    death of, 215–16
    deep ecology and, 120–21
    divorce from Susie, 122
    Esprit and, 121, 122, 124, 138, 144
    estate of, 217–19, 237
    extends line of credit to Patagonia, 138
    at Lago General Carrera retreat, 212–16

# INDEX

legacy of, 250–51
luxurious lifestyle of, 120–21
McDivitt and, 155–57
organic cotton and, 144
pessimism of, 211
philanthropy and, 123, 133
"A Plea for Responsible Consumption" ad,
113, 114
pressures Chouinard to sell Patagonia,
124–25, 133, 184
views capitalism as unsustainable, 212
Tompkins, Kris McDivitt. *See* McDivitt, Kris
Tompkins, Quincey, 217
Tompkins, Summer, 217–18
Tompkins, Susie. *See* Buell, Susie Tompkins
Tompkins Conservation, 219
Tools conference, 168–75
Topa Topa (brewery), 272
Topatopa Mountains, 161
touchmark, 82
toxins, 143–44, 153, 199. *See also specific toxins*
trade shows, 102–3, 223
transcendentalists, 22
Tripp Lite, 253
Trott, Byron, 245
Trump, Donald J.
election of, 220, 222
national monuments and, 222–23, 224
Patagonia's partisan political action after
election of, 232–36
Patagonia's resistance to, 224–25, 232
Patagonia sues, 224–25
spars with Chouinard, 226
wins second term, 267
Trump administration, 220–25, 232–36, 236
tsampa, 270
T-shirts, 178
Tuolumne River, 92–93
Turkey, 195
Twitter, 226, 233

UC Berkeley, 40
Umbro, 66
underwear, 70–71, 98, 101, 200. *See also* long
underwear
Unilever, 243
unions, 78–79
United States, 175

University of California, Santa Barbara, 64
Ural Mountains, Russia, 79
US Bureau of Land Management, 225
US Congress, hearings on climate change, 106
US Department of Defense, Chouinard
Equipment for Alpinists and, 176
US Department of the Interior, 222–23
US Forest Service, 225
US House Committee on Natural Resources, 226
US Marine Corps Mountain Warfare Training
Center, 175–76
US military, 99, 175–79
Utah boycott, 222–24
Utah Republicans, 222, 223
*Utne Reader*, 113, 114, 115, 205

Valley Cong, 30
Vancouver, Washington, 136
Ventura, California, 3, 7, 42, 46, 60, 62, 64, 76,
79, 108, 119, 120, 130, 136, 161, 165, 172,
185, 193, 200, 220, 230
conference for suppliers in, 153–54
firestorm in, 225–26
local politics and, 110–11
plan for new CSU campus in, 110–11
Ventura County, California, 88
Ventura River, 62–63, 64, 83, 97, 186
Verité (independent labor chain auditor), 201,
208
VF Corporation, 42
Vietnam, 200
Vietnam War, veterans of, 44
Vietnam War protests, 40, 186
Vjosa River, 256
Volcan Llaima, 48
Vulgarian Mountain Club, 34

Wales, 53–54
*The Wall Street Journal*, 67, 177
Walmart, 188–97, 204, 212, 225
Walton, Rob, 188, 192
Walton, Sam, 188
Weeden, Alan, 120
Weeks, Ken, 21–22
Welch, Jack, 4
Wellman, 152
wetsuits, 263–64
Whillans, Don, 43

# INDEX

White House, 223
whitewater kayaking, 92–93
Whole Foods, 272
wildfires
  "let it burn" approach, 105
  Thomas Fire, 267
  at Yellowstone National Park, 105–6
Williams, Kate, 187
Wind River Range, 20, 21
winning back the wild, 105–31
women, in leadership roles, 91 *(see also specific women)*
wool, 98, 99, 100, 112, 115, 153, 201–2, 263
Woolyester, 153
workday, rethinking, 62
World War II, 11, 14, 276
Worn Wear, 204
Worumbo Woolen Mill, 12, 36–37
Wright, Jonathan, 95, 96, 212, 216, 217

Wyoming, 1, 7, 20, 21, 60–61, 106, 169, 185, 191, 235
Wyoming Resource Providers, 170

Xinjiang region, China, 266

Yale University, 175, 178
Yellowstone National Park, 105–6, 168, 185
Yeung, Johnny, 147–48
Yosemite Climbing Club, 30
Yosemite National Park, 28, 29–30, 59, 110, 169
Yosemite Valley, 21, 36–40, 41, 43, 52, 104, 111, 143. *See also* Yosemite National Park
Yulex (textile), 263–64

Zen Buddhism, 4, 5, 211
Zero Population Growth, 142
Zinke, Ryan, 223, 225, 226